ASSASSIN!

ASSASSIN!

J. BOWYER BELL

ST. MARTIN'S PRESS
NEW YORK

Library of Congress Cataloging in Publication Data

Bell, J. Bowyer, 1931–
Assassin.

1. Assassination.   2. Political crimes and
offenses.   3. Assassination—History.   I. Title.
HV6278.B44   364.1'524   79–17823
ISBN 0–312–05773–3

IN MEMORIAM

Seamus Costello
Maira Drumm
Eduardo Mondlane
George Curtis Moore
Kamal Nasser

This book has been written under the auspices of the Institute of War and Peace Studies Columbia University

A man who goes forth to take the life of another he does not know must believe one thing only—that by his act he will change the course of history.

Itzhak Yizernitsky-Shamir,
CENTRAL COMMITTEE STERN GROUP

contents

preface

My original intention to write this script arose during the traumatic years of the American assassinations—the Kennedys, King, Malcolm X, the Nazi Rockwell—when there was a rush of analysis, often if not always based on the premise that such deeds are done by the aberrant, which in America they largely are, and are futile if not counterproductive, which is moot. From my study of political violence, assassination in many parts of the world was not only a normal political act, rational, explicable, but also often effective, perhaps in some cases taking fewer lives in the transfer of power than an election. Certainly, there were all sorts and kinds of assassination—personal, psychopathic, authorized—but the most spectacular surely was revolutionary assassination, the effort to change history by recourse to murder. Alas, despite the best intentions, I spent the next ten years studying other aspects of political violence, traveling to far wars and distant coups, interviewing guerrillas in the Horn, bombers in Belfast, and kidnapped victims in Italy, producing a great many pages. Finally, at the prodding of Tom Dunne of St. Martin's, I have returned to this special study of treacherous violence.

Over the years my academic concern with political violence has been pursued in quite unacademic ways; in fact, this book opens with one of the very few chapters I have written about people whom I do not know personally. One purpose, at least, is to begin so far back that the people, issues, and the treacherous violence involved in the murder of King Henry IV will not engender the indignation and anger in the reader that more contemporary political murders usually do. After that, however, in a great many cases I am, indeed, writing about people I know, the perpetrators, the victims, the conspirators, and those who have escaped. In time some of the assassins have become my friends, just as some of their victims were. The book is, in fact, dedicated to five such victims. They, of course, might find the other company uneasy: four men —a radical Irish revolutionary leader, the president of *Frente de Libération de Moçambique* in Africa, an American Arabist diplomat, and the spokesman for the Palestine Liberation Organization —and one Irish woman, a vice-president of the Provisional Sinn Féin. And beside the retrospective discussions of political murder with hundreds of the involved over the last ten years with this work in mind, although never privy to a conspiracy, I have appeared from time to time at likely sites: Cyprus in 1974 immediately before the coup against Makarios, Italy in 1976 when the prosecutors Vittorio Occorsio and Francesco Coco were killed, and in Dublin when the British Ambassador Christopher Ewart-Biggs was assassinated by a culvert-bomb. There have been those who check my itineraries in order to vacation elsewhere. And in the end, before the typewriter, there is neither the romance of a violent and spectacular subject nor the horror and anguish that treacherous violence brings when the victim—or for that matter the murderer—is more than a name in a headline. The people I have studied at first hand for twenty years are engaged in a deadly game; the attrition rate is often high, and the power fleeting. Like Grand Prix drivers and bullfighters, they live with death for the benefits it may bring them and their cause. The revolutionary game is a dangerous one: victories are rare and the risks disproportionate. But in large areas of the world, it is the only game that can assure radical change. In Ethiopia or Spain or Cyprus, assassination, as a first or last choice, becomes a simple and ordinary, if frightful, tool of the rebel. And now there are rebels who operate not in the outback or the bush but kill in Germany, strike at the heart of the state in Italy, detonate car bombs in Washington. They murder ambassadors in Paris and Vienna, and each other in London. If the past is prologue, assassination is to be with us yet—or at least with some of us, some of the time.

Since the book rests on hundreds of interviews, thousands of hours of discussions on revolutionary matters with the involved and threatened, it would be hopeless to attempt to thank all of those over the years who have in one way or another added to my stock of knowledge. Some undoubtedly will disapprove of the result. Many of the involved—obviously—want to remain anonymous: the subject is for them hardly academic. For my academic colleagues who have given aid and comfort some of the same problems exist; but at risk, their risk, one or two special thanks are in order: to Dottore Alessandro Silj in Rome, to Professor Carlo Schaerf, who has thrice brought me to his International School for Disarmament and Research on Conflict in Italy to discuss such matters, to the indefatigable Oliver Snoddy in Dublin, and, most important, to my Columbia colleagues, especially Werner Schilling, director of the Institute of War and Peace Studies, and the irreplaceable Anna Houri.

Rome
New York
Dublin
Dr. J. Bower Bell

prologue

"I've Been Stabbed!"
The Assassination of Henry IV of France

On Friday, May 14, 1610, Paris was bustling with preparations for war and the arrival of Queen Marie de Médicis, who was expected to enter the city two days later. King Henry IV was preparing to march on the lower Rhine with an army of thirty thousand to thwart what appeared to be a Spanish Hapsburg plot to usurp three small German duchies. Henry, as always opposing the power and the pretensions of the Hapsburgs, intended to intervene in support of the two Protestant claimants, the Elector of Brandenburg and the Count Palatine of Neuburg. After decades of religious wars, Henry, himself once a Protestant, put the national needs of France ahead of any sort of alliance with the good Catholic Hapsburgs—to the horror of many good Catholic Frenchmen. Thus, more often than not France was allied with the Protestants for reasons of state. In fact, Henry IV's kingdom was a precursor of the new wave: absolutist, increasingly centralized monarchies fighting national wars rather than religious crusades. Whether the claimants were Protestant or not and whether the issue was worth a war were less important to Henry than France's need everywhere to match Hapsburg initiative. He would march on the Rhine and leave Marie de Médicis and the heir to the Bourbon fortunes, the future Louis XIII, who in 1610 was still only nine, in Paris to maintain the authority of the crown. To increase

5

the queen's prestige, Henry had seen to it that she was crowned in a dramatic ceremony at Saint-Denis the previous day. On Sunday she would be in Paris and the way cleared for Henry's war.

Soon after two on Thursday afternoon, the king announced that he wanted to confer with the Duke of Sully, his chief financial minister, who for years had sought to centralize France's confused fiscal affairs and devise means to defray the increasing costs of the state. Like Henry, Sully was an early architect of royal absolutism and his financial maneuvers made possible Henry's military ones. Sully was across Paris in the Arsenal, so the king ordered up a coach and prepared for the short trip through the streets. In Paris, however, short trips were not necessarily quick. The city was still medieval, walled, cut with twisting alleys and without the grand boulevards and parks of later centuries. In fact, Henry had ordered the construction of the Palace Royale, the first great open breathing space in the old city. That, with the Pont-Neuf, then the newest and now the oldest bridge across the Seine, was his major contribution to the structure of the city. But the Palace Royale was still unfinished and the city remained crowded around the Ile de la Cité and Ile St. Louis. Other than the palatial Louvre and a few churches, the buildings were crammed together without order, without elegance, and without any of the facilities of a modern city. Open ditches cut through the streets were filled with refuse and sewage. The lanes and alleys were filthy, dark, and dank, teeming with all sorts and conditions of people—beggars in rags, tradesmen and clerics, animals and housewives, unemployed soldiers, the diseased, the leprous, the various. The city stank. From the air it would have appeared almost circular, with few buildings outside the walls, the fields pushing in, mottled walled squares pocked by windmills, the land on which the "central" city would rise a century later.

The city's unorganized growth of the past century was all too apparent. Even the few straight thoroughfares were cluttered with shops and stalls spilling across the cobbles in violation of the law. As early as 1554, Henry II had ordered all the shops and stalls to be pulled down along the Rue de la Ferronneire to prevent traffic jams, the curse of medieval cities built more for sieges than for commerce. Such regulations seem never to have been enforced, and for decade after decade further efforts to clear the streets faltered—royal absolutism was still the course of the future, despite the efforts of Henry and Sully. Consequently, any coach trip, even that of the king, could be a trial. Around three P.M. Henry got into his awkward square carriage along with the Dukes of Epernon and Montbazon and Marshal Lavardin. He told the captain of the guard not to bother with an escort; "I wish to be left alone."[1] A king was never alone, but only a few nobles on horseback, along with several footmen, accompanied the coach out of the Louvre and along the Croix-du-Tiroir.

Henry was on the left, with Epernon on his right and Montbazon and Lavardin seated opposite. It was a glorious spring day and the king pulled back the heavy leather curtains so that as the carriage rumbled down the Rue Saint-Honoré he could observe the preparations for the entry of Queen Marie de Médicis. The coach swung into the Rue de la Ferronnerie, which ran alongside the Saint-Innocent cemetery. The street, narrowed by the usual shops and stalls, was jammed with people and carts. The king's coach came to a halt as a wine cart and another loaded with hay almost totally blocked the street. The king's few horsemen pushed between the two carts and pressed on through the traffic. Most of the footmen soon scrambled over into the cemetery and wound their way among the graves up to the end of the Rue de la Ferronnerie to wait for Henry's coach, still blocked in front of the premises of the notary Pontrain. One of the two remaining footmen moved off to see if he could move the two carts or find their drivers. Inside the coach, Henry, who had left his glasses back at the Louvre, asked Epernon to read a letter aloud. The duke unfolded the petition and began to read. The wait was awkward. The coach was at something of an angle; one of the right wheels had run off into the gutter that ran down the middle of the street, so that the opposite left wheel was raised and the four men sat on an angle. Tilted, Epernon continued to read. The last footman leaned down and began to retie his garter.

Without warning, a tall, stocky, red-haired man pulled himself up on the wheel beside the open window. Intent on the letter, the king and the three nobles hardly noticed. Then the red-haired man struck out and down twice with a knife. One cut was a four-inch slash on Henry's left side that tore across the second and third ribs and along the pectoral muscle but without cutting into the chest cavity. The other wound was lower down, between the fifth and sixth ribs, a stab rather than a slash. The knife cut through the lung and severed the aorta an inch above the heart. It was a mortal blow. The attack was so swift, so unexpected, that the men in the carriage barely understood what was happening. Henry cried out, "I've been stabbed!"[2]

The assassin then struck again, a third time, and his knife slipped, ripping through the sleeve of the Duke of Montbazon. The red-haired man then stepped back off the wheel and stood silently clutching the bloody knife. Henry was ashen, blood pouring from his mouth. He never uttered another word. His life was pumping out through the gash in his heart.

For another moment there was utter silence in the coach. The three nobles were still stunned. If the assassin had dropped the knife and walked off, they would have been unable to recognize him. Their attention was focused on their maimed king and the blood gouting down his chest. The one footman had seen nothing. The street crowd had paid no attention. The assassin still did not move. Finally, one of the king's household, Saint-Michel, realized what had happened and rushed forward toward the red-haired man with his sword drawn. Epernon recovered his senses and called out, "Don't kill him if you value your life."[3] Still holding the bloody knife, the assassin was seized. Epernon threw a cloak over Henry and told the gathering crowd that the king was not seriously hurt. He ordered the coach back to the Louvre, and Henry bled to death on the way. His body was taken to his dressing room and placed on the bed, and a small shocked crowd began to gather in the room. Cardinal de Sourdis and Chaplain Boulonge began the prayers customary at the point of death. But the real moment of death for Henry came as soon as the knife of the red-haired man severed his aorta and changed the course of French history.

At the moment that the prayers began over the king's blood-stained body, the assassin, François Ravaillac, was being questioned at the Hôtel de Retz, close to the scene of the crime but safe from the angry crowd that sought to kill the murderer of the king. On the day of the assassination, he was tortured and put through a preliminary interrogation. Torture was an essential component of any such interrogation. On Sunday, May 16, he was moved to the Conciergerie on the Ile de la Cité and questioned again. He was examined twice on Monday, again on Tuesday morning, and a fourth time on Wednesday. On May 25, he was once more put to the torture and warned by the clerk of the Paris Parlement to tell the truth if he valued his salvation in the world to come. Ravaillac repeated the same story—he had acted alone without aid or accomplices. For all the interrogators this was difficult to believe. They were concerned not so much as to Ravaillac's motives but rather as to the existence of a conspiracy—were the Hapsburgs involved, or Henry's French enemies, or perhaps the Jesuits? It seemed inconceivable that anyone from such a humble background could have acted without external aid. At the very least he must have had the devil's aid. Ravaillac replied that such a course would have been a sin. He insisted he was a good Catholic. It gradually became clear just what sort of Catholic he had been—and this only confused his interrogators further.

In 1610 Ravaillac was thirty-one years old, an unmarried barrister from Angoulême. His career at best had been marginal; he had been in prison for debt and existed mainly by giving religious instruction to the young in Angoulême. Often the parents of his eighty pupils paid him in kind—bacon, grain, wine, or meat. Six years previously, first his father and then his sisters deserted the household, leaving him the sole support of his mother. Food was often short and luxuries nonexistent. Ravaillac, despite or perhaps because of his material difficulties, remained deeply pious. He was at one point received into the religious order of the Feuillants but his monastic career proved exceedingly brief. After six weeks he was asked to leave "because he had seen visions during his private devotions."[4] The Feuillants, like the Church in general, had grave doubts about any private visions, the product most often of unbalanced minds rather than revelation. Ravaillac then tried to join the Jesuits, who turned him down officially because he had been a member of another order but surely in part because of his manner and his visions. After hearing his confession, the Jesuit d'Aubigny suggested that "he had hallucinations rather than visions, which were the result of the mental confusion clearly visible in his face. What he needed was to go back home, follow a wholesome diet, tell his rosary and say his prayers."[5] Ravaillac could not or would not follow such a sensible regime. Increasingly in the grip of his visions, he was obsessed with the necessity of killing the king if Henry did not change his policies. In 1609 Ravaillac had failed to give a prophetic message to the king and decided that Henry must die. Henry was making no effort to convert the Calvinist Protestants to the one true apostolic Catholic and Roman Church. He planned to make war on the Pope. He refused to punish Huguenots but imprisoned Catholics. He must die in an act prepared for God. And he had. Ravillac felt he had behaved as a truly devout Catholic.

Under questioning, he finally accepted that he was guilty of an appalling crime but "inasmuch as he had done it for God, that He would grant him grace to remain until death in a state of faith, hope and perfect charity."[6] He then realized that he had decided to commit murder of his own free will in opposition to the will of God. On the morning of May 27, the Paris Parlement declared him "guilty in fact and in law of the crime of treason to God and man, principally on account of the most wicked, abominable and detestable parricide committed on the person of our late King Henry the Fourth."[7] The sentence had been a foregone conclusion from the moment Ravaillac had been bundled into the Hôtel de Retz, and the sentence for such parricide was indeed frightful. First, however, he was tortured once again in a last hope that he would reveal his accomplices. A clumsy metal boot was put over one of his legs and one after another three screws were turned down gradually, slowly crushing his joints. He fainted as the third screw was turned. He had still revealed no accomplices. He was taken from the rack and placed on a mattress until noon. He was then moved to the chapel, where two doctors from the Sorbonne heard his confession. An hour later, he was brought out of the chapel and taken to the prison gates. When he came out of the gates of the Conciergerie to climb into the cart, a huge crowd screaming and shouting pushed forward to get at him. He was stoned on the way to the main door of Notre-Dame, where he was propped up in his long shirt to hold a lighted candle and confess to his crime. The howls of the mob prevented anyone from hearing the confession. He was then taken to the scaffold on the Place de Grève for the final dreadful act.

In the midst of the huge roaring mob, Ravaillac stood on the scaffold and begged forgiveness of the king and queen. His arm, the arm that had committed murder, was then plunged into burning sulphur. Ravaillac screamed out to God and Jesus Maria. Next, with red-hot pincers, pieces of his chest, arms, thighs, and calves were torn off. Molten lead, boiling oil and resin, and a mixture of molten wax and sulphur were poured into the gaping rips, cauterizing the blood and wounds in an excruciating operation to keep him alive for the next stage. No one could hear the wounds sizzle for the crowd howled on, urging that no prayers be said, that his death be a lingering one—"let his soul trickle away drop by drop."[8] For over an hour Ravaillac had been torn and burned before the executioners brought up four horses and tied them to his arms and legs. The four horses were then pulled in different directions, often tugged along by the mob to increase the pressure. A new horse was brought up. The rider, after replacing one of the leg horses, gave the mount a slap, and the jerk sideways broke Ravaillac's thigh bone. Finally, after ninety minutes, broken and burnt, Ravaillac died. The crowd rushed forward and began hacking and ripping at the body with knives and sticks and swords. The limbs were torn from the executioners and dragged through the streets. The bits and pieces were burnt all over Paris and the ashes scattered.

All Ravaillac's property was confiscated and taken by the king. The house in which he had been born was pulled down and an order issued that nothing could be built on the site. In Angoulême, his mother and father had two weeks to leave France and risked summary execution if they ever returned. None of his relatives would be permitted to use the name of Ravaillac. The punishment of one who had killed by treacherous violence was awesome. And yet despite the dread shadow of the scaffold, the cauldrons filled with the glowing pincers, the seething oil and reeking sulphur, despite the four horses and certain dismemberment, Ravaillac in the grip of his special obsession had not been unique in a determination to kill the king. In fact, his was the twentieth attempt to murder Henry IV.

Not only the France of Henry IV but also much of Western Europe had for decades been an assassination zone. In 1588 Henry, Duke of Guise, had been murdered at Blois, and the next year Henry III was killed by Jacques Clémert. In England there had been the Gunpowder Plot to blow up King James in Parliament, and the swirl of conspiracies around Mary, Queen of Scots. In Venice the spiritual leader of the resistance to Papal authority and the interdict of 1605–1607, Fra Paolo Sarpi, bore an assassin's scar on his face. In fact, so did Henry, who had been attacked on December 27, 1594, by a twenty-year-old student, Jean Chastel, who, unable to end his own life, suicide being abhorrent to God, sought to perform a great deed punishable by death and thus while contributing to the common good also shorten his stay in purgatory. Striking at the king's throat, Chastel had only slashed Henry's lip and broken a tooth. He, like Ravaillac, had simply stood with his bloody knife until he was discovered and arrested. He, like Ravaillac, felt it was permissible to kill kings. And he, like Ravaillac, suffered the penalty, the preliminary torture, the burning pincers and molten sulphur, the four horses and a lingering death. Subsequently, in supposedly more rational times, there was a tendency to see the lone assassin as a maniac, disturbed by visions, possessed not by Satan but hallucinations. Matters were not so clear to those who questioned Henry's assassins. Everyone believed in the powers of the devil, in the reality of witches and the obsessions of a dark world. For nearly two centuries witches would be burned, and the powers of the devil remain with us yet. Thus the judges in the cases of Chastel and Ravaillac did not discount the diabolic component but sought most closely for a political conspiracy—who was involved, who would gain, who had broached the idea, where was the plot? Mostly, it seemed, the lone assassin appeared to be just that—a solitary citizen who had killed not as a murderer but as a just instrument of fate, acting in God's name for God's purpose. And the assassins acted within a social context where the ideas concerning the legitimacy of tyrannicide had wide currency, wide enough to convince failed monks and young students.

Throughout the sixteenth century, an era of brutal religious wars between warring armies who could imagine but one true religion, the question of legitimacy had a special place. The defenders of the faith simply assumed that their opponents represented institutionalized evil, bewitched or misguided or dedicated to heresy. All must be converted or killed. Increasingly, this proved impossible. Some Protestant bastions could not be reached or crushed. Other Catholic powers could crush their own heretics but their crusades abroad faltered. Religiously divided countries such as France remained gripped in bloody civil wars and were subject to constant outside interference. It was little wonder that the theologians were concerned with the problem of tyrannicide.[9] Two of the most influential, Juan de Mariana, a Jesuit, who wrote *De rege et regis institutione,* and Jean Boucher, who published two works on the subject, were widely read. Mariana's work was in fact republished in 1610. Although both, among other scholars, produced tomes studded with classical examples and often extensive digressions, the basic problems were relatively easy to understand. Certainly Jean Chastel and Ravaillac found the ideas then current easy to grasp.

Essentially, there was general agreement that there were two kinds of tyrants, those of usurpation and those of oppression. In the first case the ruler came to power illicitly; in the second, he misused his power, however gained. The first problem for both assassins and theologians, however, was what was the appropriate response to such a tyrant. And since the sixteenth and seventeenth centuries seemed in certain eyes to abound in tyrants, it was a most important question. As always, there was no consensus, but certainly a considerable number of the knowledgeable had argued that even a single individual can strike down such a tyrant— others, of course, argued that the monarch as God's representative, no matter how tyrannous, was not subject to earthly justice. For those involved in the twenty attempts on Henry IV, the crucial point was not whether or not tyrannicide was a valid act— obviously they accepted that it was—but how to define a tyrant. And they all agreed that Henry IV of Navarre was both a tyrant by usurpation and a tyrant by oppression.

When Henry III had been assassinated in 1589 by the good Catholic Jacques Clément, even moderate Catholics were appalled to realize that the Protestant champion, who had once accepted the Roman Church and then recanted, was next in line by blood—but not very next. Distant relatives had come to the throne before, but always within the traditional consanguinity of the tenth degree. Henry IV was twenty-two degrees removed from the dead Henry III. His opponents claimed immediately that the line had lapsed and a new king should be chosen by the Estates General. In any case, *any* Protestant as the king of France would be a ruler by usurpation. Even when Henry abjured the Protestant faith on July 25, 1593, many doubted his sincerity—he had used the ploy before. And many pointed out that his religious policies in no way reflected his newly proclaimed faith. He allied France with the Protestants against the Catholics. He refused to allow the writ of the Council of Trent to run in France. He refused forcefully to convert French Protestants. Worse, in 1599 he issued the Edict of Nantes, which formally tolerated their existence. All this was for the good Catholics evidence that Henry of Navarre had no right to the crown of France, and was a tyrant by usurpation.

For both good Catholics and those disgruntled by the demands of the new absolutist system haltingly constructed by the king and Sully, there was equally ample evidence that he was a tyrant by oppression as well. Certainly his religious policies convinced many militant Catholics that a heretic sat on the throne of France. Others were equally convinced that the new centralizing methods of Henry and Sully that changed old ways, eroded old liberties, and rewarded a new official class were facets of tyranny. The nobles deplored Henry's ingratitude, and the peasants and the less well-off often complained not only of the changes but also that the rising power of the new officeholders was used to strip them of their lands and humble feudal privileges. The growing current of absolutism was a revolution imposed from the top, that is, oppression by the king if you and yours did not benefit. While few theologians agreed that a single individual had the right to kill a tyrant by oppression, the consensus was that revolt was then legitimate. And thus there were those who added oppression to the king's calender of sins. No matter that in 1610 Henry and Sully seemed to have solved France's fiscal problems, that within a few years the rapacious policies of his successors would turn him into Good King

Henry, that change does not equate with oppression; for his enemies his guilt was patent. He was a tyrant. And so Ravaillac struck him down.

Ravaillac acted out, in fact, a small but vital role in an age of conspiracy. Europe seemed filled with tyrants, heretics, apostates, atheists, and traitors. The assassin had become a legitimate tool of politics, his deed consecrated by the purity of motive and the evil of the victim. Regimes and their servants conspired, urged the enthusiastic to violence, hired the skilled, subverted the hesitant to violence. Ambassadors, when admitted, were viewed as suspect, seats of subversion, and usually justly so. Thus the first reaction of Henry's advisors and officials after his death was that Ravaillac had been a tool of a grander political vision. This did not appear to be the case, for by 1610, many accepted that an individual could kill a tyrant. Ravaillac's own somewhat halting explanations were general ones—Henry was pursuing an anti-Catholic policy and was illegitimate. Ravaillac's main goal, then, was to punish the apostate, remove the tyrant. It is to be assumed that, if he gave the matter much thought at all, he assumed matters would thus be improved. Henry's successor, forewarned, would pursue a different, more pious course. He, Ravaillac, would have acted upon history even as his body was being burned and torn apart on the Place de Grève. And centuries later the dispassionate and disinterested would largely agree that "with that blow, the whole pattern of European politics changed."[10] He was, in a sense, a great success.

In 1610 Spanish Hapsburg power seemed to have crested. Spain had been driven out of Ireland and forced to make peace with England, where James VI of Scotland became king. In 1609 the armistice with the Dutch rebels had been forced on a reluctant Philip III. In Italy Charles Emmanuel of Savoy had signed the Treaty of Brussalo, agreeing to attack Milan and giving France an Italian ally. In England King James I had agreed to participate in Henry's war plans. Everywhere Henry IV had been a constant menace to Philip III, to a Spain that could not afford war and yet longed to fight, to a Spain with wasting assets and an indolent and arrogant leadership. Ravaillac's blow was thus the saving miracle for the House of Hapsburg. During the next decade French power and prestige crumbled. Europe was dominated in a Pax Hispanica. In France the great nobles used the minority of Louis XIII to undo the changes of the king and Sully, the Spanish subverted enemies of the king, and pious Catholics formed a Spanish party and arranged that Louis XIII and the heir to the Spanish throne would marry each other's sisters in 1611. In Italy Savoy was humbled; Venice made peace; Pope Paul V was the Spanish candidate, and anti-Spanish sentiment evaporated. Spanish influence returned in the Palatine, and England and the Netherlands were quiescent. There was a decade of Spanish hegemony with Philip III as Monarch of the World, Spanish manners and models predominated, and everywhere was the binding of the Jesuits under the Pax Hispanica.

There were deeper tides at work. On Philip's death in 1621, the decade of Spanish peace found Spain weaker. Somehow the wicked had flourished. The Dutch were wealthy, the English successful. The old opponents in Italy reappeared. Spain at peace had lost ground and soon Spain at war would lose more. The nobles' brief triumph over absolutism was undone. The French center continued to absorb control, transform old ways and old privileges, raise new tactics and new forms—not without protest. But in the short run, Ravaillac's blow had transformed Europe—and in the long run, as the saying goes, all are dead. For ten years France no longer challenged the Hapsburgs. The power of French Protestantism ebbed, due as much to the restrictions of the Edict of Nantes, which was ultimately revoked, as to new and pious directions. The new oppressions of absolutism eased. Ravaillac had his reward. He had changed history.

The murder of Henry IV on that May afternoon in Paris in 1610 is in many ways an ideal case study of the nature of political murder. First, no one today can be emotionally involved in the death of a monarch three centuries ago, or even terribly concerned about the results. No one but students and specialists care about the problems of seigneuries or tax farms, although the complicity of Jesuits in any conspiracy still intrigues some. Second, the death of Henry IV contains in one form or another most of the vital ingredients of a political assassination. Who murdered, and why?

Was Ravaillac a maniac or not?[11] Was he a child of his times or an aberration? And was the course of history changed by the deed? After three hundred years matters are still not entirely clear. Some consider Ravaillac a madman, others do not. Certainly, at the twentieth attempt on Henry's life, such deeds were hardly novel, but Ravaillac hardly comes through the mists of time as a hired killer or an agent of reasoned conspiracy. Rather, he was clearly a religious fanatic, if nothing more—in a time when Europe abounded in religious fanatics, some commanding armies and others sitting on thrones. And, perhaps most important, rational or no, the impact of his deed can be parsed but, as always with cases of "what might have been," with no assurance of rigor. Still, in the short run things appeared to change, events unfolding that would have seemed improbable in 1610 and unlikely if Henry IV had lived. And in the long run, the direction, perhaps even the speed, of European events seemed little affected. France moved toward absolutism and Spain's penury. The English and Dutch flourished. A religiously divided Europe came to terms with itself. Ravaillac had lived and died very much in an era of transition. He had killed for the past, the old ways, the pure faith, the Pope, and piety. And for a decade under Philip, there was the pious peace of Pax Hispanica, the last Spanish illusion, and then Europe moved on and Ravaillac and Henry became irrelevant, part of the past, linked only for that May afternoon in the history books.

NOTES

The major source for the prologue is Roland Mousnier's *The Assassination of Henry IV, The Tyrannicide Problem and the Consolidation of the French Absolute Monarchy in the Early 17th Century*, London, Faber and Faber, 1973, slightly updated from the original French work published in 1964. Mousnier has included a highly detailed bibliography, pp. 393–414, largely, as is to be expected, in French. An excellent collection of sources on the problem of tyrannicide can be found in Walter Laqueur's *The Terrorism Reader*, Philadelphia, Temple University Press, 1978, and in a paperbound edition by the New American Library; and see the earlier study by Oscar Jaszi and John D. Lewis, *Against the Tyrant: The Tradition and Theory of Tyrannicide*, Glencoe, The Free Press, 1957.

1. Mousnier, *The Assassination of Henry IV*, p. 24.

2. *Ibid.*, p. 25.

3. *Ibid.*.

4. *Ibid.*, p. 31.

5. *Ibid.*, pp. 34–35.

6. *Ibid.*, p. 32.

7. *Ibid.*, p. 50.

8. *Ibid.*, p. 52.

9. See Laquere's *Reader*.

10. H. R. Trevor-Roper, "Spain and Europe 1598–1621," *The New Cambridge Modern History*, Vol. IV *(The Decline of Spain and the Thirty Years War 1609–1648–59)*, Cambridge, Cambridge University Press, 1970, p. 268.

11. Roland Mousnier, "The Exponents and Critics of Absolutism," op. cit. p. 106.

part I

MURDER OF
THE MIGHTY

Every man has the right to kill a tyrant and a
nation cannot take away this right even from
one of its citizens.

ST.-JUST

1

Killing No Murder

> . . . only we under God have the power to pull
> down this Dragon which we have set up. And
> if we do it not, all mankind will repute us ap-
> provers of all the villanies he hath done, and
> authors of all to come. Shall we that would not
> endure a king attempting tyranny, shall we
> suffer a professed tyrant?
>
> SIR EDWARD SAXBY, urging the death of
> Cromwell, in *Killing No Murder*

History books have long been intrigued with assassins and with
all those questions Ravaillac's deed engenders. Murder has been
with us since Cain and Abel, and murder for political reasons
nearly as long. The litany of the slain includes the powerful, the
benevolent and the wise, the vicious and the degenerate. Yet the
act that ties the sprawled and bleeding body of Henry IV together
with the slaughtered emperors of Byzantium, the poisoned Italian
princes, the heretical revolutionaries and martyred presidents, is
little understood. Assassination has, through the centuries, retained an atmosphere of awe and terror, so that even today—
perhaps particularly today, in an era of institutionalized violence,
mass murder, and almost indiscriminate slaughter—the deed engenders anguish rather than reasoned analysis. Like any spectacular and violent novelty, the assassin has attracted considerable
attention and perhaps at no time greater than during the dread

epidemic of American murders: the two Kennedys, Martin Luther King, Malcolm X, and George Lincoln Rockwell—and the maiming of George Wallace. The threats still exist. The vulnerability of the powerful and prominent, in America, continues.

Despite the continuing prevalence of political murder and a concomitant popular and academic concern, there is little agreement even on a general definition of "assassination." Those who murder in the service of the state and those driven by fantasies are often lumped together with the gunmen of urban guerrilla organizations or even organized criminals. When social scientists, always alive to rigorous distinctions and special categories, have sought to fashion a satisfactory definition, they have not been able to satisfy all of their colleagues, much less the less rigorous writers who insist on using the word as they, not the scholars, see fit. The ever-faithful dictionary definition—choose any dictionary—is seldom sufficiently precise.

> *as·sas·si·nate* vt 1 : to murder by sudden or secret attack
> 2 : to injure or destroy unexpectedly and treacherously
> *syn* see KILL

Most see that the deed is sudden, probably treacherous, and certainly murderous. The element of fanaticism as a motive is often introduced. After that you are on your own. Again, those concerned with such matters are inclined to trace the origins of the word itself. The term came from the Arabic *hashshāshin* (those who use hashish), the name for a Shīite Ismā īli sect in the Middle East during the eleventh and twelfth centuries that murdered its opponents, reputedly using agents under the influence of drugs. In the West the first use of the word came in Dante's *Inferno*— *"lo perfido assassin"*—and implied those who murdered for money, precursors of Murder Inc. and the Mafia contract soldier, rather than Lee Harvey Oswald or the gunmen of the *Organization Armée Secrète* of the Algerian war.

Presently, there are a variety of factors arising from the problem of defining assassination. Although the word is sometimes used to mean simply killing, in most cases the victim is a public figure, a prominent man possessed of political power.[1] Just *how* powerful and *how* prominent remains a moot question. Thus, in some of the carefully collected lists of contemporary political scientists some lesser officials are included and some ignored, in part because the sources used, such as *The New York Times Index,* are not all-inclusive. That is, you are more likely to make the *Index* if you are shot in London rather than in Tibet or Yemen. Still, there is general analytical agreement that the victim is prominent and powerful and a political figure. The second difficulty is why the assassins kill. The death of a political figure, of course, has a political impact, but the killer's motive may have little or nothing to do with politics. In South Africa in 1966, for example, one Demitrios Tsafendas felt that he was gradually being consumed by a gigantic, serpent-like tapeworm, a worm that no doctor could find and yet Tsafendas knew existed. Gripped by this fantasy, certain that the doctors were to blame, he decided on vengeance. On September 6, 1966, he entered the South African Parliament, where he worked as a messenger, walked up to Prime Minister Henrik F. Verwoerd, and, in full view of the members, stabbed him to death. Verwoerd was known as "The Doctor" and that had been enough for Tsafendas. Verwoerd was one of *them.* That Verwoerd was also the symbol of the apartheid system, an architect and advocate who had already survived an attempt on his life six years before on April 9, 1960, was irrelevant; for Tsafendas he was "The Doctor" and *they* would do nothing about his tapeworm. He was declared insane and confined for life in Pretoria.

And finally, the most uncertain area of all is the impact of the deed. No matter *what* the assassin intended—to act out his fantasy, kill for profit, or spark a revolution—the death of a political figure has some political impact. What impact is often moot—Verwoerd's murder did not and does not appear to have changed the course of history, but what of French and European events after the murder of Henry IV? What if Gavrilo Princip had not shot and killed Archduke Francis Ferdinand, heir to the throne of Austria-Hungary, on June 28, 1914? Thus what is an assassination is less important than why there is an assassination, and both much less so than the actual impact of the deed.

THE ROOTS OF POLITICAL MURDER

In any case, it is generally agreed that the murder of the mighty has had a long and often spectacular history, and not solely in the West. In fact, for centuries after the rise of feudalism and the establishment of the medieval monarchies and Roman Church, political murder was largely absent from the West. At times elsewhere such political murders were also noticeable by their absence—during much of Chinese history, for example. Still, more often than not, and however narrowly defined, assassination winds like a thread through modern Western history, except for the long recess of the medieval era. For present purposes, a history of assassination is mainly concerned with the evolution of the idea and the increasing practice under changing historical conditions.

Assassination is simply a violent crime with political implications. The nature of the deed seems to have changed little; the problems of definition, of motive, of impact, and of prevalence remain constant. A *history* of assassination is thus only relevant in that such deeds are analyzed. Simply to string together in chronological order the more spectacular murders of Western civilization tells little of the context, little of politics, less of the concept. For example, the instances of tyrannicide are interesting but the evolution of the idea in Western thought is important. Assassination as we know it became a technique of politics simultaneously with the transformation in institutions, ideas, and values associated with the "Renaissance"—one of the categories into which historians for convenience divide up the past. Concurrently there was a concern that such deeds be attacked or defended, explained or authorized, or fitted into the great chain of Western political thought.

The Roman Empire can, for convenience's sake, if not accurately, be said to have ended on a specific date, but the birth of the West is blurred. Certainly, however, by the ninth and tenth centuries, there were recognizable princes, established institutions, and a special, if limited, view of the world. From this time until the beginning of the "Italian method"—political murder as a tool of the city or state—assassination, especially of princes, was rare indeed. Even then, there were few clear cases. On June 9,

1208, Count Otto of Wittelsback murdered King Philip of Swabia, but he was motivated by a private grudge. On October 29, 1268, Conradin of Swabia, the last Hohenstaufen emperor, was captured, tried, and beheaded in Naples, along with his male friend Frederick of Austria, by Charles of Anjou; but at best this might be considered a judicial murder. The same was true when King John of England captured Arthur, his nephew, and executed him. There were a few classic cases, for examples. Wenceslas III of Bohemia was murdered in 929 as a result of a conspiracy hatched by his brother, Boleslav, and in 1308 the Habsburg Albert I was murdered by his nephew John "the Parricide." But assassinations of princes were few, and the most spectacular assassination was that of the Archbishop of Canterbury, Thomas à Becket, by the king's courtiers in what might be called an excess of zeal. In contrast, in the Byzantine Empire during the 1,058 years between 395 and 1453, there were 107 emperors: 8 were killed in war, 12 abdicated, 12 died in prison, 18 were mutilated and dethroned, 23 were assassinated, and 34 died natural deaths. In the fifteenth century the West would also enter an age of assassins; but for the bulk of the medieval period, assassination—even out of personal spite or hot blood, and certainly for political purposes—was rare.

Obviously the elite of the day knew of the concept of tyrannicide even if contemporary instances were unusual. Increasingly the classical authors of Greece and Rome were discovered, largely in Latin text, by the scholars of the cathedral schools. These texts that seemed to foreshadow Christianity, works inspired by God, included discussions of the nature of tyrannicide. There was a Western interest in the concept that extended as well to Biblical examples. Perhaps the most famous advocate of the virtues of tyrannicide was John of Salisbury, who in 1159 completed *Polycraticus,* a work widely read in subsequent centuries and reissued during the reign of Henry IV. He apparently felt that either tyranny by usurpation or tyranny by oppression should be answered by the sword. The tyrant had violated God's law and was thus guilty of treason against God. A great many scholastics subsequently pondered the problem and many came to quite different conclusions. St. Thomas Aquinas advised against tyrannicide even if such tyranny was excessive and intolerable. In any case, the complex and often abstruse analyses of tyrannicide were almost entirely based on classical examples and Biblical citation, thus creating a history of the dead. The Old Testament produced a whole variety of examples: Ehud murders the King of Moal, Joab kills Absalom, and Jehu shoots the tyrant Jehoram through the heart, orders the tyrant Ahaziah to be killed, and has Jezebel thrown out of a window. While the various murders were variously interpreted, the medieval scholastics recognized that in the pagan world of the Greeks and Romans various writers—Aristotle and Cicero and Seneca—viewed tyrannicide with general approval. Seneca was in fact credited with the formula that no sacrifice was more pleasing to God than the blood of a tyrant. As in the case of the Bible, the classical world abounded in examples. Some Greek democracies even arranged for a town crier to wander the streets offering a reward for the assassination of any citizen whose conduct appeared to foreshadow the seizure of power as a tyrant. And Roman history was threaded with the blood of emperors slain in the name of liberty, in fear, in lust for power, and in the name of order: Caesar and Caligula, Domitian, Caracalla, Aurelian, and, even on into the dim last centuries, Valentinian II in 392 and Valentinian III in 455.

Not all these classical examples parsed for clues to the nature of tyrannicide were quite what they seemed. Even the meaning of tyranny became transformed in the cause of advocacy, for the word was to the Greeks not necessarily pejorative but simply a label for a kind of government. One of the great historical examples of the use of assassination to rid citizens of a tyrant and restore the liberties of the city was the murder of Hipparchus by the Athenians Harmodius and Aristogeiton. For two thousand years the advocates of tyrannicide cited this deed that liberated Athens from oppression, but in reality matters were considerably more sordid and the "liberation" difficult to discern. In 527 B.C., the Athenian tyrant Peisistratus died and was succeeded by his eldest son, Hippias. His younger brother, Hipparchus, powerful and influential but *not* the tyrant, fell deeply in love with a young man called Harmodius, who repelled his erotic advances and told in turn his own lover Aristogeiton. He in turn feared that Hipparchus, in order to woo away Harmodius, would use the power of the ruling family, perhaps resorting to force. Consequently Aristogeiton began to consider force himself. Matters became more intense when once again Harmodius refused the advances of Hipparchus, who then publicly insulted the young man's sister. Both Aristogeiton and Harmodius were now determined on "tyrannicide"—they would kill Hippias and his brothers and the crowd would rise to seize their liberties and the two could continue their passionate affair without the advances and insults of the rejected Hipparchus. A few conspirators were added to the plot and the date set for the festival of Panathenaea when the citizens of Athens could carry arms. The attempt collapsed when the two became alarmed that they had been betrayed, but not before in rage and frustration they came upon Hipparchus near the Lecorium and, according to Thucydides, ". . . falling upon him with all the blind fury, one of an injured lover, and the other of a man smarting under an insult, they smote and slew him."[2] Harmodius was killed on the spot and Aristogeiton soon captured. Hipparchus was dead. Hippias, fearful of other assassins, became increasingly oppressive. The two lovers had brought Athens not liberty but further repression. They had killed not nobly but out of base passion, sexual jealousy, and spite. No matter. They entered history as admirable assassins who killed the foul tyrant Hipparchus and restored the liberties of Athens.

The classical legends, the Biblical citations, the learned discourses of the clerics took place largely on a high and very theoretical plane, insomuch as tyrants appeared rarely on the medieval ground, and their murders still more rarely. True, increasingly in Italy, along with the transformation and blossoming of the arts, the revival of learning, and the new styles of architecture, the use of violence for political purposes flourished as well; but elsewhere the prince was largely inviolate. Then on November 23, 1407, the Duke of Orleans, brother of the mad French king, Charles VI, was murdered by eighteen masked men as he left the residence of Queen Isabella of Bavaria. Two days later John the Fearless, Duke of Burgundy and cousin of both Orleans and the King Charles, accepted responsibility for the murder. He had wanted to rid himself of a rival in the king's council. He escaped and briefed John Parvus to conduct his defense. On March 8, 1408, Parvus defended John the Fearless by resting his entire case on the legitimacy of tyrannicide, with recourse to numerous classical and Biblical examples. The Duke of Burgundy, for reasons that had little to do with Parvus's eloquence, was acquitted. This, however, was not the end of the matter, and ultimately the Council of Constance condemned the murder of a tyrant by a private individual. There was continuing confusion as to an absolute ban and regular dissent by philosophers and theologians. And increasingly, in the fifteenth century, there were assassins moved by varying motives who would rid the world of tyrants or rivals.

Certainly in Italy there had been no dearth of tyrants, those by usurpation and those by oppression. Increasingly the assassin became a tool of the state, poisoners available for hire, murderers paid by uneasy princes. Lacking the confusions and concerns of the theorists examining the moral justification of tyrannicide, the Italians killed pragmatically, for political purposes, for fear of usurpation, for power. Yet even in the fierce and brutal politics of the Italian Renaissance, the moral assassin was not absent. In the fifteenth century few Italian princes had as sordid a reputation as that false and ferocious man Galeazzo Maria Sforza, Duke of Milan. There came together three men determined to rid Milan of the tyrant. One, Carlo Visconti, was motivated by tradition; the Sforzas had stolen Milan from the Viscontis. The other two, the students Girolamo Olgiati and Gian Andrea Lampugnani, perhaps owing to their study of the classics, loved liberty and despised tyranny. They would be the Harmodius and Aristogeiton of Milan. So while they practiced with their daggers they read the classics, seeking inspiration in Sallust and Tacitus. On December 26, 1476, St. Stephen's Day, they stabbed and killed the Duke in St. Stephen's Church. Visconti and Lampugnani were killed by Sforza's bodyguards. Olgiati lived to be tortured to death. He refused to repent: "My death is untimely; my fame eternal, the memory of my deed will endure forever."[3] The modern assassin had arrived on the European stage. There would be philosophical advocates for tyrannicide, such as the Jesuit Mariana and the Venetian Paolo Sarpi with his face scarred by an assassin's knife. There would be practitioners acting in the name of a higher order, such as Olgiati, or for more narrow political purposes, such as Visconti. Some would be gripped by an obsession like Ravaillac's; some would be demented.

With the collapse of the universal church in the West and the long drawn-out wars of religion, wars that ended only with a toleration from exhaustion, Europe lived in an era of conspiracy and murder. There was a decline in legitimacy—every prince was someone's usurper. Imposed authority could be and was resisted by recourse to tyrannicide. With the rise of monarchical absolutism and the uneasy acceptance of religious diversity, there was relative calm—but the long invulnerability of the medieval prince had gone. This does not mean the age of absolutism was without incidents of assassination, although the horror that arose when Damien struck at Louis XV once with a penknife indicates a surprise at such treacherous violence that did not exist when Ravaillac struck at Henry IV. There were, however, no long-lived conspiracies, no real institutionalization of assassination, no "history" —rather incidents imbedded in special places, processes, and personalities. The modern assassin, as an individual, as a co-conspirator, as an agent of the state, may, like the advocates of tyrannicide, appeal to a higher law; he may, like the Italians, act out of greed or for vengeance; but his deed, with its purpose and rationale, arises not from the experience of the French kings or Italian despots but from the ideas and responses to the concepts of the Age of Reason, from the implications of the French and American revolutions, and from the impact of the industrial revolution. In order to kill Jean Paul Marat, Charlotte Corday did not need to look to the example of Ravaillac or the litany of classical examples. Marat had betrayed the revolution and that was sufficient. Thus for historical purposes the idea of assassination as a legitimate—or for some illegitimate—deed entered the West in ancient garb long before real assassins begin to kill in Italy, a sign of modernity and declining legitimacy. After that, in turbulent and uncertain times or within uncertain and vulnerable governments, the assassin was never completely absent from European events. With the spread of the ideas of the Age of Reason and the vast transformation engendered by industrialization, with the decay of absolutism and the vulnerability of new princes, Europe (as it had in Henry's time) entered another era of assassination. Once again some deeds were by the demented; many were by the lone killer acting in the name of a higher authority; but during the nineteenth and twentieth centuries there were long periods when assassination was as much a tool of revolutionaries as prisons and guillotines were of the threatened. Assassination became part of the political fabric of the West. In 1897 King Humbert of Italy narrowly escaped the dagger of the anarchist blacksmith Pietro Acciarito. After evading the knife, the king ordered his coachman to drive on—"*Sono gli incerti del mestiere*"—"These are the risks of the job."[4] And for almost two hundred years this has been the case. Just as Henry IV failed to survive the twentieth attempt and William of Orange the sixth, so too did modern kings and presidents remain repeated targets. In the nineteenth century Louis Philippe of France evaded eighteen attempts and in the twentieth century Charles de Gaulle survived at least thirty.

During the past two centuries there have been strands or currents of assassination, some very long-lived and some the fashion of a single decade. There have been repeated murders by confused and muddled assassins driven by obscure and improbable obsessions. On January 30, 1835, President Andrew Jackson escaped death when the two pistols of Richard Lawrence misfired. Lawrence, who at times imagined himself to be King Richard III of England, felt that Jackson was involved in a conspiracy to hold back money due him from the United States government. He was tried, was found not guilty by reason of insanity, and spent the remainder of his life in a mental institution. There were those lone murderers on the brink of reason, caught up in some luminous political idea. In Paris in 1892, the police arrested a young man called Ravachol for two political bombings and then uncovered a whole series of crimes including grave robbery and the murder of a ninety-two-year-old woman. "See this hand?" he said. "It has killed as many bourgeois as it has fingers."[5] A practitioner of the *culte de moi,* an Ego Anarchist, he believed that all was permitted, that society was evil incarnate, that there were no innocents. There was as well the lone assassin who chose a victim with care and carried out the deed with skill, who was driven not by fantasy or self-serving slogans but by reasoned analysis. As often as not the lone assassin acted in the midst of a revolutionary campaign at a time of revolt or repression. On Sunday, July 29, 1900, Gaetano Bresci, who had saved expense money from his job in a textile plant in Paterson, New Jersey, shot and killed King Humbert of Italy. His anarchist friends in the United States approved of the deed, and in New York Emma Goldman said, "We have never plotted for the death of the monarch, but the assassin has our sympathy."[6] Bresci was sentenced to life imprisonment. "I shall appeal after the coming revolution,"[7] he declared, but reportedly committed suicide in prison ten months later. If Bresci were not part of a revolutionary conspiracy, many others were. In Ireland there were the Fenians, in Russia the People's Will, in the Balkans the Black Hand, and throughout much of Europe the anarchists. Some campaigns of assassination would flare up for a few years and then be snuffed out by repression or an acceptance of the futility of murder. In a case such as Ireland, for generation after generation there was the cycle of revolt and repression and quiescence.

And in special places, political assassination became endemic— in Haiti since 1806 twenty-eight presidents, presidents-elect, or former presidents have been murdered. At special times assassination has been one of the risks of power—between 1894 and 1914 six heads of state were assassinated by professed anarchists: President Carnot of France in 1894, Premier Canovas of Spain in 1897, Empress Elizabeth of Austria in 1898, King Humbert in 1900, President McKinley in 1901, and Premier Canaljas of Spain in 1912. Such murder, legitimized by the revolutionary as a moral act in defiance of institutionalized oppression or undertaken as a practical means to a desired end, became during the nineteenth and twentieth centuries an integral part of the political process. And these murders in most cases were political in intent, even if the politics, like those of the Frenchman Ravachol, were grotesque.

> *It will come, it will come,*
> *Every bourgeois will have his bomb.*
> *"La Ravachole" (French street song)*

Besides the reasonable bombers and gunmen there were the psychopaths prattling at times popular slogans—Richard Lawrence, "King Richard III of England," felt that killing Jackson would permit the Bank of the United States to be rechartered. Although no country appeared immune to the psychopathic assassin, the United States appeared especially vulnerable, with the presidency a magnet for the mad. The attacks on Presidents Jackson, Lincoln (possibly), Garfield, McKinley, Theodore Roosevelt, Franklin Roosevelt, John F. Kennedy, and Gerald Ford were by individuals who appeared to be seriously disturbed—and this was true with many of those who attacked other major American political figures or who were satisfied with threats or plots. While there can be some correlation between external events—divisive issues or political turmoil—a history of the psychopathic assassinations must focus on psychic phenomena rather than on a political process. The murderer Ravachole was a facet of a French political process. "Richard III" was irrelevant to American politics. Although a history of assassination has to consider the role of the psychopath, not to mention those who are authorized to murder for the state or take upon themselves as vigilantes the responsibility of using violence to protect a threatened system, the most politically significant deeds have been those arising from reasoned conspiracies with definable aims open to subsequent analysis—the attempt on President Harry S. Truman by Puerto Rican nationalists, or the murder of Spanish Premier Admiral Luis Carrero Blanco in Madrid on December 20, 1973, by members of the Basque organization ETA. Perhaps the most spectacular of all modern assassinations, at least in regard to the apparent impact on the direction of events, was the murder of Archduke Francis Ferdinand of Austria-Hungary on June 28, 1914.

During the century before World War I, if there was any clear direction in Balkan events, it was the continuing and largely successful challenge to the multi-ethnic empires by various nationalists. The Ottoman Empire, supposedly the sick man of Europe, had been losing ground since the beginning of the Greek war of independence in 1821. In recognition of the aspirations of the Magyars, the Austrian Empire had in 1867 become the Austro-Hungarian Empire; but this did little to satisfy the ambitions of the Czechs, the Slovenes, Serbs, Croats, or Italians within imperial boundaries. And outside the empire the Slavs, encouraged by the self-interested Russians, the independent existence of the tiny state Montenegro, and the Greek success, tended to see the major enemy of the new nationalism as the Ottomans—the Turks were alien Islamic occupiers who kept the Christians in misery and degradation, ruling by intimidation and repression.

Two of the most primitive and miserable of the Turkish provinces were Bosnia and Herzogovina, an isolated land of rugged mountains and narrow fertile valleys. The Turks had been content to rule by collecting tribute from the conquered Slavs, who, hidden away from the bustling European world of the nineteenth century, continued in the old peasant ways. In Bosnia, society for the Christians (the Eastern Orthodox Serbs or the Roman Catholic Croats) remained structured by a family association—the *zadruga*—that in turn was part of a clan with a feudal overlord. Between the direct tribute paid to the Ottomans and the feudal dues paid to the clan lord, the peasant-serfs—Serbian *kmets*—eked out a miserable and uncertain existence without hope or prospect of comfort. In 1875 the *kmets* of West Bosnia revolted. The women and children fled to sanctuary in Austria-Hungary and the men, even those who had served Turkish authorities, harassed and held off the Turkish army in the rugged mountains for two years. The war spread to Serbia and Montenegro, then to Bulgaria; but the crucial moment came when, for a variety of imperial reasons, Russia attacked Turkey. Beset by escalating nationalist risings throughout the Balkans, directed by incompetents and corrupt leaders, unable to halt the Russian advance, Turkey appeared on the edge of collapse. Such a collapse would most assuredly transform the precarious European balance of power. Britain dispatched a fleet to Istanbul. Austria-Hungary mobilized the army. No one cared much for the Turks, who in 1876 had crushed the Bulgarian rising with such ferocity that their reprisals became known as the Bulgarian Atrocities; but the Balkan ambitions of the various major powers had to be carefully balanced to fill what appeared to be a growing vacuum as the Terrible Turks collapsed. This was done at the Congress of Berlin, far from the escarpments of Western Bosnia.

To a degree the Turks were everyone's second choice—would an independent Bulgaria be a Russian pawn or a center for subversive nationalism? Was it time for full Romanian independence, and would this lead to irredentist demands? And what of a free Serbia? The solution, as far as Bosnia and Herzogovina were concerned, was both cunning and irrelevant to the aspirations of the rebels. The Turkish Sultan retained sovereignty over the two provinces, but Austria-Hungary would occupy and administer them. The rebels had exchanged one imperial oppressor for another. The dream of an independent South Slavic state including Serbia and Montenegro remained unrealized. So in the wild up-country the *kmets* continued a sullen, low-level, irregular campaign of resistance to the authorities, to the tax collector, to conscription.

In August 1907, Gavrilo Princip enrolled at the Merchants' School in Sarajevo instead of the military academy as originally planned—better a rich merchant than a Hapsburg officer who might have to make war on his own people. Princip came from the turbulent West Bosnia; his grandfather Jovo had been a Turkish policeman—*a zaptije*—had resigned, had fought in the rebellion after 1875, and had been killed while shooting ducks during the irregular war. His father would have preferred that Princip stay bound to the land and the ways of the past, but his uncle and his mother insisted that he go to school. As a boy he was a great reader and made good grades, receiving a prize; but when pressed, he became violent and aggressive at any slight, intimidating the older boys. In 1907, at thirteen, he traveled to Sarajevo and the Merchants' School. He would board with the widow Ilić, sleeping in a room with her son Danilo, who was seventeen.

After the death of his father, Danilo had been forced to scramble to help his mother make ends meet. He had sold newspapers and worked as a prompter and handyman in a theater, a laborer, railway porter, quarryman, longshoreman—anything available—before finally graduating as a teacher in 1912, five years after Princip had shared his bedroom. Danilo and after him Princip were typical examples of the new Serb. They had scrambled out of the misery and isolation of the mean peasant villages of the empire because of talent and drive, because of parental ambitions, because of the help of Serbian educational institutions. Each scraped and scrimped through school, half shepherd, half scholar, suddenly consumed by the variety and power of contemporary ideas. The great outside world of the universities opened a bewildering series of doors—socialism and anarchism, nationalism, idealism and radicalism, the words of Marx or Bakunin or Mazzini. The deeds of distant revolutionaries became as familiar as the exploits of the *kmet* guerrillas. Some went very far afield. Ilić traveled to Switzerland to meet with the Serbian nationalist Vladimir Gaciović and his Russian Menshevik friends. Ilić, like Gaciović, was dedicated to revolution, to change brought about by violence, for he believed there could be no liberation for the South Slavs as long as Austria-Hungary existed. And it had been made abundantly clear that the Hapsburgs intended to thwart the separatist dream —in 1908 Vienna had formally annexed Bosnia and Herzegovina. There had been talk of a federated empire—and instead of the dual Austria-Hungary arrangement, the aspirations of the Czechs and Slavs might be recognized. Gradually, there was less hope of change. The old emperor Franz Josef, who had come to the throne in 1848, lived on and on without interest in change. His latest heir, Archduke Francis Ferdinand, grew older too, more conservative, less open. Even the moderate Serbs lost hope in constitutional change. And increasingly the young nationalists had no time for moderation.

Between 1903 and 1906 the Croatians forcefully resisted their Magyar overlords in Hungary but to the disappointment of the Hapsburgs showed no more loyalty to Vienna than had the Slavs. And there were riotous demonstrations in the Slavic provinces favoring the Croatians. In 1906 Franz Ferdinand paid an official visit to the Slavic provinces, where he was received by the crowds in sullen silence and, in Dubrovnik, with insults. Whatever lingering sympathy the archduke might have had for his Slavic subjects evaporated. In Bosnia and Herzegovina the industrial workers came out on strike for a nine-hour day and regular wages. They were joined by the *kmets* and the free peasants. The landowners and industrialists appealed to Vienna. The army was dispatched and the strike broken forcefully. There would be no concessions to Slavs. In 1908 Bosnia-Herzegovina was formally annexed. Vienna wanted to make it quite clear that there would never be a greater Slavic state.

Slavic, especially Serbian, nationalism could not so easily be suppressed, and with the growing rigidity in Vienna, repression was the empire's only option. Within the Slavic provinces an increasing number of the moderates responded by either joining existing secret nationalist cells or forming new ones. These were murky and uncertain organizations, variants of the nineteenth-century movement of Young Bosnia. They split and merged, dissolved and reappeared, always under romantic names, always replenished by the dedicated young, the new generation of high school and college students. And with rare exception they looked for aid and comfort to Belgrade, capital of a free Serbia. There the key figure in the nationalist conspiracy was Colonel Dragutin Dimitrijevic, known as Colonel Apis, and the secret *Ukendinjenje ili Smrt* organization.

Colonel Apis was no novice at conspiracy or in the practice of violence. In 1903 he had played a major part in the army coup that killed King Alexander and Queen Draga. In fact, when the two dozen officers broke into the palace, Apis had been wounded by a bodyguard. Fearful that the coup would fail, he had waited with a revolver to his head while his fellow officers searched the palace for the royal couple. Eventually a secret room behind the royal bathroom was discovered. There the king and queen, crouched in fear, looked up and quickly promised reforms. The officers paid no attention, emptied their revolvers into the pair, and then mutilated the bodies with their sabres. Apis lowered his revolver; suicide would be unnecessary. The king and queen were thrown out of the window into the courtyard while the elated officers cried, "The tyrants are no more." And now Apis felt that there could be no greater tyrants than the Hapsburgs. He opened up lines into the empire, keeping in touch with the secret societies remaining in the background, feeling for the most effective string to pull, seeking the most spectacular plot to strike at Vienna. In the increasingly charged atmosphere of Serbian nationalism, individuals decided for themselves to strike a blow. On June 3, 1911, Bogdan Zerajdic, a twenty-three-year-old son of a peasant, borrowed a revolver from a student and prepared to kill the Emperor Franz Josef as he visited Sarajevo. He did not fire. Twelve days later, with his borrowed revolver, he stood in front of General Marijan Varesanin, governor of two provinces, and shot him five times and then shot himself dead. Varesanin survived. Zerajdic, whose last words were "I leave my revenge to Serbdom,"[8] was buried in an unmarked grave.

Assassinations by Balkan nationalists by 1911 were hardly rare —in fact, only the revolutionary anarchists had fashioned a longer butcher's bill. Emperor Franz Josef had been close to violence for much of his career. Crown Prince Rudolf and his mistress Marie Vetsern died in a suicide pact at the palace at Meyerling. The next heir, Archduke Karl Ludwig, while on a pilgrimage to Jerusalem, had sipped the waters of the Jordan and died of typhus, leaving Franz Ferdinand as heir-apparent. The emperor's brother Maximilian von Hapsburg had become involved with Napoleon III in a Mexican adventure and was executed by Juárez. Maximilian's wife spent the remainder of her life in an asylum. There had been attempts on the imperial couple. As early as 1853, the Hungarian Janos Libenyi had knifed Franz Josef, who barely recovered. There had been a campaign of assassination in Vienna in 1884. Then, on September 10, 1898, Empress Elizabeth was killed on leaving her hotel at Geneva to take the lake steamer. Luigi Lucheni, a former soldier in an Italian cavalry regiment, discharged the year before, had decided to kill someone for "anarchism." Too poor to buy a stiletto, he had honed down a file and hovered outside the hotel until the empress emerged. He rushed up, peered under the parasol to make sure of his victim, and then stabbed Elizabeth through the heart. He was "delighted" that her death played a part in the war on the rich and the great. It was small wonder that the Hapsburgs grew remote, withdrawn, and increasingly repressive after years in death's shadow.

There was little doubt that Colonel Apis and his conspirators, the mysterious *Ukendinjenje ili Smrt,* the volunteers in the Young Bosnia cells, the lone gunmen like Zerajdic, the itinerant collectors of revolutionary ideas such as Danilo Ilić or Vladimir Gaciović and their young converts like Gavrilo Princip, saw the Hapsburgs as the target. In 1912 and 1913 during the two Balkan wars, the Turkish position in the Balkans collapsed and Slavic ambitions increased. It seemed certain that in a third war the suzerainty of Hapsburgs might be ended and a united Slavic state—Yugoslavia —established. And what better way to begin a war than with the death of a tyrant, a Hapsburg. And so inside the empire and in Serbia the plots went on, secretly, often without any contact or cooperation with other nationalist societies. Even at the center of the net, Colonel Apis could not keep track of all the threads of conspiracy. Then in March 1914, it was discovered that Archduke Francis Ferdinand would visit Sarajevo, capital of Bosnia, during military maneuvers to be held in June. His presence in Bosnia would be a warning to Serbia that Belgrade's victories in the two Balkan wars had not transformed the situation in Bosnia-Herzegovina. In Belgrade three young men decided that this was their opportunity to strike.

Gavrilo Princip had received the word in a newspaper clipping sent by City Hall in Sarajevo to avoid the censor. Since his arrival in Danilo Ilić's house in 1907, Princip had led a confused student's existence. After three years at the Merchants' School, his increasing concern with Serbian literature and history made a career as a rich merchant less attractive and he had switched to the Classical High School in Tuzla after passing a stiff examination in Latin and Greek. He then transferred to the high school in Sarajevo, where he would need to finish two more grades to graduate. By 1912 he was deeply involved in Serbian nationalism and joined at least one of the Young Bosnian societies. He dedicated himself to the nation, refusing to drink, avoiding girls and those who had no ideals. He read constantly—Serb-Croat literature, Slavic history, the new ideas of socialism and anarchism. In 1912 he took part in a public demonstration against the Austrian authorities and was promptly expelled from school. He walked to Belgrade and led the hand-to-mouth existence of an expelled student, sleeping in doorways, begging in the streets, cadging an occasional meal from the local monastery, but always reading on revolution, talking to the dedicated. He was increasingly determined to perform a great deed. And in 1912 when Serbia went to war he rushed to join the army —and was refused as too small and weak. Frail, intense, with a sallow complexion and burning blue eyes, he looked more like the poet he hoped to be than the soldier the Serbs needed. He returned to high school to finish the last two grades, embittered but no less determined. The arrival of the newspaper clipping from Sarajevo suddenly and unexpectedly opened the door for Princip; there would be a chance to change history, to perform the great deed, to kill the enemy of the Serbs, Archduke Francis Ferdinand.

The heir to the Hapsburg throne was fifty in 1914, a large stolid man, morose, heavy, and gloomy. He abhorred the disloyal Slavs, distrusted the Magyars, suspected a Jewish conspiracy behind the rise of both finance-capitalism and socialism. He had become an arch centralist, profoundly opposed to any change, a social reactionary and a man without need for affection or admiration beyond his family. At least at home, there was a continuing trace of spirit, for despite family opposition the archduke had married the love of his life, Czech countess Sophie Chotek von Chotkova. At the insistence of Franz Josef, the union was a morganatic one, so that the archduke's son would not inherit the throne; but it was also an extremely successful one. Although many felt the Duchess of Hohenberg to be vain, excessively religious, and even ambitious of becoming empress, Francis Ferdinand was delighted. In 1914 after fourteen years of marriage, the archduke at fifty and the duchess at forty-six remained happily married, the parents of two sons and a daughter. She had always been a resolute supporter in troubled times, and insisted on accompanying him on his visit to Bosnia, a visit that caused certain doubts about the heir's security. The province remained turbulent and hostile; security officials were aware of the existence of various nationalist conspiracies; there was serious tension with Serbia. Friends advised him not to go, and he talked jokingly about the prospect of bombs being thrown. But as Inspector-General of the Army he would, of course, go. And his wife the Duchess of Hohenberg would, of course, accompany him. The two would arrive at Ilidze Spa south of Sarajevo on June 25 to meet the governor, General Potiorek. Army maneuvers would begin the next day.

Well before the archduke set out for Bosnia, Princip had begun preparations for his arrival. He had first gone to his friend Nedeljko Cabrinović, the nineteen-year-old son of a cafe proprietor, who agreed to make an attempt on the archduke. Next to be recruited was Trifko Grabez, Princip's former roommate at school. This was the basic *troika*-cell. They approached known nationalists who in turn supplied them with four revolvers, six bombs, and cyanide pills, all probably donated by Colonel Apis. Princip took his Browning revolver to an isolated section of Kosutujak Park to practice marksmanship. The three then slipped across the border into Bosnia. At this stage Princip's old roommate

Danilo Ilić became the coordinator of the operation and a second *troika*-cell was organized: Mehmed Mehmedbasić, a Moslem; Vasco Cubrilović, who was only seventeen; and Cvetko Popović, another member of an ultra-nationalist secret society. They were all very young (even Ilić was only twenty-four), very dedicated, steeped in a long litany of grievances and the history of Hapsburg oppression. Yet there were doubts, especially on the part of Ilić, who was not sure Bosnia was politically prepared for such a deed. Princip was unswerving. The time for the deed had come. Even a last-minute message that Colonel Apis had doubts did not sway him. The other conspirators agreed to go ahead on June 28, when the archduke's limousine would move down Appel Quay along-side the River Miljacka. On the morning of the twenty-eighth, Ilić stationed his two *troikas* along a three-hundred-yard stretch: first Mehmedbasić with a bomb, then Vasco Cubrilović with a Browning and a bomb, then Cabrinović with a grenade, then Popović, with himself as a back-up, and finally Princip with a Browning near the Lateimer Bridge and Grabez further along the quay.

The archduke and the duchess left the Hotel Bosnia at the Spa Ilidze, and took the train to Sarajevo. There they would motor down Appel Quay to be received at the town hall, go sightseeing in the capital, and then have lunch at the Governor's Palace, followed by visits to the museum, the mosque, and the Army inspectorate headquarters. It was to be a typical imperial set-piece, formal and stolid. The couple left the train and arranged themselves in a long, open, Viennese sports car. The archduke, with his elongated cavalry mustaches, his huge green-plumed hat, and his elaborate three-starred general's uniform, looked like a storybook heir-apparent. The duchess, now plump, wore a white silk dress with fresh flowers in a red sash, a huge white picture hat, and a cape of ermine tails thrown across her shoulders. She carried a white parasol to ward off the sun. The six-car caravan moved out at a quick pace, passing the rows of Austrian flags and the red-and-yellow emblems of Bosnia. Portraits of the archduke were gar-landed with national colors and the crowds were reasonably sympathetic.

The six cars swept past Mehmedbasić, who hesitated to throw

his bomb while a policeman stood next to him, and then it was too late. The cars were going too quickly for second thoughts. They came abreast of Cubrilović, who recognized the royal couple but could not bring himself to shoot with the duchess in the car. At this point, ten minutes after ten, the next in line, Cabrinović, leaned over and asked a policeman which car carried the archduke. The policeman told him. Cabrinović hurriedly knocked the pin out of his grenade against a lamppost and began counting the recommended number of seconds. The archduke's limousine suddenly loomed up alongside him. He tossed his grenade. It arched up, bounded behind Francis Ferdinand's head and tumbled off the folded hood onto the road. The archduke's car kept going. No one in it had noticed. The grenade detonated under the next car, injuring several of the escorts. The other cars hurriedly stopped. There was considerable confusion. Cabrinović swallowed the poison, which was only to burn his mouth, and leaped into the Miljacka, which was so low that the security men had no trouble in pulling him back over the parapet. When asked who he was, he replied, "A Serbian hero."

The first car, with the mayor and chief of police, drove on to the Town Hall to prepare the official welcome. The archduke, noting that no cars were following, had the chauffeur stop and sent back an aide to find out what was the matter. The news was that about twenty civilians and three Austrian officers had been injured. The archduke then ordered the limousine on to the Town Hall. It drove on down Appel Quay past Princip, who did not recognize the archduke until it was too late to fire his revolver, and then Grabez hesitated to throw his bomb near the swirling crowd. At the Town Hall, ignoring the bomb attack, the mayor proceeded with his prepared flowery welcoming speech, stressing the loyalty and devotion of the Bosnian people. The archduke was not amused. "Herr Bürgomeister, what is the good of your speeches? I come to Sarajevo on a friendly visit and someone throws a bomb at me. This is outrageous."[9] It also appeared to have been futile. The ceremonies proceeded. At the duchess's insistence, the good Bürgomeister continued his welcoming address from the point where he had been interrupted. The wives of the Moslem notables trooped by the duchess and Francis Ferdinand chatted with Bosnian officials. The governor assured him that there was no danger of any second attempt. Francis Ferdinand, however, decided to change his program, and instead of going along Franz Josef Street to visit the museum he would drive back along Appel Quay, now cleared by security forces, and visit the wounded officers in the Military Hospital. Once again the cortege started out, led by the governor's car and then that of the archduke. Inexplicably the governor's chauffeur turned off Appel Quay on to Franz Josef Street—the cancelled route. In turn the archduke's limousine followed. In the first car the governor ordered his driver to stop. Francis Ferdinand's driver followed suit. The archduke's limousine was crawling along, the motor idling, just in front of Moritz Schiller's delicatessen, almost at the corner of Appel Quay and Franz Josef Street. It had been less than ninety minutes since Cabrinović had tossed his grenade. The huge royal car had almost stopped beside Princip, who had been loitering on the corner to see if the procession would return.

Princip recognized the archduke. He saw a lady sitting next to him. "I reflected for a moment whether I should shoot or not."[10] He raised the Browning revolver. A security policeman saw the revolver and rushed at the young man, but an out-of-work actor named Pusara spontaneously shoved him, giving Princip a moment. He took it and aimed at the archduke and fired "twice, perhaps more, because I was so excited." He did not know if he had hit Francis Ferdinand. A second volunteer, Ferdinand Behr, punched the policeman in the stomach to allow Princip to escape. But he stood beside the limousine in a daze as someone else, a man named Velic, knocked away his revolver. He was bundled into custody. In the limousine Princip's first shot had ripped through the side of the car and into the duchess, who sat on the archduke's right side barring a straight line of fire. The second bullet, fired a bit higher, almost at once smashed through the high collar with the three general's stars, cut the archduke's jugular vein, and lodged in his spine. The duchess cried out to Francis Ferdinand, "For God's sake, what has happened to you?" She slumped forward and sank to her knees, her head in her husband's lap. He looked down and said, "Sophie, Sophie, don't die. Live for my children." She was already dying. A noble from the escort reached the side of the archduke and asked if he were in pain. He replied, "It is nothing. It is nothing." And he died. The bodies were taken to the governor's walled residence and pronounced dead. At half past eleven, the bells of Sarajevo began to toll in mourning. They tolled not simply for an archduke and his duchess but for an era, for Europe; the fuse to the Balkan bomb had been lit.

The immediate order of business for the authorities was to seize the conspirators, to try them, and especially to punish them. Even those only remotely connected with the conspiracy were arrested. Between October 12 and 27, some twenty-five Serbians were tried. The defendants' principal argument in court was, in effect, that such a killing was no murder—the archduke was a tyrant by usurpation, a tyrant by oppression. Princip said, "I do not feel like a criminal because I put away the one who was doing evil. Austria as it is represents evil for our people and therefore should not exist." Serbia required the death of the Hapsburg as an act of vengeance, as an act of state. And so Princip and the others had acted. Most of the conspirators escaped hanging because they were under twenty. Actually Princip was just twenty, but an error on the birth register saved him. Three were executed, including Danilo Ilić and the brother of Vasco Cubrilović, who had hesitated to fire with the duchess in the car. Vasco received sixteen years in prison, Popović thirteen. Cabrinović, who had thrown the bomb, was sentenced to twenty, as were Princip and Grabez. Of the thirteen imprisoned, only five survived the ordeal of an imperial prison. Ill-fed, ill-clothed, without proper medical attention, despised by the wardens, they shuffled out the years in dank cells. Princip, Cabrinović, and Grabez, besides the years of hard labor, were also required to fast once a month on a hard bed in a darkened cell. Within two years Cabrinović and Grabez died of tuberculosis and malnutrition. Princip lost an arm to the same disease and then, on April 28, 1918, his life. When the authorities discovered his ravaged body curled on the cot, they found on the wall in his handwriting his own epitaph.

> Our ghosts will walk through Vienna
> And roam through the Palace,
> Frightening the lords.

At the end of the year, when the surviving prisoners were released, including Cubrilović and Popović, Vienna was indeed filled with ghosts. The Hapsburgs had gone. There would be a Yugoslavia but no end to Slavic assassins. There were tens of millions dead on the battlefields of Europe, no Emperor, no Kaiser, no Tsar; the specter of communism threatened Europe, as did starvation. Europe and the world had been changed, utterly changed, in a tidal wave of violence that flowed from those two unsteady shots fired just after ten on the morning of June 28 in the then obscure Bosnian capital of Sarajevo.

Although the assassination at Sarajevo was certainly the crucial precedent of the European war that the conspirators had sought, it was not *the* historical cause. Nearly sixty years later Vaso Cubrilović, who as a historian had taught forty years at the University of Belgrade, insisted that the seven young men were not responsible. "The outbreak of the war had nothing to do with individuals. The war had deep roots, including the disruptive effects of rapid industrialization in old feudal societies."[11] True, they had wanted a war. "Experience in the Balkans had taught us that a state can be born in war, and also can be destroyed in war. We wanted to destroy Austria-Hungary." Years before, Andre Zhelyabou of the executive committee of the Russian revolutionary organization People's Will had said that "history moves terribly slowly, we must give it a push." Cubrilović and the others felt they had given history a push. The implication is that war was, if not inevitable, at least impending, so that the assassination acted as a lever, prying the various powers into predictable paths.

At various times in previous decades there had been seemingly as serious diplomatic crises—in fact, since the establishment of the largely fulfilled German Empire of the Hohenzollern and the Italian Kingdom of the House of Savoy after the Franco-Prussian war, European history had been one diplomatic crisis after another. What was special about the summer of 1914 was that this time those responsible felt that the very existence of their state might be in jeopardy, not simply prestige or colonial possessions or special advantages. The Hapsburgs had grown increasingly despondent over the course of Balkan history since the Congress of Berlin had recognized the independence of Bulgaria, Romania, and Serbia. The new nationalities were on the march. Turkey had gone and the existence of the empire was at stake. Thus there were those in Vienna, although not the emperor, who seized on the assassination as the ideal provocation to smash Serbian pretensions. The Germans, troubled at home by a variety of ills, were fearful that Austria-Hungary, their only real ally, would be unable to prevail over nationalist demands. As soon as he heard of Sarajevo the Kaiser wrote: "The Serbs will have to be straightened out, *and soon.* "[12] So on July 5, he assured Franz Josef of German backing, which meant that the Austro-Hungarian ultimatum sent to Serbia on July 23 was so severe that Belgrade could not really accept it and remain an independent state, although the Serbs did concede practically everything. If Serbia were crushed, Russia would be humiliated, her word useless, her posture as defender of the Slavs proven hollow, and the decay of power already so obvious after the humiliating defeat by Japan in 1905 irreversible. So when Austria-Hungary attacked Serbia on July 28 after a brief delay, Russia two days later ordered mobilization—which in effect meant war, and almost certainly war with Germany, Vienna's pledged ally. On August 1, Germany declared war on Russia; but because all mobilization and war preparations—the Schlieffen Plan—had prepared the empire for an attack first on France, there would now be a two-front war. On August 3, Germany declared war on France, and at midnight the following night the British ultimatum demanding German withdrawal from Belgium expired. Europe was at war. None of the attempts by the well-meaning or the reluctant along the way had been effective.

One certain reason the crisis led to general war was that the quality of European leadership left much to be desired. Many of the monarchs and politicians were prey to the devices and desires of their own hearts, believing what they chose even when told differently. Both the Tsar of Russia and Kaiser Wilhelm II were very limited men and many of their ministers were more so. Franz Josef was very old. A second key reason for the slide to war was that almost no one considered war unthinkable. This war would be like the last: a war of military campaigns, probably relatively brief—over by Christmas—that would have certain political consequences on boundaries and alignments. All felt these adjustments to be crucial, but none foresaw that the entire European system would be swept away—even Colonel Apis and his friends might have drawn further back if they had realized the cost that Europe and the Slavs would have to pay. All of these conditions in the summer of 1914 seemed likely to continue for some time —first, the dangers of Serbian nationalism, the concerns of Vienna and Berlin, the fears of St. Petersburg, the Schlieffen Plan, and the Anglo-French detente with Russia; second, the caliber of political leadership; and third, the concept of limited military war. Thus, although speculation is more entertaining than enlightening, if Princip had not fired his two unsteady shots, perhaps, sooner or later, history would no longer have needed a push. Maybe.

Sarajevo is certainly a most typical political assassination in many ways. In some form most of the components of political murder can be found, and most of the problems of analysis. In the Balkans in general and in the Slavic provinces of the Austro-Hungarian Empire, murder was an acceptable political act. Just as Ravaillac believed he had the right to kill a tyrant, so too did Princip. Vaso Cubrilović emphasized, "We knew it was not possible to defeat a strong state like Austria-Hungary by peaceful means. The only way to achieve change was by violence."[13] The revolutionary Friedrich Stapsz insisted, "To kill you is not a crime but a duty." So Sarajevo was a legitimate act that took place during an era of assassinations. There had not been as many attempts on the Hapsburgs as on the life of Henry IV; but assassination in the decades before 1914 was *normal*—a risk of the powerful, as King Humbert said. The archduke was certainly a highly visible symbol of all the Serbs detested; his death would be just in itself but, more important, might have considerable effect—to push history.

Then, too, the organization of the attempt—the techniques and tactics—readily reflected the considerable amount of uncertainty and the importance of the contingent and unforeseen. Many conspiracies are far less structured than historians or journalists would like. There are instead uncertain groups with shifting membership, hunted and wary people, often with the most glaring human frailties, seemingly perpetually dogged by bad luck and missed chances. Often, of course, the lone assassin acts without any aid and comfort. But even the conspiracies, with their dread-sounding names and manifestos, prove to be a handful of the most dedicated, sometimes with strings out to others, sometimes not. In the case of Sarajevo, various forms of the Young Bosnian movement were involved—Colonel Apis and his friends and perhaps others —but the conspiracy was more than anything else the response of a few people to an opportunity in the midst of a highly charged political atmosphere. And it was better organized than many— killing, live and close up, is not easily taught; the assassin learns on the job, and usually there is going to be but one job. Princip practicing with his Browning revolver in Kosutujak Park was unusual and, given his uncertainty when he fired, not terribly useful. Still, Ilić had his six people neatly in place and even got the proverbial second chance. It was not *simply* luck that Princip was standing in front of Moritz Schiller's delicatessen. Ilić had deployed not one but six men, and there had already been one narrow miss with Cabrinović's bomb. They had come to kill and they waited, seeking any opportunity. When it came, Princip was ready.

The Sarajevo events do indicate that even when the deed is legitimate in rebel eyes, when there is a period of violence, when the victim is available and appropriate, when the planning is the best possible, when the conspiracy is rational, structured, and long-lived, when there is outside aid and comfort and good intelligence and functioning weapons, and when there are properly trained, willing, and determined volunteers, matters do not always work out as planned. Someone does not or will not shoot. The plans change at the last minute. The gun misfires or the bomb explodes too soon or too late. Or nothing happens at all. There are a great many more missed assassinations than dead bodies, and a great many attempts abort long before the gun misfires while pressed to the victim's chest. And yet the archduke *was* dead and the European powder keg was lit.

NOTES

1. The *New York Times,* March 7, 1978, called the stabbing of Man Bun Lee, the unofficial "mayor" of New York's Chinatown, "an unsuccessful assassination attempt."

2. Thucydides, quoted by Edward Hyams in *Killing No Murder, A Study of Assassination as a Political Means,* London, Nelson, 1969, p. 43.

3. Bernhardt J. Hurwood, *Society and the Assassin, A Background Book on Political Murder,* New York, Parents' Magazine Press, 1970, p. 27.

4. Robert Katz, *The Fall of the House of Savoy,* New York, Macmillan, 1971, p. 136, and Barbara W. Tuchman, *The Proud Tower, A Portrait of the World Before the War: 1890–1914,* New York, Bantam, 1972, pp. 119–120.

5. Tuchman, *op. cit.,* p. 91.

6. Katz, *op. cit.,* p. 152.

7. *Ibid.,* p. 153.

8. Brian McConnell, *The History of Assassination,* Nashville, 1970, p. 172.

9. Hyams, *op. cit.,* pp. 134–135.

10. The best source for the Sarajevo events is Vladimir Dedijer's *The Road to Sarajevo,* New York, Simon & Schuster, 1966, which makes use of the trial records (Nachlass Erzherzog Franz-Ferdinand, *Prozess in Sarajevo,* Haus-Hof Staatsarchiv, Vienna).

11. *New York Times,* May 27, 1973 (interview with Raymond H. Anderson.)

12. V. R. Berghahn, *Germany and the Approach of War in 1914,* London, Macmillan, 1973, p. 187.

13. *New York Times,* May 27, 1973.

2

Killing as Murder

At least I was on the Walter Cronkite show.
—Arthur Bremer, after maiming Governor
George Wallace

When Princip stood on the corner of Appel Quay and Franz Josef Street, behind him stretched a long series of decisions that had culminated in the Browning revolver in his pocket and the determination to perform a killing—but no murder. The same is true with every political assassination from the religious obsession of Ravaillac to the vague, recently digested ideas of anarchism that led Luigi Lucheni to hone down a file and stab Empress Elizabeth. Even those murders of the mighty carried out for personal motives, for private gain or vengeance, and especially for the muddled and uncertain "reasons" of the psychopath, have a political impact. A murder by a man in the grip of an obsession, babbling of anarchism or the people's power, is seldom dismissed by the public solely as an aberrant act—a natural calamity—as would be a fatal heart attack or death from cancer. The public in general and the involved in particular usually feel that such a murder has a greater meaning than the replacement of one man by another. Vulnerability to assassination may be one of the risks of the monarch's job, but this alone indicates something of the nature of that job and of the times. And not all anarchist assassins were demented. In any case, a crucial aspect of the murder of significant

49

political figures remains the motive of the assassin—*any* such murder will have a political impact beyond the change in personnel, and some appear to have had a profound impact on events.

No matter what results the murder of a political leader may have, some of those murders are motivated only by the most traditional of personal reasons. In 1859, for example, United States Representative Daniel Sickles discovered that he was being cuckolded by Philip Barton Key, a District of Columbia district attorney. In a passionate fury he killed Key in Lafayette Square. In 1867 L. Harris Hiscox, a delegate to the New York Constitutional Convention, was shot and killed by another irate husband. Political leaders have been killed over the publication of scurrilous articles, property litigation, and assumed slights, and by discarded mistresses—Judge A. P. Crittedon of California was shot dead by Laura D. Fair: all quite run-of-the-mill or at least conventional murders. Classic murders, especially of the Agatha Christie variant, are quite rare, and politicians apparently are no more likely to be victims of outraged fathers or embittered debtors than are any other group. The American examples of personal motives have largely been minor officials, but this is not always the case. Various Latin American presidents have been killed out of personal hatred and private revenge, by an outraged brother of a mistress, in vengeance for business losses. All these were quite reasonable personal motives that resulted only in the replacement of one El Presidente by another. At times maximum leaders are not so easily replaced, often fortunately. In April 1972, Sheikh Abeid Karume, the president of Zanzibar, was assassinated.

KILLING AS A FAMILY MATTER: SLAUGHTER ON ZANZIBAR

"Everybody knew Humud would kill one day. When he was sober he was polite, shy, and kind. But when he was drunk he began thinking about his father and became very violent."

Zanzibar, a delightful island in the Indian Ocean off the coast of East Africa with a single crop—cloves, exported to flavor Indonesian cigarettes—had an uneasy political history for the decades previous to 1972. Under the British the island had been dominated by the small Arab elite. In 1955 the British decided to reserve a number of seats in the legislative council on a racial basis. The Arabs were outraged at any dimunition of their traditional privileges to the benefit of the Africans. They decided to boycott the council. Then, in November 1955, a retired police inspector, Sultan Ahmed el-Mugheiry, decided to attend a session. A week later he was stabbed while walking down the street. Seriously wounded, he was rushed to the hospital. There another Arab appeared, wrapped in long robes. He soon filled the hospital room with lamentations of dismay. Leaning over the bedside of Sultan el-Mugheiry, he pulled out a dagger and killed the wounded man. He was discovered to be one Mohammed Humud; and although there was considerable Arab sympathy, he was charged, tried, convicted, and sentenced to death. The sultan commuted his sentence. There the matter rested, with the assassin in prison, the sultan in power, and the Arabs still dominant. In December 1963, the British withdrew from Zanzibar, handing over power to the sultan and the Arab elite. Thirty-two days later, on January 12, 1964, the Africans rose, seized power, and slaughtered their Arab enemies. Out of the bloody coup came a new leader, Sheikh Abeid Karume, a sixty-two-year-old former merchant seaman descended from Malawian slaves. He had a limited education but an unlimited thirst for power. His Afro-Shirazi Party absorbed the militant pre-revolutionary Umma Party, and Zanzibar became a one-party state ruled by a revolutionary council dominated by Karume. Three months later Zanzibar merged, rather less than more, with Tanganyika, to become Tanzania; but Karume, as vice-president of the new nation, continued to rule his island. Increasingly more erratic, his peculiar decrees—forced marriages between Arab women and African men—and brutal repression made him an embarrassment to Africa. He was far more like the unsavory Arab slave-trading sultans than the leader of a revolutionary council with advisors from Russia, China, and East Germany.

Despite his behavior there were those who benefited from his rule—certainly the assassin Mohammed Humud, released after the coup—but from the first there had been plotting. In 1969 Karume claimed that fourteen people had been conspiring against his government, and announced that four had been executed by a firing squad. It became difficult to tell who was actually plotting and who was the victim of Karume's suspicions and whims. Little news came out of the island—and the courts had been abolished. In May 1971, there were reports that nineteen men had been charged with plotting a revolution and sentenced to work as cowherds for periods of three to ten years. One was the released assassin Mohammed Humud. The nineteen had in large part been convicted on the testimony of an Army officer— Ahmada Mohammed Ali was committing perjury to please the revolutionary council. Lieutenant Ahmada became Captain Ahmada. And the nineteen disappeared into prison. That was the last heard of them—the only news out of prison was usually word of execution or the appearance of the released. Then Karume announced that not only the courts but also all prisons had been abolished. Hundreds were released. The son of Mohammed Humud, who had long feared for his father's life, thus learned that he had been tortured and killed in prison. Lieutenant Humud Mohammed Humud decided on revenge: Karume would die. He approached Captain Ahmada, who had given false testimony against his father. It was not such a strange choice, for Ahmada had not wanted to lie and after the trial had made it clear that he resented his role. They were joined by two others, a corporal and a private. Friday evening at six o'clock, on April 7, 1972, the four appeared at the door of the Afro-Shirazi Party headquarters, where Karume and his colleagues were conferring. They opened a barrage of fire with submachine guns. Karume was hit six times in the chest; his heir-apparent, Sheikh Komboa, secretary-general of the party, was seriously wounded, along with another founder-member of Afro-Shirazi, Ibrahim Sadala. Karume's bodyguards, stunned by the barrage, finally did manage to shoot and kill Lieutenant Humud Mohammed Humud on the spot. The other three gunmen and a driver in a getaway car apparently headed for the Party Youth Headquarters a half-mile away, where the Chief Political Commissar of the Army and Youth Leader Colonel Seif Bakari was in his office. He was Captain Ahmada's other target. The pursuit built up too fast and the getaway car swerved out of the built-up area and disappeared. The police soon captured the driver of the abandoned car, but the three assassins had disappeared. A huge cordon-and-search operation went through the island house by house until the three were located at Bumbwini village, sixteen miles from Zanzibar town. The police opened fire and killed the two African soldiers. Captain Ahmada shot himself to avoid capture. Radio Zanzibar announced that the assassins had been identified as enemies of the country intent on overthrowing the government. There were widespread arrests on the island and the mainland. Armed guards patrolled the streets. President Nyerere of Tanzania was in constant touch by telephone and sent an investigation team to Zanzibar. Nothing else happened.

The assassins had intended nothing more to happen. Karume and his friends had been punished for the murder of Lieutenant Humud Mohammed Humud's father—the assassin—and for the humiliation of Captain Ahmada Mohammed Ali. Of course, and fortunately for the island's population, no one could replace Karume; but no one tried to overturn the revolutionary council. There would no longer be strange decrees, whimsical murders, the brutality and arbitrary repression. But there would be no new direction, no firm new leadership by the revolutionary council that had already baffled the advisors sent by East Germany and Russia and continued to confuse the Chinese. The administration would be as chaotic, the people as wretched, the future as uncertain. But Karume was gone, and by general agreement he had from the first been an archetypal tyrant—by usurpation, by oppression—bloody, cruel, wanton; but he had not been killed because he was a tyrant but because he personally was blamed for the death of the old assassin Mohammed Humud and the humiliation of Captain Ahmada. And so matters stood; the revolutionary council ruled, the people, slightly less threatened, were no less miserable, the Chinese were no less confused by revolution *a la* Zanzibar, and President Nyerere was considerably less embarrassed by island events.

MURDER, A MATTER OF MONEY

QJ/WIN . . . had been recruited earlier . . . for use in a special operation in the Congo (the assassination of Patrice Lumumba). . . .

—CIA Inspector General's Report

Like many murderers driven by rage or frustration, denied passion or simple vengeance, Lieutenant Humud and Captain Ahmada had gotten what they wanted, although at some cost. There are, however, those who kill not for personal reasons but solely to turn a profit. All private murders are, of course, crimes, but some crimes lack passion, a personal touch, and are purely and simply for gain. Some groups within organized crime circles maintain the division of profits, the allotment of territories, the discipline of subordinates, or the powers of peers by recourse to murder. The fabled Mafia in its manifold forms tends to kill its own, despite the notoriety of Murder, Inc., where the knowledgeable could go to purchase a killing on demand. Given the occasional interrelation of crime and politics, it is not surprising that from time to time a politician is killed not because of his politics but because of the profit motive. In America during the golden age of gangsters, several Illinois politicians were shot and killed—Jeff Stone, mayor of Culp, in 1926; Thomas J. Courtney, state's attorney, in 1935; and J. M. Bolton, state legislator, in 1936—allegedly by underworld figures. There are elsewhere those who kill to acquire or maintain the political power to make profits. There are presently and have often been in the past countries that are in effect family-owned businesses—Nicaragua, Haiti, even Saudi Arabia, although in the last case it is a very large family and, of course, a very large business. When there is such a close identification of profit and political power, the motive for murder is mixed, but is more easily classified under the rubric of political assassination than as crime for profit. Sometimes those who kill for profit—organized criminals—branch out into purely political matters. In New York on January 11, 1943, the anarchist Carlo Tresca, editor of a polemical newspaper, was killed, it was believed, on the orders of Vito Genovese, who as a loyal Italian-American wanted to eliminate the enemy of his friend Benito Mussolini. The gunman was never discovered, although a well-known gangland suspect, whose car was found two blocks from the scene, was questioned. This was a rare excursion into politics, for most murders by the Mafia are for discipline or profit.[1]

One of the great contemporary legends is that there are real assassins for hire—such as the antihero "the Jackal" in Frederick Forsyte's novel, who was hired to kill General Charles de Gaulle. No matter what the motive of the employers, the killer kills for profit. Generally most revolutionary movements would prefer to do their own killing—the man that can be hired can be rehired by a more generous employer, and they usually have an ample number of volunteers at their disposal. Governments, with a monopoly on arms and numerous trained men, would supposedly not need a Jackal. This is not necessarily the case, for there is often a desire to place some distance between the gunman and the employers. There is thus a small, often profitable, but highly dangerous, marketplace for such a skilled craftsman, or in some cases not-so-skilled craftsman. In present circumstances a more appealing alternative is to find an ideological mercenary who can be hired with a slogan to kill for a cause rather than to turn a profit. The Palestinians have found a variety of such transnational revolutionaries—Japanese, Germans, Latin Americans—who are eager to kill for almost any trendy cause. The most famous is Illich Ramirez Sanchez—Carlos, or, to the media, the Jackal—a twenty-nine-year-old (assuming he is still alive) Venezuelan who drifted in and out of several revolutionary camps and coteries. After several close escapes and three murders, he directed one of the most elegant of all terrorist operations, the kidnapping of an entire international organization—the ambassadors and much of the staff of the Organization of Petroleum Exporting Countries—and their transfer to Algeria and Libya when a massive ransom was paid by Austria, Iran, and Saudi Arabia.[2] Carlos and most of his colleagues are rather too spectacular for most governments that need a quiet murder done on the side. They tend to look for someone more reliable, if hardly more savory, and this, as the CIA experience in the Congo proved, is not so easy.

During the first half of the century, there had been almost no viable opposition to Belgian control of the Congo, which was until 1908 the absolute possession of the Belgian monarch. It was an almost classic example of imperial exploitation, with colonial monopolies making use of forced labor draining out immense wealth—gold, ivory, copper, tropical produce—and investing only in the necessary exploitive infrastructure. Few of the winds of change blew across the Congo—there were missionary schools, government schools, clerical openings for the natives, and a relatively high standard of living for Africa, but no preparations for self-government. There were few trained people in any profession, especially in politics. One of the rising generation excited by the rapid decolonization elsewhere in Africa and typical of the new men with new ambitions was Patrice Lumumba, born on July 2, 1925. He was one of the rare ones who went through secondary school. In 1954 he was a postal clerk in Stanleyville; in 1957 he moved to a brewery in Leopoldville and soon became the commercial director. He had always been deeply involved in politics —when and if possible. He belonged to the *Cercle Libéral* and became provincial president of a workers' association, and went to Belgium to study. After October 1958, he became one of the most active leaders of the *Mouvement National Congolais,* or MNC, a key nationalist movement. In December 1958, he attended the Pan-African Conference at Accra and adopted the idea of active neutralism—hardly popular in the West in the midst of the cold war. In 1959 he left the brewery to dedicate all his time to the MNC. Congolese political agitation continued to escalate, spurred by the African decolonization and the realization that Belgium did not have the resources or perhaps the will to hold the Congo. On November 1, 1959, Lumumba was arrested, but widespread protest forced his release. Suddenly, unexpectedly, independence was simply a matter of time, very little time. There was a joint round-table meeting in January-February 1960. Although Belgium sent in more troops in May—Lumumba protested—independence was on the way. Lumumba, an advocate of a strong central government in opposition to the federalist proposals of Joseph Kasavubu, was elected from Stanleyville district with a huge majority of 84,602. He would obviously play a major role in the new nation. On June 30, 1960, at the independence ceremonies, King Baudouin realized "with joy and emotion" that the Congo had been granted independence. Kasavubu, as president, spoke of his responsibility with "profound humbleness." Lumumba neither dismissed the past—"We have known that the law was never the same for whites and blacks"—nor neglected the future struggle—"We shall show the world what the black man can do when he works in freedom."[3] It was almost the last happy day for the Congo.

Four days later the chaos began. The national army, the *Force Publique,* mutinied; they killed the available Belgian officers and began indiscriminately looting and raping; houses were burned and civilians robbed, beaten, and shot. In a panic, the Belgians began fleeing the country while they could. On July 9, Belgium intervened militarily in Elizabethville. The violence, cruel, wanton, ruthless, continued to spread. On July 11, in the mineral-rich province of Katanga, Premier Moise Tshombe declared independence—why share the wealth with distant tribal enemies? On July 14, the United Nations Security Council decided to intervene, and troops were hurriedly dispatched. In the West there was fear that the Russians might exploit the disorder. There were too few UN troops to cope. The Congo began to come apart. Albert Kalonji proclaimed the independence of Kasai Province. For the Belgians the man responsible for the disaster was Lumumba, as well as his ministers, who "acted like primitive savages and imbeciles or like Communist creatures."[4] Yet in August 1960, at the Pan-African conference held in Leopoldville, Lumumba received considerable support. But the Congo was filled with rumors; Soviet planes were spotted in Stanleyville and Czech technicians in Leopoldville. There was news of massacres in South Kasai by the ANC and rumors of a Lumumba coup. Then, on September 5, Kasavubu announced that he was replacing Lumumba with Joseph Ileo. Lumumba claimed that this was illegal, and on September 13 got a majority in parliament on his request for full powers. In the midst of the confusion and massacres, full powers meant little— Lumumba had an armed guard of a few hundred, and the national army was busy slaughtering the Baluba of Kasai. The United Nations had frozen all airports and communications. Joseph Ileo was unable to form a government. The Belgians were determined that Lumumba—a charlatan, an agitator, probably a Communist— should be put "in a position where he cannot cause trouble."[5] On September 14, at 8:30 P.M., Colonel Joseph-Désiré Mobutu "froze" politics and turned what political power existed over to a board made up of Lumumba's enemies. Attempts at a reconciliation between Kasavubu and Lumumba failed. His enemies wanted him in jail. Mobutu appeared reticent, the United Nations uncooperative; the Guinean and Ghanian contingents apparently supported him. Finally, the *Armée Nationale Congolaise* threw a cordon around Lumumba's house, but his safety was assured by a second United Nations cordon closer to the house. There for the moment matters stood, the prime minister inside, his enemies outside, and much of the Congo in chaos.

During the slide into anarchy, Western observers had watched in horror the massacres and madness ineptly directed by unknown men with incredible names. Of all the actors on the bloody Congo stage, the one most suspect—a black Trojan horse for Communist intervention—remained Lumumba, even though sealed in his house by the army. On August 18, five days after Lumumba had demanded the removal of all white United Nations troops, the United States National Security Council met in Washington. President Dwight Eisenhower indicated such forceful concern that something should be done about Lumumba that the Director of the Central Intelligence Agency, Allen Dulles, assumed that he had authority to assassinate Lumumba. Although the Congolese prime minister had come to Washington in July and received pledges of economic aid from Secretary of State Christian Herter, few in the American government trusted him. From the CIA Station Chief in Leopoldville, Victor Hedgman, on August 18, had come a cable: "EMBASSY AND STATION BELIEVE CONGO EXPERIENCING CLASSICAL COMMUNIST EFFORT TAKEOVER GOVERNMENT. . . ."[6] He warned that there was little time to act to avoid another Cuba. At this point, both in Washington and the Congo, matters became vague and remained vague. In the government there exists the practice of "plausible denial"—the construction of an alibi, for instance, "no one ever told *me*"—in case of disclosure, by means of euphemisms and circumlocutions. It was appropriate or proper or necessary, or even vital, to kill Lumumba—but no one must actually say so. "Strong action" to one official meant political manipulation, and to another authorization to kill. Thus, after Mobuto's coup, with Lumumba still feared, CIA Station Chief Victor Hedgman was advising a Congolese effort to "eliminate" Lumumba: "ONLY SOLUTION IS REMOVE HIM FROM SCENE SOONEST."[7]

The circumlocutions came to an end, more or less, when Joseph Scheider delivered to Hedgman a packet of a toxic substance that would produce a fatal disease indigenous to the Congo, along with accessory materials—hypodermic needles, rubber gloves, and gauze masks. After confirmation from CIA headquarters, Hedgman began to explore the possibilities. Various agents could not manage access to Lumumba in his guarded house. There was some hope of luring him out so that he could be arrested by the Congolese army—at least one of those involved thought that this was all that was being contemplated—an assassination at second hand, so to speak, since Lumumba's enemies probably would have few doubts about the meaning of "eliminate." And there was concern that whoever attempted to put the toxic substance in Lumumba's food or toothpaste should not be an American. In Europe the CIA discovered just such an "asset"—designated QJ/WIN.

QJ/WIN was a foreign citizen with a criminal background—among his other problems he was under investigation for smuggling; judged to be a man of not too many scruples, he was ideal for a dirty job. In November 1960, QJ/WIN was dispatched to the Congo to undertake a mission that "might involve a large element of personal risk." He was considered on his record dependable and quick-witted by Michael Mulroney, who had known him previously and wanted to involve him in the plan to draw Lumumba away from protective United Nations custody. QJ/WIN was supposed to report directly to Mulroney, but Hedgman soon involved the "asset" in a plan to pierce both Congolese and United Nations guards, but only to escort Lumumba out of the residence. The toxin remained in the background, the asset QJ/WIN unused but in place. On November 27, Lumumba slipped out of his residence in Leopoldville in an attempt to reach Stanleyville. On December 1, he was arrested by Mobutu's soldiers and returned to Leopoldville. Two days later he was transferred to Camp Hardy in Thysville. There seemed no more use for QJ/WIN, but the Americans still were not sure that Lumumba was well and truly eliminated.

At this time another asset arrived on the scene. In September agent WI/ROGUE had been recruited and apparently trained in demolitions, small arms, and "medical immunization." He was to be a utility agent in the Congo available to organize and conduct a surveillance team, to intercept packages, to blow up bridges, and to be available for other assignments requiring positive action. WI/ROGUE was a much more romantic agent than QJ/WIN. Essentially a stateless soldier of fortune, knowledgeable about the Congo, he was also a forger and former bank robber who "learns quickly and carries out an assignment without regard for danger."[8] The CIA provided WI/ROGUE with plastic surgery and a toupee so his old friends or enemies, as the case might be, would not recognize him, and he was dispatched to meet with Hedgman in Leopoldville on December 2. Hedgman now had an asset who, according to CIA's Africa division, ". . . will dutifully undertake appropriate action without pangs of conscience. In a word, he can rationalize all action."[9] Hedgman told him to build cover during an initial period and to spot potential agents, especially in the province where Lumumba's support was strongest. WI/ROGUE then went off to register in a local hotel and "build cover."

While QJ/WIN, still kept in place as an asset, appeared taciturn, waiting for instructions to carry out the mysterious mission that might involve great risk, WI/ROGUE immediately began to play the game. He scrounged around the hotel and came to the immediate conclusion that an ideal agent would be the mysterious QJ/WIN. He began sounding out QJ/WIN, who immediately reported to Hedgman that WI/ROGUE smelled like an intelligence operator. QJ/WIN was told that the CIA knew nothing about him. It was clear that his idea of an intelligence operative came from "reading a few novels or something of the sort."[10] Obviously, WI/ROGUE was having a marvelous time. He again approached the wary QJ/WIN on December 14 and offered him three hundred dollars per month to participate in an intelligence net and be a member of an "execution squad." QJ/WIN demurred. WI/-

ROGUE pushed on, offering bonuses for special jobs. QJ/WIN went back to Hedgman, who still said he knew nothing about any WI/ROGUE. He certainly had no idea what WI/ROGUE would do next—"I found he was an unguided missile."[11] Hedgman was in the curious position of having one bought-and-paid-for asset attempting to outbid him on his other bought-and-paid-for asset to undertake a mission that was best swept under the "plausible denial" rug. WI/ROGUE did admit to Hedgman that he knew QJ/WIN, but insisted that he had not tried to recruit him. This was at a time when Hedgman knew that WI/ROGUE had told QJ/WIN that he was working for the Americans. It was all too much for the professional Hedgman and he sent off his two assets separately, WI/ROGUE to whatever boneyard accepts criminal, stateless soldiers of fortune, and QJ/WIN back to a mysterious CIA project.

QJ/WIN had first been used in Europe to spot individuals in the underworld who could be used for various (unstated) purposes. He had reported back a variety of information, including the fact that a leader of a gambling syndicate in the Middle East had on tap an available pool of assassins. As far as his own "capability" was concerned: "If you needed somebody to carry out murder, I guess you had a man who might be prepared to carry it out."[12] This "capability" had made him an ideal recruit for project ZR/RIFLE, which was intended to give the CIA the general "capability of the clandestine service in the field of incapacitation and elimination."[13] More clearly translated, the CIA wanted stand-by assassins, and under the auspices of ZR/RIFLE agent QJ/WIN was supposed to spot them. His talent scouting, however, had been interrupted by his abortive African adventure, and on his withdrawal from the Congo ZR/RIFLE was phased out, more or less. Given QJ/WIN's background, there was reason to believe that his advent in the Congo was not simply as a spotter, and the early training of WI/-ROGUE in "medical immunization," given the vials of toxin in the Station Chief's safe, could not be considered simply fortuitous. Be that as it may, both agents were paid and protected and useless. The Congolese took care of their own.

On January 17, 1961, at 4:45 P.M., an Air-Congo DC-4 landed at Luano in the State of Katanga. On board were Lumumba, Maurice

Mpolo, and Joseph Okito. They had been delivered to their enemies. The three were dragged from the plane and beaten with rifle butts. Witnesses reported that it was obvious they had already been badly beaten. The prisoners left the field in an armed convoy. After that there is considerable mystery but no doubt about the outcome. Sometime that evening or the next, the three were killed by guards acting under the orders of Minister Godefroit Munongo. The finishing shot into Lumumba was by a 9-mm P.G., a gun not carried by the ordinary Katangese police; but the particular assassin mattered little—Kasavubu and Mobutu had rid themselves of a potential danger courtesy of Tshombe and Munongo in Katanga. And they, unlike the Americans, did not have to pay for the operation.

In a real sense the American "assets," hired assassins, were typical, also revealing a continuing innocence by those who should know better. Stolid, reliable QJ/WIN—never tested, of course—descends from the Mafia, who, it is assumed, must know their business since they make money at it. The soldiers and buttonmen, the enforcers, go about their business with no more *élan* than would salesmen or shoemakers—trades that they might have undertaken but for an unexpected opportunity—and often with no greater success. Given the fact that most law enforcement officials are delighted to discover gangster victims, that it is unlikely there are going to be witnesses, and that most victims are small-time and unsuspecting, there are still a great many botched organized-crime jobs—the most notable being an execution in Brooklyn where two enforcers sitting on opposite sides of a victim seated in the front seat of a car managed to shoot each other. Still, there remains the popular belief that the hit man knows his job and, like QJ/WIN, would be nice to have on hand as a capability. WI/ROGUE, on the other hand, much like the notorious Carlos, loves his job and enjoys the money. He plays his part out of thrillers and bad movies, appalling the professional but delighting the audience. The WI/ROGUEs and Carloses of the world are charming, amusing, absolutely deadly, without qualm or scruple, a danger to all they touch—especially their own. No one likes a hired killer, and a hired killer who savors his work is even more unpalatable.

MURDER AS PERSONAL THERAPY

This country is a mess. This man is not your President.
He's not a public servant.
—Squeaky Fromme after her attempt on Gerald Ford

There are those who kill neither for pleasure nor profit, not even
from passion or in revenge, but rather while in the grip of a
strange obsession exorcised only through recourse to violence. On
May 11, 1812, John Bellingham stepped from a small group of men
waiting in the lobby of the House of Commons, raised a pistol, and
shot Spencer Perceval, First Lord of the Treasury, Chancellor of
the Exchequer and Prime Minister of Great Britain. He then
turned and walked to a nearby bench, still holding the warm
pistol, and sat down. In confusion and horror the witnesses gathered around the fallen prime minister. He was bleeding from the
corners of his mouth, and within minutes there were almost no
vital signs. His eyes were still open but his pulse was scarcely
perceptible, and by the time a surgeon arrived he was dead. Members of Commons and Lords, visitors, and witnesses suddenly realized that there was a killer in the lobby—sitting on the bench.
Seized and shaken, he announced, "I submit myself to justice.
. . . My name is John Bellingham: it is a private injury—I know
what I have done. It was a denial of justice on the part of the
Government."[14] He was utterly calm and remained so. He had
been *forced* to kill the prime minister because the government,
after endless petitions, had done nothing to right the wrong done
to him by the Russian government. In the summer of 1804, he had
sailed to Archangel from Liverpool. After two bankruptcies, in
1797 and again in 1804, he hoped for a turn of luck. Instead he
became involved in a claim case. He denied he owed the debt and
spent much of the next five years in one form or another of detention. He returned to Britain in December 1809, burning with
resentment over being abandoned by the British government. He
knew he was entitled to legal redress for his suffering. No one else
thought so. His carefully prepared petitions were received at one
official office after another by one bored official after another, filed,

and forgotten. And calmly, without rancor, Bellingham went on dispatching his petitions and letters. At last he felt all recourse had been exhausted, all petitions denied, all offices closed; there was nothing to do but kill the prime minister. He did. He saw no wrong. Calm and collected or not, Bellingham was obsessed by his claim—"no person can have heard what the conduct and demeanor of this man have been since he committed the crime, or can have read his defense, without being satisfied that he is mad. ...."[15] He was, nevertheless, charged, tried, and convicted, and on Monday, May 18, he was hanged at Newgate. Thirty years later another assassin tried to kill another prime minister of Britain, murdering his secretary instead. Excluding the Irish efforts, there has been only one other "serious" attempt at political assassination in Great Britain in this century, when Alice Wheeldon, Alfred Mason, and Winnie Mason concocted a plan to kill Prime Minister David Lloyd George by stabbing him with a needle dipped in curare. They were conscientious objectors who blamed him for the loss of life in World War I. Although certainly exotic, the plot was inept, and they were arrested; on March 10, 1917, they were sentenced to various prison terms at the Central Criminal Court. The assassin Daniel MacNaghten, who had missed Sir Robert Peel, was tried, but his explanation was not accepted as rational—pursued by "a parcel of devils" and victim of a Tory-Catholic conspiracy. Sane on some points, he was mad in that "he is not under the restraint of those motives which could alone create human responsibility." From the trial came the MacNaghten rule—one received at the time, and later, with indignation. Neither Bellingham nor MacNaughten had known right from wrong.

Bellingham and MacNaghten were hardly singular examples of the psychopathic assassin in the nineteenth century or the next. Often, of course, it was difficult to determine the degree of insanity—since almost inevitably the popular reaction to assassins is that they *must* be mad to have done such a horrible deed, but that they must be punished anyway. Some surely were mad: Richard Lawrence, who failed to kill Andrew Jackson, was sure that he was Richard III and that the President had prevented him from obtaining large sums of money; Demitrios Tsafendas killed South African Prime Minister Verwoerd because the doctors would not remove his "giant tapeworm." Often, however, the "explanation" relates not to a personal obsession or grievance but rather to the political or institutional climate of the times. On November 27, 1970, a thirty-five-year-old Bolivian painter, Benjamin Mendoza y Amor Flores, attempted to stab Pope Paul VI at the Manila Airport. He had been trying to kill the pontiff for years. He was disappointed because he had failed. He would try again—"It's gonna be a pleasure." The Pope represented for Mendoza a monstrous evil—organized religion.

> Because it's time to break down any kind of superstition and I believe my conviction was planned a long time ago in favor of people showing perhaps, a better way for living and a better world, thinking there is a reality at two times, is something different, totally different. Crimes, crimes such as Vietnam, nobody can punish, never, perhaps, they will be punished. Power is helped by great superstition which is the Christian religion.[16]

He babbled on and was diagnosed as suffering from systematized paranoia by a government psychiatrist.

In the nineteenth century, when there were neither systematized paranoia nor psychiatrists, there were still scientific explanations concerning the mad assassin. On November 17, 1878, the new king and queen of Italy, Humbert and Margherita, entered Naples during their first triumphant tour of the realm. There were banners and flags. There was a huge crowd. Every citizen had been taxed one penny to share the honor of contributing to Margherita's gift. The carpet at the door of the train had been especially painted by Morelli. The procession of carriages moved forward under a shower of flowers and to sustained cheers. Naples, despite everything, loved royalty. The royal carriage turned slowly into the Palazzo Carrera Grande, crammed wall to wall with loyal, cheering subjects. Humbert and Margherita were side by side in the open coach. Opposite them was Benedetto Cairoli, the prime minister, and the *principino*, little Victor Emmanuel. Suddenly, a pallid young man began running toward the carriage, his hand covered with a red cloth. He was Giovanni Passanante, an unemployed cook who had previously been arrested for pasting signs on the walls of Salerno that read "Universal Revolution." He leaped on the running board and the cloth fell away, revealing a dagger. He raised his arm. Queen Margherita screamed to Cairoli to save the king. This he did by leaning forward so that when Passanante brought the dagger down it plunged into the prime minister's thigh—a deep but not serious wound. Little Victor Emmanuel huddled stunned in the corner of the seat. The king, slightly scratched, began to pound Passanante over the head with his sheathed sword. Margherita slapped him in the face again and again with her small bouquet of flowers. At last the police arrived and dragged Passanante off. The carriage with Humbert and the wounded Cairoli moved on toward Palazzo Reale. The king's only comment, made a few days later to his guests at dinner, was, "Let us be seated and let's not keep the cooks waiting; you have seen, ladies and gentlemen, what they are capable of."[17]

It was almost immediately apparent that this cook was insane, his motive being that "From what I read, I gather that kings spend too much."[18] The medical specialists, however, based their conclusion on seemingly more solid evidence. The circumference of his skull was 535 millimeters—the same as found in the criminally insane in the proportion of 25 percent. His brain, they estimated, weighed ten grams less than average and they "observed" the obliteration of the central canal of the spinal cord, which was why his madness was symptomless. Sigmund Freud was at the time a fourth-year medical student in Vienna, so the specialists had to make do with these arithmetical means and intuitive observations. Passanante did not agree and refused to plead insanity. He was promptly judged both sane and guilty by the jury and sentenced to death.

Passanante was an almost classic case of the lone, psychopathic assassin. He did not have a private injury like John Bellingham, nor was he pursued by a parcel of devils like Daniel MacNaghten, and unlike even Mendoza's obsession with religion, his motive was the fashion of the moment. For almost a century the demented as well as the rational would kill for "anarchism" or the ultimate republic, would believe that the death of kings and presidents would solve the world's problems and, in the case of the demented, their own. For over a century one of the risks of the American presidency has been the magnetic attraction the office has for psychopathic assassins who kill for the cause of the day—Richard Lawrence as Richard III began the series somewhat out of synch, although, as noted, he did manage to include the burning issue of the Bank of the United States in his litany of grievances. After that, with the exception of the Puerto Rican attempt on President Truman and Congress, apparently all of America's major assassinations have been psychopathic, not political. Presidential assassinations show a century-long consistency. Although in the eighteenth century, before presidents, a rational Tory conspiracy to murder General George Washington in 1776 in New York by sprinkling poison on his favorite dish, green peas, was discovered.

On April 14, 1865, John Wilkes Booth stepped into President Abraham Lincoln's box at the Ford Theater while Lincoln's body-guard was refreshing himself at the bar. He shot the President in the head with a single-shot derringer, leaped on the stage shouting *"Sic semper tyrannis"*—perhaps, Winston Churchill felt, the most dramatic moment in American history—and then, his leg broken, hobbled off the scene. Twelve days later, in a burning barn sur-rounded by Union troops, he was shot and killed, probably by his own hand. He had feared Lincoln wanted to be king and he, Booth, had acted as an agent of God. His tiny band of fellow conspirators managed to wound Secretary of State William H. Seward but missed Vice President Andrew Johnson. All were cap-tured, quickly convicted, and executed. Booth, the driving force, had led a disorganized and unsuccessful life. Surrounded by a family of actors, his own career had drawn poor notices: potential great talent but no capacity for application. His life had been one long failure: high school left unfinished, no lasting relationship with a woman—except near the end, with a practicing prostitute —no channel for his ambitions, and then his voice had begun to fail, a disaster for even an unsuccessful actor. He became increas-ingly immersed in politics, taking the road that led from the Ford Theater to a burning barn.[19]

On July 2, 1881, Charles J. Guiteau shot and killed President James A. Garfield.[20] God had wanted Guiteau to save the country from ruin by removing Garfield so that the Stalwart section of the Republican Party could come to power in the person of Chester A. Arthur. At his trial he insisted he was an agent of God and guiltless. He was declared guilty and sane and hanged before a large, unruly crowd. His life had been, if anything, more disorganized than Booth's. There had been mental illness in the family; his mother had died when he was seven and his father, a devout Republican, accepted the tenet of the Oneida utopian community that the second coming of Christ had occurred in 70 A.D.—but otherwise led a blameless life. His son wandered in and out of schools, joined, left, and joined again the Oneida community— leaving once more and urging criminal proceedings against it. He started a newspaper—the *New York Theocrat*—"I am in the employ of Jesus Christ and Co., the very ablest and strongest firm in the universe." It failed. He married a sixteen-year-old girl. The marriage failed. He tried to sell insurance and could not. He lived by selling religious tracts and running up bills he could not pay. He wrote a speech in 1880 for Ulysses S. Grant that went unused, and when Garfield received the nomination Guiteau switched his allegiance. After Garfield's election he anticipated being ambassador in Vienna, or at least consul in Paris. He became too insistent and was barred from the White House. It was then that God "told" him to shoot Garfield. After several aborted attempts, he did.

On September 6, 1901, Leon F. Czolgosz shot and mortally wounded President William McKinley, who was about to shake his hand at a reception in the temple of music at the Pan-American Exposition in Buffalo. McKinley died eight days later, and four days after the funeral, in a trial lasting just under nine hours from impaneling to verdict, the jury found him guilty. "I killed the President because he was the enemy of the good people—the good working people. I am not sorry for my crime."[21] He was electrocuted immediately after this statement. There had been suspicion of an anarchist conspiracy but no evidence, although in an unsuccessful effort to persuade the jury that he was insane one of the psychiatrists hinted at a female conspirator because there was a female touch in Czolgosz's covering the pistol with a handkerchief. Czolgosz, too, had lived a confused and uncertain life. His mother died when he was twelve. He was shy, pious, compulsively neat, a man who abhorred cruelty, and a steady worker in a wire mill until he was twenty-three. By then he had broken with the Church—God had not answered his prayers—and became remote and moody. He suffered a nervous breakdown at twenty-five and stayed on the family farm, brooding. He did not get along with his father or stepmother, kept to his room, prepared his own food, and suddenly became interested in anarchism after the assassination of King Humbert I in 1900. He tried to join an anarchist group, but his strange behavior alarmed them and they suspected he was a police spy. They immediately published a warning to this effect. Five days later Czolgosz shot McKinley.

On October 14, 1912, in Milwaukee, John N. Schrank shot former President and Bull Moose candidate Theodore Roosevelt in the chest. The bullet tore through Roosevelt's metal glasses case and a fifty-page speech manuscript that was folded double in his pocket, and bore into his chest and upward for about four inches, fracturing his fourth rib. The ex-President was able to make his speech—"It takes more than that to kill a Bull Moose"—despite the wound. The assassin had twice been visited by President McKinley's ghost, once in 1901, when the spirit told him that Roosevelt was guilty of the assassination, and again on the eleventh anniversary of his death, when Roosevelt was campaigning as a Bull Moose. Schrank was concerned with not only the plea of McKinley's spirit but also the possibility that Roosevelt would be a *third*-term President—this, as Schrank had explained to his satisfaction in various essays, was crucial—it was vital that there never be a third-term President, so surely the visions meant he was an agent of God. He began to follow Roosevelt's campaign tour and in twenty-four days, in eight states, managed to be in the same city as Roosevelt only three times—the last in Milwaukee. After the shooting he was arrested, examined by five psychiatrists, and declared insane. He spent the rest of his life in a Wisconsin mental institution. Schrank, born in Germany, had lost his father almost at once and was raised by an uncle and aunt. He came to the United States at the age of thirteen, tended bar for his uncle, and eventually, at twenty-eight, became owner of the bar. He was polite, reserved, without friends—"I never had a friend in my life"—except for one girl who was killed in a steamship accident. At thirty he sold the saloon and began reading, writing—on the third term—and wandering around New York without steady work. He attracted almost no attention until October 14, 1912, in Milwaukee, when he acted as an "agent of God."

At Bayside Park, in Miami, Florida, on February 15, 1933, Giuseppe Zangara suddenly leaped up on an empty chair—he was only five feet tall—and opened fire on President-elect Franklin Roosevelt and the mayor of Chicago, Anton Cermak. He missed Roosevelt but hit and mortally wounded Cermak, who was standing by Roosevelt's car. He showed no remorse. In his jail-written autobiography he insisted, "I go content because I go for my idea. I salute all the poor of the world."[22] Born in 1900, Zangara had served just after World War I in the Italian army. At that time he bought a pistol in order to assassinate the king of Italy, but could never push through the crowds—his problem in Miami. In 1923 he came to the United States and worked as a bricklayer. Solitary, he showed no interest in girls, friends, or entertainment, only in his constant stomach trouble. Occasionally he expressed resentment over the privileges of the rich. In 1931 he quit his job and moved south in hopes of curing his stomach condition. During the winter of 1932–1933, he decided to kill President Herbert Hoover, but postponed acting because of Washington's winter weather. When he heard that Roosevelt was coming to Miami, he changed targets—he felt no ill will toward either man, and once Hoover had left office he would have had no further interest in killing him. On the day of his execution, sitting in the electric chair, he was enraged that no "lousy capitalists" had come to take his picture. His last words were "Go ahead, push the button."[23]

Excluding the Puerto Rican attempt on President Truman's life at Blair House in November 1950, the next presidential assassination was the murder of President John F. Kennedy and the wounding of Governor John Connally of Texas on November 22, 1963, in Dallas, Texas, by Lee Harvey Oswald. Unlike the other assassins Oswald pleaded innocent, and any later explanation was impossible, for he in turn was shot and killed by Jack Ruby—on national television. In all other particulars he fit the pattern. His father had died two months before he was born. His mother remarried when he was five, but that lasted only three years. Oswald was a loner with few friends, and while at public school in New York City was diagnosed as an "emotionally quite disturbed youngster." He became involved in various organizations and causes—he joined the Marines at the earliest possible age, but was resentful of authority and managed an early discharge. He attempted to defect to the Russians, who would not accept him as a citizen or, apparently, make use of him as an agent. His Russian wife taunted him because of his sexual inadequacies. On his return to the United States, he could not hold a job. He tried to assassinate General Edwin A. Walker, who was associated with the extreme Right, and became interested in the Cuban revolution. He was the sole member of the Fair Play for Cuba Committee. He was resentful that his Marine discharge had been changed from honorable to general after his attempted defection, and complained to former Navy Secretary John Connally. He purchased a 6.5 Mannlicher rifle by mail order and fired the shots into the President's car.[24]

The dead President's brother, Senator Robert Kennedy, was a candidate for the Democratic presidential nomination. On the evening of June 4, 1968, after addressing a tumultuous crowd on California primary day, he pushed his way through the hotel kitchen to reach his car. In the swirling crowd a young man named Sirhan Bishara Sirhan pushed his way forward and fired into Kennedy's head at point-blank range. The senator died on the kitchen floor. Sirhan, twenty-four, was a Palestinian national. Nervous and withdrawn, he had done well in school and always wanted to "be someone." He made few friends, was quarrelsome and hostile but certain of his ultimate importance. He was increasingly concerned with the Palestinian cause, and anti-Jewish—and, after the June 1967 war, he was depressed. Then, too, time was passing him by and he was not "making his mark." On June 24, 1968, his name became, at least briefly, a household word.

On Friday morning just before ten, September 5, 1975, President Gerald Ford left a breakfast meeting with one thousand prominent citizens to walk to an appointment with Governor Jerry Brown at the California state capitol. As he made his way through a cheerful crowd of supporters and spectators, suddenly, at 9:57 A.M., he stopped short. Two feet away was a slender, red-haired young woman dressed in a long robe. She had a .45 auto-

matic pointed directly at him. Secret Service agent Larry Buen-
dorf lunged forward and snatched the gun before the woman—
Lynette Alice Fromme—could fire. She shouted, "This country is
in a mess. This man is not your President. He's not a public servant." While being hustled from the park, she shouted again, "It
didn't go off. Can you believe it? It didn't go off."[25] Of all the
presidential assassins, Squeaky Fromme was the most bizarre.
After a violent argument with her father, a well-to-do aeronautical
engineer, she had run away from home, leaving college before the
end of her first semester, and was picked up by Charles Manson
on a beach. She joined his strange cult in 1967.[26] The strange
mixture of drop-outs and the desperate lived in a promiscuous
commune on the proceeds of robbery, addicted to a variety of
drugs and the whims of Manson—"Father and God" to his "Children." In 1969, several members, including Manson, were involved in the wanton and brutal murders of actress Sharon Tate
and Leno La Bianca. They had been killed to please Charlie Manson and to start off some vague race war—"Helter Skelter." To
some on the ultimate fringe of the New Left, the murders had a
special attraction. Bernadine Dohrn of the Weather Underground
was impressed: "Dig it, first they killed those pigs, then they ate
a dinner in the same room with them, then they even shoved a
fork into a victim's stomach! Wild!"[27] And for the six years since
Manson's conviction in 1969 Fromme had been drifting through
an equally wild life, a thousand acid trips, no real job, an appearance at the Manson trial with a shaved head and an X gouged in
her forehead—she had been regularly arrested, once for murder,
and had recently taken to wearing long red robes. When ar-
raigned, she gave a rambling explanation of the evils of the pollu-
tors of the water and earth. To others she indicated that her act
was based on the same sort of logic that led Bellingham to shoot
Prime Minister Perceval. "Well, you know when people around
treat you like a child and pay no attention to the things you say,
you have to do something."[28] So she did. And her face was on the
cover of *Time* magazine.

Seventeen days later in San Francisco, on September 22, Sara
Jane Moore, a forty-five-year-old woman, pulled out her pistol
and tried to shoot President Ford. Her aim was joggled at the

last minute and she missed, wounding a bystander. Moore was less bizarre than Squeaky Fromme, but no less disorganized. She was a divorcee who had used various names and undertaken various jobs, unsuccessfully. In 1974 she had a job as an accountant in order to support her nine-year-old son. When the Symbionese Liberation Army, with Patricia Hearst as a hostage, forced a food-giveaway program, she announced that God had sent her to work with the program. She was fired from that job almost immediately; but, attracted to the strange fringe world of radicals and militants, she persuaded the F.B.I. to take her on as an informer on "terrorists." She bought a revolver, became more interested in being a "terrorist" than informing on them, and tried to join a radical group. As in the case of McKinley's assassin Czolgosz, the radicals decided she was too strange for them. So she shot at President Ford. In February 1979, she escaped from the Federal Reformatory for Women at Andersen, West Virginia, but was captured a few hours later. She said the attempt was "to keep my sanity."

Collectively, then, an assassin's profile can be fashioned—even through the Fromme and Moore attempts eliminated one constant. All those involved in such attempts came from disorganized and broken homes. James Earl Ray, who killed Dr. Martin Luther King, had a family that produced two brothers with criminal records and a sister with severe mental problems; his parents had little money, and were shiftless and prone to use alcohol as a solution to their problems. Often what raw talent existed could not be organized—Sirhan was quarrelsome, Booth avoided the discipline his art required—and life became a series of failures, lost jobs, new starts, and regular plunges into organizations that might supply coherence—Oswald into the Marines, Guiteau into Oneida. They were marginal people; they did not fit into society easily at all, and often were immigrants or declassé. Their sexual lives were unsatisfactory—they might have none, like Arthur H. Bremer, who shot Governor George Wallace; or be unable to stay with any one woman, like Booth; or be derided for their failures, like Oswald; or be available to the commune or Manson's whims, as in the case of Squeaky Fromme. They were all lonely, even and particularly in the midst of crowds. Few could make or keep friends, or maintain any kind of normal personal relationships—for Fromme the Manson cult supplied an alternative to mature relations; for most of the others there was no alternative to their quiet desperation. They were all possessed by private miseries, by an inability to communicate, and often by a sense that while worthy—perhaps even important—they would always be frustrated, life was passing them by, and, like Sirhan, they had not made their mark. Each transforms the clutter, the anguish and misery, of his or her life into a public posture. Each becomes the agent of God, the victim of a conspiracy of the powerful, and transfers his own misery into a visible individual or institution. Each becomes a volunteer under a fashionable banner, from the cause of the Confederacy for Booth to the protection of the environment for Squeaky Fromme. And in so doing they are assured of their worth. They have acted on history—"Do you want my autograph?" said Bremer, as he was hustled off the scene of his flawed murder attempt. They are all asterisks in a history book. They have transformed those lives of quiet desperation into public declarations. For them, it is better to be wanted for murder than not wanted at all.

Not unexpectedly, psychoanalysts and psychiatrists, sociologists and psychiatrists, practically everyone concerned with the aberrant, have sought not simply a profile, on which there is general agreement, but more rigorous explanations. Everyone agrees that "the individuals most dangerous to the safety of the President are those socially isolated persons who adapt to stress by symbolizing their problems in a political idiom and who identify with the President in terms of violence and death. . . . the act . . . is perceived as a stroke of national policy or patriotic heroism."[30] After that the specialists tend to diverge according to their methodological-academic postures and positions—the President is a father-figure or a mother-figure. The Adlerians have one explanation and the Jungians another. Worse, putting aside the deeper explanations, the accepted profile fits far too many people. The Secret Service has a list of fifty thousand persons who may be a danger to the President and there are surely more than that in America who have backgrounds little different from that of Oswald or Ray or Sirhan. While it is possible to make up a profile of the potential psychotic aircraft hijacker (who wants, in any case, to be caught) and filter him out at the check-in booth, potential assassins do not appear at a check-in booth but out of a crowd, in a reception line, next to the limousine. And until then, they were usually not very different from others with chaotic, unsatisfactory lives—even Squeaky Fromme's weird cult was not unique, only more brutal, more pointless, more senseless than most.

In fact, over the last ten years, one of the more striking phenomena in the assassin's world has been the ability of these disorganized and driven people to coalesce, creating, if briefly, their own organization of despair. Manson's group had only the most marginal political interests—Helter Skelter. Others, such as the Weather Underground, had intensive political concerns, although not assassination, but their "revolutionary careers" can easily be explained by psychologists. Two recent American groups were composed of driven and confused, self-destructive volunteers, leading miserable, unbearable lives, who strike out in murderous violence to ease their own anguish. They collectively remain self-destructive and self-loathing; but unlike the poor, lonely confused Ray or Oswald, they have sought out and found comfort in a symbiotic relationship with others. In the case of the Black Liberation Army, the attraction was a conspiracy to murder the most convenient symbol of a despised society that had brutalized black men, kept them in prison, denied them a future. So with but a single recruit outside the ranks of prison graduates—Joanne Chesimard from New York's City College—they embarked on a disorganized national campaign to kill cops, whether black or white—"targets blue." None of their victims was powerful, no attempt was made to murder the mighty. Patrol cars were blasted with submachine-gun fire, a desk sergeant was shot point-blank with a shotgun, police officers were shot down on patrol or at roadblocks. And in time the Black Liberation Army disappeared, the members killed in shoot-outs, or captured and convicted. Chesimard was sentenced to life for the murder of a New Jersey state trooper. There were no new volunteers. There had not really been any conventional "assassinations," but only murders out of rage.

Of all the conspiracies of violence—the bombers of the Weather

Underground or the gunmen of the Black Liberation Army—only one group actually planned and carried out an "assassination." That group was the Symbionese Liberation Army, the archetype of all aberrant conspiracies, the last froth of the lunatic fringe of American radicalism. Some were middle-class university militants, driven, guilty drop-outs from reality, playing deadly war games, involved in a fantasy revolution that guaranteed the thrill and exhilaration of real danger and the sublimated prospect of self-destruction. They had coupled with the ultimate existentialist assassin: General Field Marshal Cinque, nee Donald DeFreeze, a black escaped convict whose brutal and bitter life had meaning and direction only within the SLA. They were part cult, part radical conspiracy, and most of all a means of group therapy. They could work at revolution, support each other's fantasies, lead lives not of private but public desperation. Their revolutionary deeds consisted of two bank robberies, two kidnappings—that of Patricia Hearst became the media event of the decade—a flawed shoplifting, and the murder of the black Oakland Superintendent of Schools, Marcus Foster, at the beginning of their campaign for reasons never made clear, even to themselves. The final blazing shoot-out in Los Angeles was brought to television viewers live, in color, personally, close up. The few who escaped, including Patty Hearst transmuted into Tania, girl guerrilla, drifted across the country, underground, trailing proclamations filled with ill-assorted radical verbiage, still playing at revolution. This disturbed children's crusade ended in September 1975 when "Tania" was arrested—occupation, said the charge sheet, urban guerrilla (until the lawyers arrived). These few middle-class revolutionaries in or out of the Symbionese Liberation Army or the Weather Underground had participated in "political" violence as a means of personal therapy. They were as miserable and unhappy as the pool of psychopathic assassins, but differed in that they had revolted against the comfort and success of their homes rather than the meanness and futility of a lifetime of lonely anger. They were not as deadly, except to themselves, but were really far more interesting than the bland and inarticulate American assassin. Of these, if the Symbionese Liberation Army is an archetype of the psychotic conspiracy and the only organization to undertake a "real" assassi-

nation, the most appalling of the individual assassins must surely
be Arthur H. Bremer.

On January 12, 1972, Mrs. Pemrich told Artie Bremer that her
sixteen-year-old daughter Joan did not want to see him again. Joan
was tall and gangly with lank, light blond hair and large horn-
rimmed glasses, hardly a strikingly attractive young woman, but
apparently the only friend that Bremer had made, certainly since
the death of Thomas Neuman, who, playing Russian roulette, had
shot and killed himself the year before. Bremer felt he was in love
with Joan Pemrich. She felt that "he was weird." He certainly was
not very prepossessing. At five foot six and 145 pounds, near-
sighted with a curious shuffling walk and an odd vacuous smile,
twenty-one-year-old Bremer was a janitor at Joan's school in Milwaukee. He had met her in October, first visited her home just
before Thanksgiving, and given her a bouquet of roses, a box of
candy, and a handkerchief for Christmas. She gave him a card and
a handkerchief. He put the card on the top of the refrigerator in
his apartment. "I think it was the only one he got." Most of his life,
Bremer had gotten very little. He was the son of a truck driver.
He had spent his life in a series of his parents' apartments in old
wooden frame houses in the grimy working-class neighborhoods
of Milwaukee's South Side. In 1972, one brother was under arrest
in Florida on a federal fraud charge, one was married someplace
in Milwaukee, a stepsister was someplace in California, and another brother, Roger, eighteen, was still at home. Roger noted that
Arthur "hated my ma" and did not get along with him. Arthur
seemed to like his father, who spent considerable time drinking
beer in Milwaukee taverns and playing pool. No one seemed to
know what Arthur did. The assistant dean at a technical college
Bremer attended briefly said, "He was a nondescript little guy, a
quiet little guy." And now without Joan Pemrich, he was even
quieter. There was no one to talk to—there rarely had been.[31]

On January 13, he bought a Charter Arms .38-caliber revolver
from Casanova Guns, Inc. It was the second Charter Arms revolver he had purchased. The last one had cost eighty-five dollars
and had been purchased when he left his parents' apartment on
October 15 and moved into a $138.50-a-month apartment on West
Michigan Avenue. That one had been confiscated by the police

when he was arrested on November 18 on a concealed weapons charge. The arresting officer thought him incoherent but the court psychiatrists found him sane enough to stand trial—the charge was reduced to disorderly conduct and he was fined $38.50. Now he had another Charter Arms. On the same day he bought the gun he shaved his head, leaving only his sideburns. At a dance the night of January 14, at Story Elementary School, the students kidded him about his new haircut. He stayed on there until the end of the month and then returned to his old job as busboy at the Milwaukee Athletic Club. He had already had trouble there, filing a complaint with the Milwaukee Community Relations Commission in November that he had been discriminated against because of changed duties and hours. The club indicated that Bremer had been a problem—guests complained because of his idiosyncracies, which included whistling and marching in time to Muzak. The commission found that he was a rather withdrawn young man—"appears to bottle up anger but will sometimes let it go." He had little communication with his family or friends, and was probably a borderline paranoid but conscientious in doing his job. He was sufficiently conscientious and nondescript for the club to take him back. After leaving the Sloan School on January 31, he purchased a second gun, a 9-mm Browning automatic pistol, from the Flintrop Arms Company for $114.50. Except for the blue Rambler that he had paid $795 for on September 14, it was his most expensive possession. Bremer felt that his guns and car would be crucial for his next project. Apparently, soon after Joan Pemrich had refused to see him, he had decided to kill President Richard Nixon. He began a diary, left Sloan School, bought his second gun, and on February 15, left his job at the Milwaukee Athletic Club without saying anything to anyone. He hardly ever did. His last conversation had been with Joan Pemrich. Over the next four months of his deadly odyssey he would have only one more.

Like John Schrank trailing Roosevelt, Bremer went on the campaign trail, beginning with an appearance at a Humphrey Milwaukee rally at the Capital Plaza Shopping Center on April 3, the day before the Wisconsin primary. The next day he visited Wallace headquarters in Milwaukee and then, on April 5, flew to New

York and stayed at a Howard Johnson's in the Jamaica area. He carried both guns with him. He then moved first to the Fifth Avenue Hotel and then to the Waldorf-Astoria in Manhattan, where Senator Humphrey was scheduled to spend the night of April 7.

> I thought the Waldorf was the best N.Y.C. had to offer. I was wrong. For $37 *plus* I got a room little better than the $23 Fifth Ave. joint. I took a lot of their stationary *that's* what I payed for. They spend all their money on their lobby, & hallways to a lesser degree.[32]

Whether or not Bremer knew that Humphrey was supposed to appear—his visit was canceled—his diary concentrated on his visit to a Times Square "model studio." There on the massage table, nude, he had a lengthy conversation but an otherwise unsuccessful encounter with Alga—"Though I'm still a virgin, I'm thankful to Alga for giving me a peek at what its like."[33] He flew back to Milwaukee to prepare to drive to Ottawa, where President Nixon would appear on April 13. His diary is filled with all the minor frustrations—the problem of hiding the guns (the Browning was shoved down a hole in the car trunk and lost), of getting through customs, of tire repairs and wrong turns and filled hotels. And then he had to watch Nixon's motorcade zip by without an opportunity to shoot—mostly he worried about attracting attention, and about keeping his hand warm in his gun pocket, afraid that the cold air might numb his trigger finger.

> People jumped from their cars. Would the assassin get a good view? Everyone moved in close (about 20 people). We were the only people other than cops for a few blocks.
>
> He went by before I knew it. Like a snap of the fingers. A dark shillowet, waving, rushed by in the large dark car. "All over," someone said to no one in particular.[34]

Assassination was proving as difficult as most things had been for Bremer. Once he lost a chance because he spent too much time with his "appearance and composure."

I will give very little if ANY thought to those things on any future attempts.

After all does the world remember if Sirhan's tie was on straight?

SHIT, I was stupid!!![35]

He drove down to Washington, but could not get close to the President and decided to save money—"Cheaper maybe to pay my rent $138.50 for 30 days rather than $17 per."[36] So he was back in Milwaukee on April 19—"ALL MY EFFORTS & NOTHING CHANGED Just another God Damn failure."[37] He moped around and then went to see the film *A Clockwork Orange*, and thought about getting Wallace all through the picture. His real problem with Wallace was that "he won't even rate a T.V. enteroption in Russia or Europe when the news breaks."[38] Better to kill J. Edgar Hoover. But Wallace became the next target, and on May 10, Bremer attended a Wallace rally in Cadillac, Michigan. On May 13, he was questioned by a policeman at a Wallace rally at Kalamazoo, Michigan. He missed getting close every time he tried. Wallace was leaving to campaign in Maryland. Bremer was running out of money; the blue Rambler gave him constant trouble. The Browning had been lost inside the car and his last try at Kalamazoo had aborted—"My cry upon firing will be, 'A penny for your thoughts.' "[39]

Bremer drove the Rambler to Maryland, on Wallace's trail. He appeared on May 15 at a Wallace rally in Wheaton, Maryland, wearing sunglasses and a red, white, and blue shirt decorated with Wallace buttons. He did not get close enough. He moved on to the Laurel, Maryland, shopping center where Wallace spoke again. He arrived as early as he could to get a place in the front row. Three hours later, at a little past four in the afternoon, after Wallace had left the speaker's platform and the bulletproof glass shield to walk to his limousine, Bremer shouted, "Hey George! Hey George! Over here!" A few others took up the cry and the Alabama governor came over to shake hands. Suddenly Bremer drew his Charter Arms .38-caliber revolver, stuck it between Ross and Mabel Speigle, and opened fire at nearly pointblank range. He got off five shots before Ross Speigle wrestled him to the ground.

Wallace was hit, paralyzed from the waist down; a bodyguard, a Wallace campaign worker, and a Secret Service agent were also wounded. The crowd was trying to get at Bremer, shouting, "Kill him, let's kill him." Speigle held him down until a variety of law enforcement people rushed him out of the parking lot. Bremer turned to one of the men holding him as he was being led off to jail—"How much do you think I'm going to get for my autobiography?" And he was on the Walter Cronkite news show that night —the CBS film was used at his trial, where he was convicted of various counts of assault with intent to murder and sentenced to a total of sixty-three years in prison. He has remained a loner at Maryland State Penitentiary in Baltimore. He grants no interviews, and won't even see his mother. According to Warden George Collins, "He just doesn't want to be bothered." Wallace appeared in a wheelchair at the Democratic Convention in July —a symbolic husk no longer relevant to national politics. Bremer's response to the sentencing judge's question about whether he had anything to say was, "Looking back on my life, I would have liked it if society had protected me from myself."[40]

"POLITICAL" MURDER WITHOUT POLITICS

> . . . we are savage killers and madmen.
> —Field Marshal Cinque (Donald DeFreeze) of the
> Symbionese Liberation Army

Many of those who have killed or maimed the mighty because of an obsession, vengeance, or greed would or did feel vindicated. Sheikh Abeid Karume was dead, and vengeance was served; with Patrice Lumumba dead, if by other hands, QJ/WIN and WI/ROGUE were the richer. Perceval, too, was dead and Bellingham had acted as he felt he must. The American assassins who had killed or tried to kill for a variety of causes appeared satisfied by the impact of their deed, even if few others saw the cause of the South or international anarchism or the claims of the environmentalists advanced. It is not, of course, what was intended that truly matters, but what ensued from the murder, what were the perceptions and responses of those responsible. At times little seemed to change—it is difficult to imagine that Britain would have been a greatly different place if Perceval had lived, and life on Zanzibar is still in the hands of the revolutionary council, now less wanton, and the people as a lot less miserable. Still, especially in the American instances, the violent intrusion of the assassin has or might have made real differences.

The attack on Jackson on January 30, 1835, came after he had transformed the office of the President but before he issued his specie circular that led to a disastrous panic a little over a year later. Most of the other major events—crises, confrontations, new directions, and new postures—had already occurred, and if Jackson had been killed, Vice President Martin Van Buren would have come to power a year earlier, pledged loyally to Jackson's own policies. As it was, the only fallout of the attempt was a suspicion among Jackson's supporters that Lawrence was part of a Tory plot; but with the cooperation of the prosecutor, Francis Scott Key, Lawrence was found not guilty by reason of insanity. Successful assassins usually had poorer luck with such a plea—and in the case of Lincoln's murder, everyone even faintly connected with the conspiracy was hanged. What general and what specific differences Lincoln would have made remain moot questions. Certainly, if he had pursued a policy of reconciliation instead of radical reconstruction, he would have been less vulnerable than Johnson, but perhaps no more effective.

Both Jackson and Lincoln were dynamic, strong Presidents, while the next two victims, Garfield and McKinley, were not— Garfield, of course, had little opportunity to be anything. His death, supposedly at the hand of a disappointed office-seeker, was used by the proponents of civil service reform, perhaps a movement whose time was ripe in any case. Czolgosz's self-proclaimed anarchism added a substantial penny to the growing concern about alien forces and political violence—there had been nearly a generation of labor turmoil, including the failed assassination of industrialist Henry Clay Frick on July 23, 1892, by the well-known anarchist Alexander Beckman. Despite the drama of Roosevelt's speech with the blood soaking through his shirt, Schrank's attack seemed to have little impact on the fortunes of the Bull Moose or the direction of American politics. While Congress could—and did, after McKinley's death—pass legislation adding anarchists to the list of excluded immigrants and restricting the activities of those already here, it was somewhat more difficult to pass legislation banning the appearance of the spirits of martyred Presidents.

In the case of Zangara's attempt on Roosevelt, as a failure it had no viable impact on the course of events; but if it had been a success, modern American history would surely have been transformed—how transformed remains speculation, intriguing but no more. To a lesser degree this would have been true with the death of Truman—there were still two eventful years that would have been different years under Alben Barkley and, more narrowly, there would have been a different perspective on the Puerto Rican problem. In the case of Kennedy, while we know what happened, it can only be suggested that Johnson, with a martyr to hand, was able to achieve an impressive record of domestic legislation that Kennedy might not have found as easy—and almost certainly the priorities and positions of Johnson's elective term would have been different from those of Kennedy's second term. Whether we would still have made similar commitments, like all such speculative questions, remains moot. And in the final case of Ford, if either Squeaky Fromme or Sara Jane Moore had killed the President, it seems unlikely that a Rockefeller administration would have been very different or more capable of withstanding a Reagan challenge for the nomination. And a Reagan-Carter campaign would seemingly have had a result somewhat similar to the Ford-Carter one.

It is not simply the specifics that flow from murder on the political scene that must be traced, but also the perceptions of the powerful and the public. In the violent decade after John Kennedy's assassination, there were many who felt that somehow America was to blame for the violence—the most articulate were those who urged radical social reforms to repair the injustices of the past. And they spoke to a largely receptive audience. Just as the rising anguish about the industrial turmoil, the labor wars, the massive waves of immigrants, could be personified by the Polish

Czolgosz—born in the United States four months after his parents' arrival—who killed for the working class that so much of conventional America distrusted—so, too, could Booth's deed be turned to the advantage of radical Republicans. It does not do very much good to explain to an anguished and outraged public, eager for vengeance, that there was probably not an Oswald conspiracy, no vast net of cunning reactionaries behind James Earl Ray, no sane, much less political, reason why Bremer shot Wallace. Squeaky Fromme is transmuted into a symbol for permissiveness and decayed moral standards—and the disciplinarians' assets increase. Czolgosz, as a "rational" anarchist, adds to the arsenal of the isolationists, the exclusionists, the conservative and conventional. Civil service reform is hastened in one century and civil rights in another, both because of the perceptions of those involved rather than the reality of the motive of the assassin. And such a perception is remarkably different from that when someone dies a natural death or becomes incapacitated in office—what might have been the fate of the League of Nations in the United States Senate if Woodrow Wilson had been shot down in the street instead of crippled by a stroke?

NOTES

1. In March 1978, another Mafia entry into revolutionary politics was reported by the Roman newspaper *Il Messaggero*. Thirteen days after the Brigate Rosse kidnapped former Premier Aldo Moro, the "godfathers" of mobs based in eleven cities from Turin to Palermo met and issued a threat that if Moro were not released by 4 A.M. March 30, their colleagues would suppress all Brigate Rosse people, even in jail. It was, they indicated, their patriotic duty. Police noted that crime had fallen by 60 percent because of the massive 50,000-man dragnet thrown over Italy. The deadline came and went and, alas, the conclusion of the observers was that the communiqué had been a hoax.

2. One sign of instant media success is instant clip-and-paste books (either just before or just after television specials), *cf.* Colin Smith, *Carlos: Portrait of a Terrorist,* New York, Holt, Rinehart & Winston, 1976, and Christopher Dobson and Ronald Payne, *The Carlos Complex, A Study in Terror,* New York, Putnam, 1977.

3. G. Heinz and H. Donnay, *Lumumba: The Last Fifty Days.* New York, Grove, 1969, p. 161.

4. *Ibid.,* p. 18.

5. *Ibid.,* p. 19.

6. Select Committee to Study Government Operations, *Alleged Assassination Plots Involving Foreign Leaders,* Washington, D.C., Government Printing Office, November 20, 1975, p. 14.

7. *Ibid.,* p. 17.

8. *Ibid.,* p. 46.

9. *Ibid.*

10. *Ibid.,* p. 47.

11. *Ibid.,* p. 48.

12. *Ibid.,* p. 182.

13. *Ibid.,* p. 181.

14. Mollie Gillen, *Assassination of the Prime Minister, The Shocking Death of Spencer Perceval,* New York, St. Martin's, 1972, p. 7.

15. *Ibid.,* p. 112.

16. *Boston Globe,* November 29, 1970.

17. Robert Katz, *The Fall of the House of Savoy,* New York, Macmillan, 1971, p. 85.

18. *Ibid.*

19. There is, of course, a very considerable body of literature on the Lincoln assassination—without a final consensus that Booth was or was not a rational assassin. An excellent popular account is Jim Bishop's *The Day Lincoln Was Shot,* New York, Harper & Row, 1955.

20. See Charles E. Rosenberg, *The Trial of the Assassin Guiteau,* Chicago, The University of Chicago Press, 1968.

21. Staff Report to the National Commission of the Causes and Prevention of Violence (Prepared by James F. Kirkham, Sheldon G. Levy, and William J. Crotty), *Assassination and Political Violence,* New York, Bantam, 1970—an excellent summary of American assassinations in particular to that date, *cf.* Czolgosz, pp. 67–69.

22. *Ibid.,* p. 73.

23. *Ibid.*

24. The literature on the Kennedy assassination in general and Lee Harvey Oswald in particular has reached the point where it was deemed profitable to publish a large "resource manual" simply indicating the scope of the new industry. Congress in 1978 again—still—investigated the matter, discovering some indication of a conspiracy that did not convince skeptics. Societies and conventions exist concerned with nothing else. Careers have been based on that one day. Clearly a great many Americans, many of them sensible, prefer a conspiracy to the application of Occam's razor: the simplest explanation—Oswald was a typical, psychotic assassin, American variant.

25. *Time,* September 15, 1975.

26. For a detailed account of the Manson cult see Vincent Bugliosi's *Helter-Skelter,* New York, Norton, 1974.

27. The Dohrn comment, made at the Flint War Council and variously reported in both the conventional and underground press, was the first giant step by the Weather Underground off the far side of the New Left Road.

28. *Time,* September 15, 1975.

29. For example, on April 6, 1978, Phillip Estes Reed, 37, of San Antonio, Texas, hijacked a tow-truck in Pecos, Texas, in order to drive to Washington—he threatened President Jimmy Carter's life over the Panama Canal treaties—and drove two thousand miles through Arizona, New Mexico, Oklahoma, and Missouri before being overpowered by an FBI agent in Lebanon, Missouri. The hijacking

hardly had the flair—or danger—of helicopter theft, but was typical of the unending problem of the FBI and Secret Service in monitoring presidential threats. Written threats can at least be subject to content analysis, but the hijackers and fence jumpers and lone White House protestors are regularly with us, each with a special cause and a potentially dangerous obsession.

30. Edwin A. Weinstein and Olga G. Lyerly, "Symbolic Aspects of Presidential Assassination," *Psychiatry: Journal for the Study of Interpersonal Processes,* vol. 32, no. 1, February 1969, p. 11. As might be expected, the professional literature of the problem of assassination, especially after John Kennedy's murder, is massive, often contentious, and fairly predictable. The Weinstein/Lyerly article is less time-bound, being based on material from 137 male subjects over the period 1945–1965.

31. *The New York Times,* May 22, 1972, did an immensely detailed investigation of Arthur Bremer's background, but the most fascinating source is the last half of his diary (the first part is still buried)—13 entries—the last two days before he shot Governor Wallace. Arthur H. Bremer, *An Assassin's Diary,* New York, Harper Magazine Press, 1973.

32. Bremer, *op. cit.,* p. 31.

33. *Ibid.,* p. 41.

34. *Ibid.,* p. 71.

35. *Ibid.,* p. 77.

36. *Ibid.,* p. 112.

37. *Ibid.,* p. 94.

38. *Ibid.,* p. 105.

39. *Ibid.,* p. 137.

40. *Ibid.,* p. 142.

3

Killing as Politics: War and Order, Murderous Legitimacies

Uomo morto non fa guerra.
Dead men don't make war.

Our enemies are the forces of Romanism and
Communism, which must be destroyed.
—Ulster Volunteer Recruiting Circular, 1971

There are, of course, those who organize murder in the service
of a recognized legitimacy, for the defense of the realm or the
protection of a threatened system. First and most obvious are
those authorized by a state to kill—soldiers in wartime, agents in
peacetime—and there are, too, those curious confrontations of
no-war-no-peace, irregular campaigns in the bush or partisan ambushes in occupied zones; the killer claims to act as soldier. Second, there are those without uniform or recognized standing who
kill to maintain existing institutions and customs; either there is no
state to direct their actions, or an existing state tolerates their
murders or in some instances opposes them. This is the murderous
violence of the vigilante.

Those who resort to murder when the existing and cherished

institutions won't or can't defend themselves—or have collapsed —abound under certain circumstances. In the United States immediately after the close of the Civil War, large areas of the South were without effective law enforcement, at the mercy of wandering bands of refugees, freed slaves, and outlaws. The Ku Klux Klan was founded to assure order but then evolved into an organization to counter the radical transformation the federal government sought to impose on Southern society. In decay the vigilante current of terror and intimidation remained an integral part of the rural South until recently. Soldiers answer, if at times haltingly, to real law; the lynch mob answers to the pragmatic needs of its society; thus, each is often legitimate in many eyes, unlike the revolutionary. The soldier or the night rider is for law and order, albeit the old order.

KILLING DURING WAR

Though in the trade of war I have slain men
Yet do I hold it the very stuff o' the conscience
To do no contriv'd murder.
                    —*Othello,* Act 1, Scene 1

War, regular war with massed armies and chains of command, with rules and regulations and conventions, hardly seems to come under the rubric of political violence at all. War seems mostly about killing in conventional and congenial ways, the sport of kings, the province of generals, and yet even during the battle the planning and executing of specific operations against specific individuals for obvious military and political advantage can be isolated and treated as assassination. Reportedly, at the Battle of Waterloo, Wellington turned down a soldier's offer to have a shot at Emperor Napoleon, marshalling the French troops opposite British lines, because gentlemen have no business contriving at shooting each other. It is not that generals and admirals are above death in battle; but, like their men, they tend to be killed anony-

mously. Someone like Lord Nelson may have been shot down on
his quarterdeck because he was a good and recognizable target,
but few such encounters are planned mainly or solely to eliminate
an individual leader. Remarkably few military leaders or the leaders of the military during a war are killed on purpose. None of the
involved seem quite certain whether bombing Buckingham Palace or Berchtesgaden would be productive. At the time of the
massive American B-29 fireraids that devastated Tokyo—in one
raid on March 10, 1945, 140,000 died—pilots had instructions to
avoid the Palace "since the Emperor of Japan is not at present a
liability and may later become an asset."[1] Of course, there was no
unwritten *rule* to avoid striking at individuals. The British in
North Africa, in a long penetration raid, attempted to hit Rommel's headquarters. A much more traditional assassination attempt was authorized by Adolph Hitler against the Allied Big
Three, Josef Stalin, Franklin Roosevelt, and Winston Churchill.
Operation Long John was to be a commando attack on the three
when they met in Teheran, Iran, in November 1943. Nothing
came of the attempt; most of the paratroop-commandos were
betrayed on landing and scooped up, and perhaps Hitler had little
hope that anything would happen. However, the operation was
one of the few such exercises during wartime but hardly the only
one.[2]

The Big Wars, Pop Goes the Weasel—
The Death of Admiral Isoroko Yamamoto

In April 1943, the war in the Pacific had certainly not been won
by the Allies, despite the successful offenses in New Guinea and
Guadalcanal in the Solomon Islands; nor had the Japanese lost,
despite the end of the great victories that had nearly swept their
opponents from the Pacific. Both the Japanese and Americans had
problems of priorities. General Douglas MacArthur had to compete with not only the European theater but also the needs of the
navy. Still he had managed to put together Operation Cartwheel,
a drive to begin in June against Rabaul. Japanese Imperial head-

quarters, too, had problems in the area—whether to concentrate on the defense of New Guinea or the Solomon Islands. On March 25, Admiral Yamamoto and General Hitoshi Imamura received a directive to concentrate on the former. Yamamoto was given the task of destroying Allied air and sea power in the entire area. His Operation I (I-Go) would consist of a series of massive air strikes against Guadalcanal and New Guinea. On April 7, directed personally by Yamamoto, who had moved to Rabaul from Turk, 224 fighters and bombers hit Guadalcanal, the largest air attack since Pearl Harbor. The pilots were wildly enthusiastic, although actual damage was slight. Then three big raids were launched against New Guinea, with the same results. The Japanese pilots reported that 175 planes had been destroyed, although only five had actually been lost. With I-Go over, Yamamoto prepared to return to Turk. First, however, he wanted to stop by Lieutenant-General Masao Maruyama's headquarters on Ballale Island off the tip of Bougainville to thank the men for their sacrifices on Guadalcanal. General Imamura had considerable doubt about the wisdom of the gesture—he had already had a narrow escape from American fighters over Bougainville. Yamamoto insisted.

Commander Yasuji Watanabe wrote out Yamamoto's schedule by hand and took it himself to Eighth Fleet headquarters on April 14 to be delivered by courier, eliminating any chance of interception and decoding. The communications officer told Watanabe this would be impossible, and not to worry: the new naval code had been changed on April 1 and could not be broken. Watanabe left; the message was encoded and sent. As soon as Japanese transmission began, the message was intercepted by Combat Intelligence headquarters at Pearl Harbor. The specialists worked straight through the night and at dawn had a decoded text in plain Japanese. Lieutenant Colonel Alva Lasswell, a Marine language specialist, and his staff filled in the blanks, identified the code symbols, and sent the English translation to Admiral Chester Nimitz's office by eight in the morning. Yamamoto would leave Rabaul at 6 A.M., April 18, in a Mitsubishi medium bomber with an escort of six Zero fighters, and arrive at Ballale Island at 8 A.M. The very best the Japanese had was vulnerable—"He's unique among their people

—it would stun the nation."[3] Nimitz agreed to try it and sent Admiral William Halsey instructions to begin preparations—Ballale was a long way from any American base. In Washington the mission was approved both by Secretary of Navy Frank Know and the President. On April 15, Nimitz wired Halsey "good luck and good hunting."

At 6 A.M. Tokyo time, Sunday, April 18, Yamamoto's Mitsubishi took off from Rabaul accompanied by another bomber containing his chief of staff, Vice Admiral Matome Ugaki, and several aides. The two bombers and six fighters flew at 5,000 feet for two hours and thirty-four minutes, until Bougainville appeared on the left, and the pilots began to descend to land at Kahili airfield. One minute before, exactly on schedule, a tight group of sixteen P-38 Lightnings commanded by Major John W. Mitchell arrived after a 600-mile flight over open water with only compass bearings and airspeed readings. The problem was, could the killer group of planes hit the unexpected extra Mitsubishi still gliding toward Kahili unsuspectingly? The P-38s dropped their extra fuel tanks. Almost at the same time the silver belly tanks began dropping from the Japanese Zeros—the P-38s had been spotted. It was too late. One P-38 could not get into action—the fuel tanks of one stuck—but the other two drove toward the bombers, then down so low they were skimming the jungle. Ugaki, in one Mitsubishi, could not understand what was happening. He asked the pilot, who could see only that the plane was amid a tangle of Zeros and P-38s: "I think there was an operational mistake."[4] One P-38 put a long burst into Yamamoto's plane—the right engine and wing flamed up; another burst and the tail disintegrated, and the Mitsubishi cartwheeled into the jungle and exploded. Ugaki's plane shimmered past the column of black smoke and crashed into the sea. Ugaki was the only survivor.

POP GOES THE WEASEL. P-38'S LED BY MAJOR JOHN W. MITCHELL USA VISITED KAHILI AREA ABOUT 0930 SHOT DOWN TWO BOMBERS ESCORTED BY ZEROS FLYING CLOSE FORMATION. ONE SHOT BELIEVED TO BE TEST FLIGHT. THREE ZEROS ADDED TO THE SCORE SUM TOTAL SIX. ONE P-38 FAILED RETURN. APRIL 18 SEEMS TO BE OUR DAY.[5]

The Americans did not announce Yamamoto's death, fearing that the Japanese would know their code had been broken. On May 21, the superbattleship *Musashi* arrived in Tokyo Bay with Yamamoto's body, and the Japanese people learned that he had "met gallant death in a war plane." His successor, Admiral Mineichi Koga, said, "There was only one Yamamoto and no one can replace him."[6]

The Irregular Wars, Mondlane, Cabral, and the Risked Revolution

Despite the slaughter and destruction of the Pacific war—the Bataan Death March, the Tokyo fireraids, the tortured prisoners, and the ruins of Hiroshima and Nagasaki—it was a *conventional* war, recognizable as such to the officer corps, even if they had different traditions and values. And it was largely fought in conventional ways—the killing was anonymous, Yamamoto a special case. In less conventional wars—the battles in the bush by revolutionary guerrillas or the no-warning bombs planted in the lanes and alleys of a large city by avowed revolutionaries—there is a tendency for the threatened to opt for equally unconventional tactics. In a real war the problems with killing specific individuals —everyone knew the reputation of Yamamoto or Rommel—were the pragmatic difficulties: the distance, the army between the target and the killer, the problems of accurate intelligence and ultimate access. In irregular war, especially in colonial war, the target, even if known, is elusive, deep in the bush or hidden anonymously in an attic or walking unrecognized through the streets. Sometimes the security forces are lucky and scoop up one of the wanted who can be charged, tried, convicted, and imprisoned or tortured on demand, or shot trying to escape or evade capture. In a very few cases, information received makes possible such a security operation—and in that case, the murder is not in the course of a counter-insurgency operation but is a judicial execution, another brutal category of murder. In other special cases, however, the threatened not only know who specifically threatens them but also where he lives—for when an insurgency is run from exile, usually friendly exile, security is more lax, a target more vulnerable—most vulnerable of all when the campaign is over and only the vengeance of the defeated remains.

In the 1960s the Portuguese in their three African colonies—overseas provinces of Angola, Mozambique, and Guiné—faced classic long-lived and tenacious guerrilla insurrections. Only in Guiné-Bissau, where Amilcar Cabral's PAIGC *(Partido Africano da Independencia da Guiné e Cabo Verde)* dominated the armed struggle that began there in January 1963, was opposition to the Portuguese limited to one organization. Gradually in Mozambique FRELIMO *(Frente de Libertação do Moçambique)*, under the guidance of Dr. Eduardo Mondlane, a former professor of anthropology at Syracuse University in the United States, monopolized the struggle. In Angola the revolt had begun in February-March 1968 and ultimately saw three major forces, the *Movimento Popular de Libertacão Angola* (MPLA) with in part a tribal Kimbundu base, the *União das Populaçoes de Angola* (UPA), with a Bakongo base, and *União Nacional para a Independência Total de Angola* (UNITA), based on the southern Ovimbundo tribes. Increasingly —despite splits and clashes, the rise and fall of other organizations, and normal political attrition—the struggle in Portuguese Africa was personified by Cabral of PAIGC, Mondlane of FRELIMO, Agostinho Neto of MPLA, Holden Roberto of UPA—who became less active as time went by in his Congo exile—and Jonas Savimbi of UNITA, who tended to remain in hiding in southern Angola. Each of the major movements gradually became transformed into a counter-state with headquarters and—in the cases of Zambia, at times the Congo, and Tanzania—training camps for the guerrilla army in friendly states. Legates were dispatched, conferences attended, agreements with other liberation organizations negotiated; in many sympathetic states the leaders of the movements were considered presidents-in-exile. Thus, despite occasional and often well-publicized forays into the liberated zones in the bush, Neto, Mondlane, and Cabral acted openly as political leaders rather than as operational commanders. Everyone knew who they were, what they were, and usually where they would be. Security really did not exist at FRELIMO headquarters in Dar-es-Salaam. Unknown people could, and did, simply walk into Mondlane's office unannounced. They were each tempting targets, especially since most armies fighting irregular wars are outraged at the "unfair" advantages the guerrillas have while conventional forces must keep to convention. There in various black African capitals, walking free, plotting, planning, training terrorists, were the godfathers of violence.

On February 3, 1969, Eduardo Mondlane opened a package bomb and was killed in the explosion. Almost at once everyone had a prime candidate for the assassin, depending on their own predilections and postures. Certainly the simplest explanation was that the Portuguese had arranged matters to eliminate one of their most persistent and articulate enemies. Certainly most of the spokesmen for FRELIMO indicated that the PIDE—*Policia Internacional e de Defesa do Estado*—was behind the killing. Others felt that behind the PIDE lurked the CIA. Others, however, noted that during much of 1968 FRELIMO had been in turmoil. There had been serious disturbances at the Mozambique Institute, directed by Mondlane's wife, and at party headquarters in Dar-es-Salaam. Besides the internal political bickering, there was increasing dissidence at the front, where the sacrifices were unevenly distributed on a tribal basis. Mondlane was in fact far more popular with the Western press and public than with many in FRELIMO. Weeks passed, and then months, and there were no culprits. Rumors faded and FRELIMO, under group leadership, soldiered on. Mondlane's loss was a blow, but not a fatal one; perhaps most important, the ties to the West that he had maintained had less priority as the Russians, in particular, fueled FRELIMO's guerrilla struggle.

Several years later, on January 20, 1973, Amilcar Cabral, the most successful of the African nationalist leaders, drove his Volkswagen home from an embassy reception in Conakry, capital of Guinea. On reaching the PAIGC compound, the car was stopped by Innocencio Cani, who had been found guilty of selling a PAIGC launch on the black market but had been forgiven. Cabral got out of the car, leaving his wife, and asked Cani and several other PAIGC people, each with blemished records, what the trouble was. Cani shot him in the stomach. Cabral called out for his wife to go for a doctor. The conspirators finished him off and, leaving his wife, rushed to a nearby office and dragged off Cabral's deputy, Aristides Pereira. They attempted to escape in Cani's launch but were spotted the next day by Guinean MIGs and overtaken by naval craft. This time the link between the conspirators and the Portuguese was more than a matter of speculation. It was not the first attempt, in any case, for in November 1970 a force of white and black Portuguese commandos had attacked Cabral's small bungalow and President Sékou Touré's residence with bazookas and submachine guns, unsuccessfully, for Touré was not in residence and Cabral was in Europe, although his wife narrowly escaped death. After that there had apparently been continued Portuguese planning for another attempt by releasing certain prisoners and subjoining other PAIGC people in Guinea. The plotters, infiltrators, and malcontents understood from the new Portuguese commander, General António Spínola, that after Cabral's death negotiations between a new Spínola-sponsored movement, *Frente Unida de Libertacao de la Guiné*, and Lisbon would lead to an African-manned government in Bissau with promising niches for the successful conspirators. Cabral was dead, but for all intents and purposes so was Spínola's new front group; as in the case of FRELIMO, there was no indication that PAIGC had been seriously damaged. In both cases, of course, *something* had been done, two most important pieces had been removed from the board, but the game continued and new pieces were fashioned. In time, Spínola came to the conclusion that while Portugal might not be in danger of defeat, neither were the African guerrillas, and the war could not be won. And, when he returned to Lisbon, he became involved in the conspiracy that led to the destruction of the Portuguese government and the old corporate system. The door to freedom for Guiné and Mozambique and Angola opened in Lisbon with Spínola's hand on the knob.

Partisan War, the Murder of the Man with the Iron Heart, Reinhard Heydrich

Resistance to occupation has long been recognized as a form of war—giving the Spanish term *guerrilla,* little war, to the dictionary of violence, yet the laws of war are often ignored in the case of distant colonial campaigns. Most occupiers tend to see armed resistance to their presence as absolutely illicit, a serious threat to the advantages of victory, and a provocation that must be met with overweening force or disproportionate brutality. In such matters there can be no rules—the discontent are deported, the rebellious tortured, the suspect imprisoned, and resistance met by extensive reprisal. This was certainly the policy of Nazi Germany, one that for Berlin had the added advantage of ridding large areas of the new, greater Reich of "undesirables"—Jews, Slavs, gypsies. And one of the very first non-Germanic areas occupied by the Reich had been the truncated provinces of Czechoslovakia on March 15, 1939. Unlike the Saar or the Sudetenland or Danzig or Austria, this territory was occupied, not absorbed, and the Czechs, unable to resist militarily, abandoned by their allies, began—as so many other Europeans would—to organize resistance. Those who could fled to London and set up a government-in-exile, an embarrassment to the British until they too were in the war. Those who could not go did what they could.

At first this was very little, but the war spread and German interest focused elsewhere. In time there were partisan bands in the mountains, secret printing presses, cells that collected and distributed intelligence. And perhaps the single greatest asset the Czech government-in-exile possessed was the evidence that the resistance was active, and the most valuable asset for Allied purposes was information supplied by the agent Franta to London through his controls, Lieutenant-Colonel Josef Masin and Major Vaclav Moravek. Franta was a Nazi intelligence officer, Paul Thümmel, who had worked for Czech intelligence since 1936, supplying extremely high-level information first to Prague and then to London. Other than passing on Franta's information, which required advanced radio equipment, Moravek and his group wanted parachutists dropped into Bohemia to aid the resistance and carry out diversionary action. By April 1941, the British war office gave authorization for parachute training for the Czechs. The first course began in May. There was as yet no interest in Reinhard Heydrich—the Man with the Iron Heart.

Of all the major Nazi leaders Heydrich somehow remains elusive, an iron surface covering absolute ambition and deeply hidden doubt. Heydrich appeared to be the ideal Nazi, slender, blond, cold, without scruple or restraint. He lived for power, would kill for power, and was totally uninterested in ideological rationalizations. He cared nothing for the tortured logic of Nazi theory, nothing for the wrongs done Germany, nothing for history. Yet he looked the ideal Nazi. He was a good athlete, an excellent fencer; he played the violin with apparent feeling, preferring Mozart and Haydn. He shot well; he rode well. He had insisted that Hitler allow him to fly missions on the Eastern Front —he did not want to sit out the war at a desk. And he was young, handsome, an Aryan without the crippling faults of gross Göring or the enigmatic Himmler or the twisted Goebbels. An evil young god of death who by the beginning of the war was one of the most powerful men in Germany, one that many saw as Hitler's successor. No task daunted him—and he, more than any other, was the architect of the Final Solution. Yet his colleagues and rivals suspected or knew, and Heydrich knew it, that in his background there existed a Jewish strain.

> He had overcome the Jew in himself by purely intellectual
> means and had swung over to the other side. He was
> convinced that the Jewish elements in his blood were
> damnable; he hated the blood which had played him so
> false. The Führer could really have picked no better man
> than Heydrich for the campaign against the Jews. For
> them he was without mercy or pity.[7]

And without mercy or pity he came to Prague, willing for tactical reasons to leave the center of the stage at Berlin briefly to add one more triumph to his record by pacifying the Czechs.

At once the arrests, deportations, executions began. The walls of Prague were plastered with placards listing the victims—Communists, partisans, students, Jews, suspects; 163 death sentences the first week, and 718 dispatched to concentration camps. By October 11, five thousand had been arrested. All ambitious partisan operations were suspended or postponed. Masin was arrested, the radio lost, Franta silent. Even the new parachute drops failed and the first agents were captured. In London a meeting was held where the decision was made to assassinate Heydrich on October 28, 1941, the Czechoslovakian national day. The mission aborted, but further parachute groups were sent into Bohemia to make contact with Fanta and to bolster the resistance. In March 1942, contact was re-established with London, and Franta's information that had been piling up could be passed along; but by then the Germans had all but closed in on him—he had already been arrested twice. By the time the radio worked, Franta was under arrest again. On March 21, 1942, Moravek fought a long gun battle at a Franta rendezvous and then committed suicide so the Germans could not question him. The Franta affair also threatened the various parachute groups that had been dropping since December; some escaped arrest, some made their way to the partisans, some were captured, and one betrayed his group. In April another group was dropped, this time with another assassination operation. The target was Emmanuel Moravec, who had accepted the post of Minister of Education from the Germans. The major area leader, Professor Ladislav Vanek, while agreeing that the death of Moravec would have less of an effect than that of Heydrich, still feared large-scale reprisals. The partisans radioed President Eduard Benes in London asking that the operation be called off. A Swedish courier reached Benes with another copy. On May 13, in London, a meeting was held, attended by two political representatives and two from Czech military intelligence. The army representatives insisted that a "large action" was expected. On the recommendation of the majority at the meeting, President Benes informed Vanek that a "large action" was necessary to dispel the impression that the nation was collaborating with the Germans—there must be a complete repudiation of the Nazi occupation. "In this situation an aggressive action or revolt would be highly desirable and indispensable. In international politics this would mean salvation for the nation, even at the cost of large sacrifice."[8] This meant the Heydrich assassination was on— a "large action."

Two of the paratroopers, Josef Gabcik and Jan Kubish, began the preparations—loitering on the Reichsprotector's route to the castle, collecting bits and pieces of information, codifying his routine, his personal habits, the observations of his servants. The decision was made to locate the attempt at a sharp bend in the street in the suburb of Holesovie, along Heydrich's daily route between his villa and his office in Hradcany Castle. The limousine would have to slow almost to a stop and Gabchik, who had been especially trained on the Sten submachine gun—he could assemble it rapidly with one hand—would be waiting at curbside. There would be a back-up, Jan Kubish, who had a bomb and aides in the general area to aid the escape. It was a simple plan, perfected over the previous five months. The serious problem was timing, for Prague was filled with rumors that Heydrich was planning to leave for a new assignment—which was quite true. He had pacified the Czechs, caught Franta, and in the process tamed some of his internal rivals—it was time to move onward and upward. He was to administer France.

On May 23, watchmaker Josef Novotny was called to Heydrich's office to repair an antique clock. While working on the clock, he noticed a paper on the Reichsprotector's desk outlining his personal schedule for May 27, hour by hour, including his permanent departure from Prague by plane. With Heydrich out of the room, Novotny crumpled the sheet of paper and tossed it into the wastebasket. He tidied up the clock, tested the chimes, and went on his way. Minutes later the charwoman Marie Rasnerova appeared in the office, emptied the wastebasket, and left quietly. The Reichsprotector, hard at work at his desk, took as little notice of her departure as he had that of the Czech watchmaker. The Czechs decided that the 27th would be the day—the last day for Heydrich in Prague. Those in the resistance who had hoped the operation would be postponed for lack of time were disappointed. Kubish and Gabcik had waited for five months, London had sent the order, it was time. Gabcik and Kubish, the first with the Sten, the second with a bomb, would be on the curb wearing raincoats, the weapons concealed in briefcases. There would be two women's bicycles beside them. Both would be armed with pistols for defense but neither saw the need. Rela Fafek's car would pull out slightly in front of Heydrich's when he left the villa and precede him all the way into Prague. Josef Valcik would be just beyond the curve with a mirror to flash the signal that Heydrich's car was into the turn. Around the district would be "passers-by" to ease their escape. When the car reached Gabcik he would simply step out and empty his Sten into Heydrich and the driver. Kubish would trip his bomb and exchange his briefcase for that of Heydrich. They would both ride off, lose any pursuit, and go to ground in their safe houses. They were ready.

May 27 was an absolutely radiant day—clear blue sky with a few clouds, the gardens and trees in blossom—and the morning streets filled with people. At his villa Heydrich was late—he had been playing with his three children and talking to his wife, who would soon bear him a fourth. S.S. Oberscharführer Klein waited by the side of the elegant black Mercedes limousine, growing warm in the sun. The clock struck ten—they should have been on the road or at the castle. Heydrich finally appeared, slipped into the rear seat, and sat with his briefcase on his knees. Klein drove off and began to pick up speed when he reached the main road. There was little traffic—only the single car keeping a bit ahead, driven by Rela Fafek. Heydrich ordered Klein to speed up. They were going to be late. Fafek still kept ahead of the Mercedes. And as Klein drove into the built-up zone he had to slow down still further; ahead was the sharp corner that could not be managed even at twenty-five miles an hour. Klein took his foot off the accelerator. The single car ahead made the turn and disappeared. There was a streetcar. A young man standing beside a tree was playing with a pocket mirror. There was a flash and a gleam. The Mercedes made the turn. A young man on the right-hand side of the road dashed across and Klein had to slow almost to a stop. It was 10:31. Josef Gabcik stepped off the curb and lifted the Sten from under his raincoat. The Mercedes was dead in the road. Klein and Heydrich sat stunned, hardly understanding the danger.

Gabcik squeezed the trigger. Nothing happened. The Sten had jammed. Klein and Heydrich finally reacted and drew their pistols. Kubish reached into his briefcase, pulled out his bomb, and lobbed it up and toward Heydrich, who was standing up taking aim at the frozen Gabcik, his Sten still clutched uselessly in his hand. There was a heavy roar. Gabcik began to run. Kubish was sprayed with shrapnel, and across the street there were a couple of casualties. The rear wheel and the side of the Mercedes were torn. Heydrich was still upright but he had dropped his pistol.

Kubish leaped on his bike and pedaled off. The pedestrians kept on walking, passing by the shattered car and the stunned Heydrich. "Let him walk." A trolley passed. A truck passed. No one came to his aid but a single woman, a known collaborator. Eventually she stopped a small station wagon. When Heydrich tried to move, he collapsed. The two managed to get him into the station wagon and to the nearby Bulkova hospital. There it appeared the Reichsprotector had been very lucky—the shrapnel had missed the kidneys, had missed his spine, had missed the major arteries. He had a splinter in his chest wall that was removed by an immediate operation. There seemed no reason that he would not recover, but he did not. On June 4, he died of septicemia.

> Death occurred as a consequence of lesions in the vital parenchymatous organs caused by the bacteria and possibly by poisons carried into them by the bomb splinters and deposited chiefly in the pleura, the diaphragm and the tissues in the neighborhood of the spleen, there agglomerating and multiplying.[9]

Long before then, the reprisals had begun.

Hitler immediately ordered the arrest and execution of ten thousand Czechs suspected of anti-German activities. S.S. Obergruppenführer Karl Hermann Frank, the man in charge in Prague, declared a state of siege. Himmler acknowledged this and ordered Frank to shoot immediately the hundred most important enemies of the Reich chosen from the ten thousand hostages held. On May 27, Frank flew out to report to Hitler. He advised the Führer not to demand mass executions for the moment, since they would indicate that all of the Czechs were guilty. Hitler appeared to agree, but replaced Frank. In Prague the Gestapo began carrying out great sweeps—on May 27-28, 541 persons were arrested; simultaneously there were intensive efforts to find the specific individuals involved—a combination of torture and betrayal was gradually revealing the scope of the assassination operation. The arrests, executions, and deportations continued. Czechs in the concentration camps of Terezin, Mauthausen and Dachau were systematically slaughtered. Villages—Lezaky, Bernatice, Pardubice—were surrounded, the suspects shot and the others deported. The most notorious reprisal came at the small coal-mining village of Lidice. There, on June 9, the Gestapo rounded up 198 women and 98 children and sent them off to concentration camps, where most of the women were murdered and the children parceled out among German families. All the men and boys over sixteen, 173 of them, were murdered. The village was razed. The killings went on until June 18, when the state of siege ended, and when the Gestapo at last trapped the parachutists involved in the Church of St. Cyril and St. Methodius on Norimberska Street. The seven held out for hours until they had either been killed in the gunfight or committed suicide to avoid capture—both Gabcik and Kubish were among this group. Elsewhere the resistance was devastated. On September 29, another 252 persons were condemned to death. And the killing never really stopped. All told, 936 people were condemned at Prague and 395 at Brno. The procedure to sequester the property of murdered Jews was named Operation Reinhard in Heydrich's memory. The Man with the Iron Heart, as Hitler called him during his funeral speech, seemed amply avenged—the mass graves, the rubble of Lidice, the crowded concentration camps, the impetus given to the Final Solution. Yet, Hitler bitterly complained that Heydrich's death was like a lost battle—and in the summer of 1942, Hitler and Nazi Germany knew little of lost battles.

In London Heydrich's death was similarly seen as a victory—the resistance had shown it could strike at the heart of Nazi power; the indiscriminate German repression indicated, just as Frank had suggested, that all of Czechoslavakia resisted the German occupation; and finally Lidice became a symbol of Nazi brutality and a symbol of Czech resistance. Of course, Franta was gone, the parachutists were gone, the major resistance networks were gone, the arrested and detained were gone, and others would go. In London, and not there alone, it was felt that the German's butcher bill had simply been presented early. The slaughter of the inferior, the Final Solution, sooner or later would have taken the same bitter toll. There would have been perhaps a slightly different list of innocents, but a list of the same length. At least with the death of Heydrich, the Germans had paid a price. It was very much a symbolic price. Still, if Heydrich were quite special among the Nazi leaders, there appeared to be no shortage of those who could ruthlessly and without moral reflection organize the destruction of undesirables. Heydrich might have added a grisly glitter to the holocaust as the dark angel of death with Jewish blood; but without him the millions were just as dead. But the Czechs had not killed an organizer or a functionary; rather, the Man with the Iron Heart had been blown up.

Internal War: ". . . it is an eye for an eye and a tooth for a tooth." (Carlos Marighella, September 1969)

Unlike a resistance movement or even a conventional armed force, or for that matter a guerrilla column in a liberated zone, a revolutionary (or reactionary) movement within the state poses serious problems of definition and response for security forces. The Germans did not really trust any Czechs; the Portuguese knew their enemies, even suspected that some might be in their own African forces, but seldom had doubts about other Portuguese. The Japanese and Americans in the Pacific War knew the opponent. But when the enemy is not a distant native, an occupied people, or the big battalions across the river, when the enemy can be anyone, where there are no liberated zones but only murder from a ditch or bombs in the night, the imposition of order by any means is difficult. The British army in Ulster may suspect the Catholics, the Argentine police any university student, or the Spanish authorities all Basques, but pinning down and naming specific opponents is difficult, often impossible. And without a specific target, there can be no assassination—though there can, of course, be campaigns of murder and repression: any Catholic can be interned, any university student arrested and tortured, all Basques considered guilty. Sometimes the authorities may know whom they seek and even his rounds—the chief of staff of the IRA operates, if clandestinely, in the Republic of Ireland much of the time—but confrontation is more likely to come unexpectedly in a shoot-out or successful police sweep. The recourse for those governments without restraint has been torture in order to intensify and trap the enemies of the state. Many states feel that in a choice between anarchy and brutality, the latter is preferable. So in an internal war, the target of the state is the leader whose charisma fuses the small group of rebels. He more often than not is the *foco* of armed dissent.

Almost since the liberation from Spain, the rebel vocation has been popular in Latin America. There have been civil wars, rotating elites, fighting in the bush, coups and *pronunciamientos;* the army has intervened or the countryside collapsed into random violence. After the unexpected success of Fidel Castro in Cuba, beginning with a dozen men and ending with a country, Latin American revolutionaries have parsed his experience for the appropriate means to power. Similar expeditions failed, similar rural *focos* failed—the most famous being that of Ché Guevara in 1967 in Bolivia. Increasingly, there was a feeling that there must be a better way. And at approximately the same time that Guevara was being hunted down in Bolivia, a Brazilian, Carlos Marighella, felt he had discovered the way into the future.

Marighella was an unlikely convert to the armed struggle, for as an old-line Communist he came from a current suspicious of premature adventures. He had joined the Brazilian party in 1928 at the age of sixteen. He was the son of an Italian immigrant and a black Brazilian woman, the daughter of a slave. Known as the Ebony Giant, Marighella was to spend almost his entire life underground, on the run, except for two brief periods of legality: once immediately after the Second World War, when he was a member of the Brazilian House of Representatives until the Communist Party was outlawed, and again when President João Goulart called off the police until he was ousted by the army in April 1964. In the same month Marighella, leader of the São Paulo Communist Party, was arrested while addressing a rally at a movie theater in Rio de Janeiro. In the melee the police shot him three times in the stomach. He recovered and escaped from the infirmary where he was being held. His militancy was deepened and increasingly he was at odds with the more conservative leadership of the party. Finally, in 1967, he went to Cuba to attend the Conference of Latin American Solidarity, and from Havana called for the armed struggle in Brazil. At the end of 1967, he returned secretly to Brazil and organized the *Acão Libertadora Nacional* (ALN), and in February 1968 the armed struggle began. There were at the time two or three other small clandestine groups—*Vanguarda Armada Revolucionaria-Palmares* (VAR), the *Movimento Revolucionario-8* (MR-8), and the *Movimento Revolucionario-26* (MAR), some new, some old, some based on recruits from old organizations like Marighella's people from the São Paulo Communist Party, others volunteering from the failed rural *foco* at Caparao. In 1968, although many in the underground knew each other, there was not yet an effective movement toward a single liberation front or a comprehensive ideological position—only a consensus on the need to begin. The first step in the armed struggle was the expropriation of capital. Over a hundred banks in the largest Brazilian cities were robbed by the ALN and the other *guerrilheiros*. An American army captain, Charles Chandler, was shot and killed as he left his São Paulo apartment. A proclamation accepting responsibility claimed he was a CIA agent. American-owned warehouses and companies were bombed, barracks were burned, jailbreaks were organized. Outside Brazil a minimum of attention was attracted until October 8, 1969, when MR-8, along with some ALN people on loan, kidnapped United States Ambassador Charles Burke Elbrick in downtown Rio. The *guerrilheiros* demanded the release of fifteen political prisoners. The military government complied and the fifteen were flown to Mexico. Conservative Brazilian opinion was outraged. The military government was deeply embarrassed. The security forces were determined on swift repression of the new urban guerrillas.

In point of fact, the security forces—the regular police, the political police, the army, the navy intelligence—had over several years put together a response that would prove effective not only in Brazil but also in Uruguay and Argentina. Torture had been institutionalized and judicial assassination introduced. Almost as soon as President Goulart had been deposed by the military, the police response to any kind of disorder, crime, or protest became increasingly severe. The police established "death squads" that killed known, or even suspected, criminals. In 1968 in São Paulo, police chief Sergio Paranhos Fleury was involved in eliminating crime by such means really before it was fully apparent that the bank robberies were part of an urban guerrilla campaign. Once it became clear that there was a revolutionary challenge to the new order, the security forces perfected what had become congenial and accepted means. Over the door of the army interrogation center on Tutoya Street in São Paulo was a sign that indicated the police were not alone: *Aqui nao ha Deus nem direitos*—Here there is neither God nor human rights. The state was involved in an internal war and such means were considered necessary. And for security purposes torture worked. After all, "we have to get information fast or the whole cell will be gone. Unfortunately, our policemen are not very sophisticated."[10]

The information the police wanted most concerned Carlos Marighella, who was—and properly—considered the major force behind the urban guerrillas, the man most likely to weld the small groups into a single movement. In June 1969 he had already written, in what became known as *The Minimanual of Guerrilla War,* a crucial theoretical work for those concerned with urban revolutionary warfare. He was one of the few in the underground with an international reputation—and he was an old, old enemy. Then, in October 1969, the police arrested two Dominicans who under torture revealed sufficient information about Marighella's movements for the São Paulo police to prepare a large operation. On November 4, eighty police under the direction of Sergio Paranhos Fleury ambushed and killed Marighella in a wild shoot-out. In the midst of an internal war, where suspects shoot on sight and fight on, refusing to be captured and tortured, the line between assassination and death in action is a thin one—and often the security officials would prefer to have a live prisoner who knows a great deal rather than a dead martyr. This was not the case with Marighella. He was killed in an internal war by officials of the state. And he became not the first victim but only the most famous in a campaign of repression waged by the military and police against revolutionaries, against dissent, against criminals, against the disorderly, a campaign so violent, brutal, and unrestrained, without recourse to the most elementary civil rights, that it became necessary for higher authorities to deny their own responsibility. Order was being imposed by nothing less than a vigilante movement within the security forces.

KILLING WITHOUT WAR OR THE LAW: VIGILANTES

> Who will free me from this turbulent priest?
> —Henry II of England in reference to Archbishop
> Thomas à Becket

Murder on the Right

Vigilante movements, tolerated, encouraged, or even oppressed by governments, have a long and not especially savory history. And once the Brazilian authorities had rid themselves of Marighella, the turbulent Red priest of revolution, what legal restraints that remained quickly eroded.

During the year after Marighella's murder, Brazil was an arena for a bitter urban guerrilla campaign pursued by the security forces despite increasing international protest outside the law. Up to June 1970, thirteen security people were killed and sixty-two wounded. The casualty toll for the underground would never be known for certain. Marighella's successor, Joaquin Cârmara Ferreira, another old-line Communist at fifty-seven, was killed resisting arrest—"lung failure caused by a heart attack." In September 1971, the last significant leader, Captain Carlos Lamarca, thirty-three, was killed in a shoot-out in the interior in Bahia. By then revolutionary resistance had largely been crushed. The most spectacular rebel tactics had been a series of diplomatic kidnappings that coerced the government into freeing political prisoners. The Japanese consul Nobuo Okuchi was taken on March 5, 1970, and released for five prisoners and a mother superior—a relatively modest demand. West German Ambassador Ehrenfried von Hollenben, kidnapped in June, cost the government forty prisoners, and the Swiss ambassador, in December, cost a bumper total of eighty. Between 1969 and 1971, 130 prisoners were released and flown out of the country; and with the toll in the shoot-outs and those still in prison, few were left to carry on the struggle. If, as apologists for the regime insisted, an internal war necessitated such brutal measures—certainly by 1971 such measures appeared to have been effective—there was no longer need for repression. And by the time of Lamarca's death in September 1971, the government had moved, even if at times haltingly, against the "death squads." In October there were thirty-five São Paulo policemen under legal investigation, and an official inquiry had found Sergio Paranhos Fleury guilty of taking part in the killing of three criminals in São Paulo in 1968. Despite these moves, critics of the regime insisted that torture continued and the murder of suspects remained a tactic. In January 1973, when authorities announced that the guerrilla movement was "dismantled," they also noted that six terrorists, including two foreign women, had been killed in shoot-outs. In October Mata Machado and Gildo Macedo Lacerda of the Marxist-Leninist Popular Action were shot and killed by security agents who broke into a "secret" meeting in Recife. And the "death squads" continued to eliminate undesirables (at the peak, two thousand in Rio in 1970), a steady toll of criminals, smugglers, beggars . . . to compensate for the impotency of the law and to rid society of harmful elements."[11]

In November 1974, Fleury was acquitted. In March 1975, President Ernesto Geisel announced that the government could now concentrate on economic, social, and political development because security forces had brought internal terrorism under control. The "death squads" continued to operate. In 1975, official sources disclosed that in Rio alone since 1973, 654 persons had been killed. Political prisoners continued to disappear, torture was still used—and always the spurts of killings by the "death squad." In 1977 in Rio, after a two-year lull, another five hundred had been killed by August; and in São Paulo parents of detainees suspected of left-wing activity claimed the prisoners had been tortured. Matters may have improved, as President Geisel had indicated, but not so much that the vigilantes had disbanded. They had, however, just about run out of real revolutionaries to assassinate and had to be content with the socially unredeemable.

Brazil was hardly alone as a site for the vigilantes of order, tolerated or encouraged by a state under siege. In Guatemala, where a tiny reactionary elite dominated a huge, apathetic Indian population, the radical ideas of Castro, the appalling poverty, and the inadequacies of the government coalesced in the MR-13 movement that in 1960 began guerrilla operations. For a decade a variety of rebel groups sought to create rural *focos*, to radicalize the Indians, to bring the war into the cities. The governments tended to respond with measures not unlike those favored in Brazil. And, as in Brazil, vigilante groups appeared: *Movimiento de Acción Nacionalista Organizado* (MANO, The White Hand), *Nueva Organizacion Anticommunista* (NOA), and *Ojo por Ojo* (Eye for Eye). In contrast to the Brazilian "death squads," the Guatemalan vigilantes, in a far smaller country, were responsible for a far greater total of murders—estimates for the 1966–1971 period put the total at nine thousand. Many victims belonged to suspect groups or organizations, some attended the wrong schools, some merely were in the wrong place. Many of those killed were obscure. Some were not.

Christian Democratic Deputy Adolfo Mijangos López, who was paralyzed from the waist down, was machine-gunned to death by *Ojo por Ojo* on January 13, 1971. Similar state-tolerated vigilantes appeared elsewhere in Latin America, especially in Uruguay during the campaign against the Tupamaros and in Argentina, in response to the rise of the new urban guerrillas—a response that continues.

The vigilante on the edge of the law is hardly a Latin American phenomenon alone, although the number of revolutionary leaders killed rather than processed through the criminal justice system in the last decade, beginning with Ché Guevara in Bolivia and continuing in Argentina, is massive. In Germany, for example, in the uncertainty and near-anarchy following the Armistice of November 11, 1918, murder increasingly became a conventional means of politics. Perhaps the most famous victims were Karl Liebknecht and Rosa Luxemburg. The former was by temperament an agitator with a natural niche in the barricades; emotional, tempestuous, he sought to sweep all obstacles to the revolution before him by sheer force of will. Luxemburg was an ideal counterweight in the Spartakus movement, analytical, deeply learned in Marxian dialectics, aware of the political realities and organizational obstacles. In December 1918, Liebknecht, Luxemburg, and the leaders of the newly founded German Communist Party scented the collapse of the center, the loss of control by Friedrich Ebert's Social Democratic government. The masses seemed ready to mobilize and the military, except for a few officers, to mutiny. By January, there were huge demonstrations in the streets of Berlin, recalling the November days in Petrograd in 1917. They remained demonstrations. The government decided to act, and Defense Minister Gustav Noske brought in both the army and his still not fully organized Free Corps. The Free Corps—the Iron Brigade of 1,600—under Noske arrived on January 11. Within three days all Spartakus-Communist resistance had been crushed, in some cases brutally. The alliance of the new Social Democrats and the old military had proven more effective than the militant masses.

On January 15, after order had been fully restored, officers of the Volunteer Division of Horse Guards arrested Luxemburg and Liebknecht and brought them to their headquarters in the Eden Hotel. They were turned over to Captain Pabst, adjutant of the Free Corps. That evening a group of officers escorted Liebknecht out the rear door of the hotel. As soon as he emerged a sentry named Runge brought the butt of his rifle down on his head. Liebknecht staggered and fell and was dragged into a waiting automobile. As the car drove off, Luxemburg was escorted through the door. Again Runge smashed his rifle down on the prisoner's head. She collapsed on the ground and was also dragged senseless to a waiting car. As the car drove off a Lieutenant Vogel sitting next to her drew his pistol and emptied it into her battered head. Her body was found several days later floating in the Landwehr canal. Liebknecht had been driven to an isolated stretch of the Charlottenburg Highway and pushed from the car. He was asked if he could walk. He took a few staggering steps and was shot down "while attempting to escape." Runge was dismissed from the Free Corps for leaving his post and for "improper use of his weapons."[12] He was sentenced to two years in prison. Still later, Vogel was brought to trial and sentenced also to two years in prison as a "psychopath," since he was not really responsible for his acts.

Murder on the Left

Not all vigilantes arise on the Right, although by general usage such self-proclaimed defenders of the system of the old institutions or old ways oppose change or impose appropriate order when official institutions are unable to do so. There are, however, exceptions. In 1937, one of the century's great revolutionaries, Leon Trotsky, sailed for Mexico, having been granted asylum by President Lázaro Cárdenas, who was engaged in massive land reforms and the expropriation of foreign-owned companies. Mexico was an exciting social experiment and one that had produced, stunningly and unexpectedly, a world-renowned school of painters. Diego Rivera, José Orozco, David Alfaro Siqueiros, and others created dramatic, often gigantic, murals depicting the long struggle of the Mexican poor, the foreign exploitation, and the wonders of the emerging revolution. Nearly all were members of one revolutionary party or another and saw no distinction between their life as artists and their involvement in politics. Trotsky was to stay with Diego Rivera, who had withdrawn from the official Mexican Communist Party and was delighted to open his doors to a revolutionary legend.

By 1937 Trotsky was little less than a legend. He had been Soviet foreign minister, founder and commander-in-chief of the victorious Red Army, advocate of permanent revolution, orator, organizer, and a prolific writer. On Lenin's death in 1924, he had appeared the obvious successor to guide revolutionary Russia in a hostile world. Over the next four years, the stolid Georgian Josef Stalin, brooding, secretive, and infinitely cunning, maneuvered his rivals into varying combinations that eliminated them one by one. In 1928 he exiled Trotsky to Alma Ata and, in the following year, from Russia. First in Turkey, then in France, and finally in Norway, Trotsky became increasingly irrelevant to Russian events. In 1935 he attacked Stalin in *The Revolution Betrayed.* By then the great purges were under way, forcing leading Bolsheviks to confess that they had betrayed the revolution—often, apparently, under orders from Trotsky. Trotsky, however, was in no position to give orders. He had no allies or friends in Russia, and few elsewhere. There were pools of strength—interest in an alternative to the Stalinist current; but often without any real contact with the master, as was the case in Spain. In 1937 and 1938, however, the purge trials continued, along with the involvement of Trotsky's name. In 1938 the Fourth International was founded in Paris. Even though it was a slight challenge to Stalin and orthodox Communism, the Secretary, Rudolf Klement, was murdered. Stalin wanted no challenges in Spain. Communists saw that their "Trotskyite" rivals were killed or imprisoned, Red heretics being more dangerous than Fascist pagans.

In 1939 Trotsky left Diego Rivera's house—some say because he flirted with Rivera's wife. Rivera later indicated it was all a plot on his part to put Trotsky in a vulnerable position so he could be killed. In any case, he moved into a house on the Avenue Vienna in Coyoacan, on the outskirts of Mexico City. The house was fortified: the wall built higher, a watchtower erected, and the front gate barricaded. Five or six young men, secretaries at times, guards at others, usually Americans who wanted to spend a few months at the feet of the master, were always about, as well as his wife Natalya and his grandson Seva. There were ten Mexican policemen, who kept two shifts, housed outside.

It was not only the death of Rudolf Klement of the Fourth International that prompted the security precautions on Avenue Vienna, but also the growing vituperation of the Mexican Communist press—Trotsky the little old traitor, curlike, Judas, betrayer of the revolution. A combination of embittered volunteers from the Spanish Civil War and hysterical local Communists who rigidly maintained the Stalinist line became increasingly outraged at his presence. And there was no reason to think that Stalin, who had destroyed an entire revolutionary generation of his old colleagues, decimated the Russian military establishment, and dispatched agents to eliminate other exiles, would restrain himself in Trotsky's case. For Stalin the glittering Trotsky with his facile pen, his penetrating mind, his charisma undimmed in exile, was a living witness to the brutality and betrayal of Socialism in One Country, a potential magnet for the disenchanted—and the one great foe unpunished. And besides the distant Stalin and the local Communists, there were rumors of the German Gestapo, and there could always be the single demented gunman. So the walls were heightened and a machine gun put in the tower, and the secretary-guards maintained.

All this was in vain when the threat became reality. On May 24, 1940, Trotsky was the target of a huge and elaborate assassination raid directed by the Communist painter David Alfaro Siqueiros. He gathered around him artists, foreign soldiers, militant mineworkers, and the unemployed—dedicated Communists all—including an agent of the Soviet GPU. There had been elaborate preparations. Two girls posing as prostitutes had lured off the police guard, leaving only the secretary-guards, and only one of those, the American Sheldon Harte, would be awake. Siqueiros and his twenty colleagues gathered on Cuba Street. Siqueiros was dressed in the uniform of a major with dark glasses and a fake mustache. His second in command, the painter Pujol, wore an army lieutenant's uniform. The others were suitably attired. Into four cars they stuffed ropes and rope ladders, rubber gloves, incendiary bombs, a rotary saw, huge revolvers, and at least two machine guns. They drove up and stopped in front of the house. One knocked on the gate. Sheldon Harte opened the door—perhaps as had been prearranged, perhaps just foolishly, but evidence indicates that to some degree he was implicated in the plot. The raiders moved into the yard and took up positions around the house. Everyone inside appeared still asleep. There was no sound from the guards to the rear. The group broke up into four parties and moved in on Trotsky's bedroom—one group for each side, with Siqueiros at the back with his machine gun to prevent the guards from leaving their quarters. The men were now at the windows and doors to the bedroom, only a few feet from Trotsky and his wife.

Simultaneously they opened up a barrage directly into the bedroom. The firing seemed to go on and on. The machine guns swept back and forth. The glass in all the windows was shattered, bits of plaster and wood spun into the air. Inside the bedroom Natalya and Trotsky were lying on the floor, the air above them filled with the whirr of bullets slicing through the room. There was a flare from some sort of incendiary bomb and Natalya saw a figure moving into the room during a pause in the barrage. He raised a pistol and fired eight times directly into their beds. The raiders then took Trotsky's two cars and Sheldon Harte with them and drove off into the night. One incendiary bomb had set fire to the grass on the lawn and another was burning at the door to Seva's room. Only Seva had been hurt, wounded in the toe. The bedroom was a sieve, the doors and windows shattered, the walls pocked with dents and holes. It seemed incredible that anyone was alive. There were seventy-three bullet holes around the bed alone. "A happy accident," said Trotsky.[13] In fact, it seemed incredible in the great shoot-out that the raiders had not shot up each other. It was also strange that the secretary-guards had done nothing. Strange that Harte had let them into the compound. Strange that everyone seemed so calm. Strange that twenty armed men firing several hundred bullets had been so incompetent that they could not kill an unarmed man. The Mexican Communist Party was soon in disarray, the raiders in hiding; the official line was that Siqueiros was an "uncontrolled element considered half mad."[14] The only casualty was Harte, whose body was found buried in the cellar of a farmhouse. Most of the cases against the raiders petered out after a couple of years—the suspects in Harte's murder were cleared. Siqueiros faced only minor charges, and by 1942 he was a hero permitted to jump bail and go to Chile. The whole affair was so ludicrous, more a spoiled work of art than an effective assassination, that it passed into folklore as a spectacular, a "happening," rather than as a failed murder by a gang of Communist vigilantes. Harte was forgotten and by the end of the year Trotsky would be dead at the hands of a more serious, if less romantic, killer.

The Muddled Murders of Hate

More often than not (Trotsky being a notable exception), the problem facing the vigilante assassin is the same for conventional security forces engaged in irregular or internal war: specific victims are elusive. If there is a period of relative peace, a potential victim of the wrath of the orderly—Trotsky in tranquil exile—may prove vulnerable. It was thus not as shocking that Martin Luther King was shot down and killed as it was that someone had not tried before, and that the killer fit the psychopathic rather than the vigilante profile. In Brazil the vigilante-police solved their access problem by using torture to find the target. Sometimes, however, the vigilantes do not have security protection, but, like their targets, must operate clandestinely. It is difficult, often impossible, to track down and punish—murder—specific evildoers. The alternative has often been to define larger and therefore more vulnerable groups as guilty: any uppity black, any Jew, any Cypriot Greek police officer, any university student, any Irish Catholic. Punish any one and you punish them—the disloyal and subversive—all. And inevitably the punished innocents are obscure but available, murdered instead of assassinated. It is the toll of dead that has a political impact rather than the shock of a single deed. Still, at times, the vigilantes are lucky and the prominent are insufficiently elusive.

In Northern Ireland the Provisional IRA transformed itself between 1969 and 1971 into Catholic Defenders to fend off any Protestant programs. The Provos were, however, primarily concerned not with defending but with initiating a campaign against the British presence and British security forces called into Ulster to keep the peace, that is, to protect the Catholic population. During 1971 the Provos increasingly attacked British troops, bombed in the center of towns, and set up country ambushes for wandering security patrols. There were gunfights along the border. Between April and August four British soldiers were killed and twenty-nine wounded. In August the provincial government, the British army, and the cabinet in London imposed internment —imprisoning without charges large numbers of Catholic "suspects." The IRA campaign simply escalated—few IRA volunteers had been arrested. Large sections of Derry and Belfast became no-go areas, the number of bombs went up, the number of incidents went up, the casualties went up. One day in December the IRA mounted thirty bombing operations across the province. The most the British Home Secretary, Reginald Mouding, could hope for in public was an acceptable level of violence. On January 30, Sunday, in Derry, British paratroopers firing into a demonstration killed thirteen people and mortally wounded another. None had been in the IRA. British prestige was at an all-time low. The country was flooded with foreign newsmen and network television teams. And matters only got worse. In a final surprise initiative, London abrogated the Stormont provincial parliament. The Provos claimed that they had bombed down the old system—and they continued their campaign, appetites whetted.

The Protestants, who made up two-thirds of the population, watched all this in dismay. *Their* parliament at Stormont had been destroyed. *Their* way of life was threatened—not to mention their privileges. All the trumpeted demands for civil rights had been nothing but cover for an IRA campaign to bring about a united Ireland with Home Rule destroying their liberties. The government in London refused to take sufficiently harsh measures. The ultras felt that something had to be done —the old parties, even the extremist leaders like the Reverend Ian Paisley, were insufficiently militant. The result, beginning in 1972, was the creation of a variety of organizations, the paramilitaries: the Ulster Volunteer Force, the Ulster Defense Association, the Red Hand Commandos. The base was working-class, largely from the Protestant ghettos of Belfast. At times there were newspapers and proclamations and press conferences; but essentially these were vigilante organizations—not too well organized—with shifting leadership, inflated titles, constant schism, but a very real and brutal purpose: to punish the Catholic community and defend the Protestant way of life (read "domination"). The means was the murder of the Catholics, usually men wandering in mixed areas or near Protestant enclaves, isolated and vulnerable and, as Catholics, "guilty." There was also that most brutal and random weapon, the no-warning bomb, placed in Catholic pubs. For some time no one would admit that the Protestants had taken up political murder —for over a year there would be denials. Finally the toll was too great to be ignored. Yet, with almost no exception, the victims were not in the IRA. Volunteers had more important matters than wandering near potential Protestant gunmen. The Protestants actually murdered more of their own leaders than did members of the IRA. The random murders were rather a typical vigilante campaign of murder.

The paramilitary's problem was access. With their Northern accent they could not wander around in the Irish Republic, where the IRA leaders were more accessible, although they could and did see no-warning bombs in the streets of Dublin. In the North the gradual division into Catholic and Protestant areas and the established Catholic and Protestant working-class ghettos meant that strangers, even strangers in cars, had real difficulty in penetrating either the little lanes of the old neighborhoods or the new housing districts. The British army had an equally difficult time, and the challenge was quite beyond the paramilitaries. They stuck to random murder, knowing many of their specific IRA enemies by name, but unable to reach them. Some of these enemies were notorious members of the Belfast Brigade or the IRA Army Council; others belonged to the political wing of the Provos—the Provisional Sinn Féin party. In Belfast the most prominent member of the Sinn Féin was the vice-president of the national party, one of the most articulate and vituperative orators in a city that had made rabble-rousing an art, Maire Drumm. In October 1976, at fifty-six, she and her family had been lifelong Republicans and had paid the price. Her husband Jimmy had spent much of his life in prison by 1976, more than any other living Irish Republican, most of the time without charge. Their twenty-year-old daughter, Marie Therese, had received an eight-year prison sentence in November 1975 for possession of a loaded revolver. Mrs. Drumm had been convicted in July 1971 of encouraging people to join the IRA—in court she had shouted, "I will not accept bail. God Save Ireland!"[15] The previous August she had threatened that it might be necessary to take Belfast down stone by stone. She was charged with illegal marching and spent more time in prison. A loyalist leader charged that her release was a disgrace. Then, on October 3, 1976, she entered the Catholic Mater Hospital for cataract treatment. On October 18, her husband Jimmy read her resignation as a candidate for vice-president to the annual conference of Sinn Féin held in Dublin. She gave her health as the reason, but promised to return to the "thick of the fray" when her health permitted. After nearly a month at Mater, she planned to sign out on October 30 and move to a nursing home in the Irish Republic.

The Mater Hospital is in North Belfast between the Republican New Lodge district and a Protestant area. There was minimal security—at her home in Glassmullan Gardens, Andersonstown, deep in IRA territory, there was a British army post behind wire and a corrugated iron wall. At night a spotlight lit up visitors to the Drumm house and there was always a careful British sentry to take down car tag numbers. Resented in the Republican stronghold of Andersonstown, the British post had long been a deterrent for those who might have her on their "short" list. At Mater, although her presence had been mentioned in the Belfast newspapers, there was neither the IRA nor the British. On the evening of October 28, 1976, two young men entered the hospital during visiting hours between 7:00 and 7:30 P.M. and apparently disappeared. At 10:30 P.M. a dark blue Ford Escort pulled up and parked opposite the main hospital gate. Inside the Mater, Mrs. Drumm was standing in a small six-bed side ward, next to Ward 38 on the second floor. Two young men in white coats pushed into Ward 38. One drew a revolver and without a word shot her in the chest three times. She collapsed on the floor. The two turned and disappeared from the ward. The Ford Escort soon drove off. Mrs. Drumm crawled several yards across the floor and then collapsed again. Ten minutes later she died in the operating room. There followed heavy activity by security forces. Searches and police checkpoints were maintained. The gunmen were not found. No one ever took credit for the murder. A spokesman for Ian Paisley's party said that "she died the same death meted out repeatedly to many hundreds of Ulster people by the Provisional IRA, whose so-called cause she so uncompromisingly espoused[; it] will be seen by many as a poetic irony. She was indeed a victim of her own hatred."[16]

The Republicans, of course, saw things differently; increasingly they suspected, not always without evidence, that some of the murders attributed to the paramilitaries had been tolerated or organized by British security forces. The British Special Air Service, an elite anti-terrorist group, was often active, often in civilian clothes, often using American M-16 rifles (similar to the IRA Armalite, so that any SAS killings could not be traced to the NATO rifle). Certainly over the years, at one time or another, various British spokesmen, including retired army officers, had urged that the gloves be taken off, that the army be allowed to "do the necessary job," which is code meaning to use the same irregular tactics as the IRA. Most armies involved in internal war or irregular campaigns have wanted to maximize their options— to be irregular, too; and at some level of authority very few have denied themselves.

NOTES

1. John Toland, *The Rising Sun, The Decline and Fall of the Japanese Empire*, New York, Bantam, 1971, p. 837.

2. *v.* Laslo Havas, *Hitler's Plot to Kill the Big Three*, New York, Bantam, 1971.

3. Toland, *op. cit.*, p. 500.

4. *Ibid.*, p. 502.

5. *Ibid.*

6. *Ibid.*, p. 503.

7. Joachim C. Fest, *The Face of the Third Reich, Portraits of the Nazi Leadership*, New York, Ace, 1970, p. 161.

8. Jan Wiener, *The Assassination of Heydrich*, New York, Grossman, 1969, p. 82.

9. Miroslav Ivanov, *Target: Heydrich*, New York, Macmillan, 1975, p. 178.

10. *New York Times*, June 29, 1970.

11. Agence France-Presse, "release," March 28, 1974.

12. Robert G. L. Waite, *Vanguard of Nazism, The Free Corps Movement in Postwar Germany*, New York, Norton, 1967, p. 62.

13. Nicholas Mosley, *The Assassination of Trotsky*, London, Michael Joseph, 1972, p. 40.

14. *Ibid.*, p. 58.

15. *Irish Times*, October 29, 1976.

16. *Ibid.*, October 30, 1976.

4

Killing by the State: Authorized Murder

"We have executed the executioners of the
previous regime. This was done to purify the
blood of the revolution, and to put new blood of
the revolution into circulation."
—Teheran state radio, after the execution of
four Iranian generals on the roof of Ayatollah
Ruhollah Khomeini's house

If, on one hand, the vigilante killing can be denied by most
legitimate leaders, and on the other, killing in battle can be accepted as a recognized necessity, there remains a middle ground
between the Ulster gunman and the British army paratrooper. At
times, irregular covert actions are not simply tolerated, but authorized—as were the CIA preparations to assassinate Lumumba.
Sometimes the authorities feel that exceptional challenges need
exceptional responses, that the normal judiciary system will not
work or that an avowed and distant enemy may be maimed without resorting to open war. Authorized killing is indeed assassination. Known in Europe after the fifteenth century as "the Italian
technique," such acts were hardly uncommon; between 1415 and
1767, the Venetian Council of Ten entertained ninety assassination proposals. There are many recent examples of agencies of the

121

state authorizing murder. At times, the situation has been confused and uncertain, the country in turmoil, the level of authorization unclear. At other times there has been no doubt that murder was selected carefully and rationally as a means of state policy at the highest level.

AUTHORIZED KILLING

A state under violent political challenge may simply authorize by statute certain criminal acts—possession of weapons or membership in a banned organization—as punishable by death. For example, since the unilateral declaration of Rhodesian independence from Great Britain in 1965, there has been a sporadic guerrilla campaign of liberation, intensifying after 1975. During this period, a reasonable estimate is that 320 people have been hanged, mainly for political or war-related crimes. The African nationalists consider all of these authorized murder: the killing of prisoners. A captured revolutionary leader—a traitor—has always been vulnerable to state execution, often summary execution, as was the case with Ché Guevara (the distinction between being shot down while resisting—Marighella—and after resisting—Guevara—is slight). The same is true for those whom a revolutionary captures during the process of seizing the state. Charles I was executed by the Commonwealth in what the new government considered a legitimate step (legalized tyrannicide) and the royalists an act of regicide. The same was true with Louis XVI—"Citizen Capet." In both cases the royalists considered the executioners illicit, despite their control of the territory and state machinery, and the act murder; in both cases the rebels did not. The more interesting cases occur not when a new government executes old enemies, but when any government does so covertly or when the existence of authority is uncertain.

The Great Purges of Stalin in Russia were in many cases covert—no show trials or public announcements—partly to cloak the immense scope of the executions, partly to lure more victims into the net; but certainly Stalin saw all the deaths as authorized and legitimate. In the long years of Italian Fascism, the single greatest challenge to Mussolini before the military collapse in 1944 came as a result of the murder of the Socialist leader Giacomo Matteotti in 1924. The complicity of Mussolini was assumed—and the degree has been a matter of dispute ever since. There followed an intensive wave of criticism that united all his foes in outrage and produced a spate of resignations from the Fascist Party. Despite the fright, the result was a more militant Fascist movement, increasingly authoritarian control at the center, and a rising capacity to eliminate internal opposition by legal means—imprisonment or detention if intimidation did not prevent dissent. Abroad the most articulate anti-Fascists were not always beyond the reach of Fascist Rome. Mussolini, too, had been the target of assassination plots, and ultimately in 1945 was the victim of an authorized execution so divorced from central control as to be as much revolutionary murder, during an irregular internal war, as an act of state.

Benito Mussolini: Rendezvous on Piazzala Loreto, April 29, 1945

On April 21, 1945, the Allied armies in Italy crossed the Po River. The end of the Axis was in sight. The German army was disengaging and pulling back; the German commander in Italy, General Wolff, had opened secret negotiations with the Allies in Switzerland, and the Italian pole of the Axis had dwindled to a faithful few scattered through the north of Italy, increasingly vulnerable to the savage partisan attacks. Benito Mussolini, Il Duce, once possessed of eight million bayonets, had fallen on evil days indeed. On July 25, 1943, with an Allied invasion of the Italian mainland imminent, Mussolini had been ousted in an internal coup, arrested, and imprisoned on the island of Ponza off Naples —where he had previously established a penal colony. There, in fact, Tito Zaniboni, who had failed to assassinate him in 1925, had been dispatched, and on Mussolini's arrival Pietro Nenni, the Socialist leader imprisoned by Il Duce, still remained. Mussolini was transferred in August to another island off the coast of Sardinia, and then, with the authorities still fearful of a German rescue attempt, to a hotel at Gran Sasso, a ski resort high in the Apennines above Aquila.

Mussolini might have been gone but he was hardly forgotten. As soon as he heard of the arrest, Hitler had ordered a special rescue operation. An SS team was set up under Colonel Otto Skorzeny, and a search for Mussolini's prison began. The rescue was ultimately mounted in a period of great confusion following the surrender of the Italian government to the Allies on September 8, 1943. Four days later, at two o'clock in the afternoon on September 12, Skorzeny's gliders began landing at Gran Sasso. Mussolini was flown out in a small reconnaissance plane and taken directly to Vienna. What followed were Mussolini's Six Hundred Days. First was the establishment of the Fascist Republic of Salo, allied to Hitler, while the mother Italian government in Rome fled behind Allied lines and declared war on Germany. Then came the long, brutal slog by the Allies up through Italy, the end run that bogged down at Anzio, and at last the fall of Rome in June 1944 —and the landings in Normandy. Increasingly it became clear even to the optimistic at Salo that the war was absolutely lost and that the new Fascist regime was increasingly irrelevant to the direction of events. By the spring of 1945, with the Allied columns rushing north, pushing toward Milan, as the Germans moved back toward Austria, the primary concern of most Fascists was survival. The north of Italy was filled with partisans, all of whom seemed determined on revenge, and the Germans were uninterested in most Fascist problems—in fact, they were rumored to be treating with the Allies—and the problem of "disappearing" either into Switzerland or civilian life was considerable. Mussolini faced even grimmer prospects than most of his compatriots, although he hoped he could reach Switzerland if all else went wrong—and in April 1945 most else had already gone wrong.

In Milan Cardinal Schuster had been carrying on sporadic negotiations with the Germans and had real hopes that he could arrange a surrender. The Germans led him on while preparing to recapitulate directly to the Allies. Mussolini, also in Milan, was persuaded by the cardinal to meet with the resistance leaders, the Committee of National Liberation of Upper Italy, on April 25 in the study of his palace. The committee demanded that Mussolini and Salo surrender unconditionally—and within two hours. Mussolini agreed only to contemplate the demand, and left the palace, but told the cardinal that he would have an answer "within an hour." The committee in the meantime proclaimed an insurrection in upper Italy and claimed all political power. It was also agreed that new popular courts of assize, tribunals of war, and commissions of justice were to be established for those guilty of criminal acts during the war with the patriots: Article Five included the death penalty for members of the Fascist government and hierarchy—which by something more than implication included Mussolini.

There was no answer from Mussolini "within the hour." He had left Milan, giving no one orders or answers, and moved north, perhaps to rally a final Fascist resistance, perhaps to find a way to Switzerland, perhaps he did not know. At the head of a small column, he reached Como at nine that evening. No one knew what to do next. Mussolini did not favor military action. The next day it was clear that there was no way into Switzerland and the column moved on up the west bank of Lake Como. He spent the night at Menaggio, where his mistress Claretta Petacci arrived. On the next day, April 27, Mussolini's caravan attached itself to a German antiaircraft unit and moved north toward Merano in the Tyrol. At 7:30 A.M. the column was halted at Musso by partisans who had set up a roadblock. "Pedro," Count Bellini della Stelle, the leader of the Fifty-second (Garibaldi) Brigade, found that the Germans were not interested in fighting, which was fortunate since he had very few partisans near his roadblock. He stalled for time and eventually took the German commander on a six-hour trip to negotiate with other partisans. By early afternoon there were eleven new roadblocks ahead of the German column and substantial partisan reinforcements in the area. Bellini now insisted that while the Germans could continue up the road first to Dongo and then to Ponte del Passo to await further discussions, all Italians must be turned over to the Garibaldi Brigade. Some of the Italians at the rear of the column were collected, and then the trucks moved out. In a German overcoat and helmet Mussolini went unnoticed. The column stopped at Dongo and a search

began. Shortly after 5 P.M. Guiseppe Negri, the shoemaker of
Dongo, looked into the cab of one of the trucks and spotted a
familiar face—"Cavaliere Benito Mussolini."

Bellini sent off word to Milan that Mussolini had been taken
along with many of the Salo ministers, put his famous prisoner in
the *Guardia di Finanza* barracks at Germaisno, and then late on
the night of April 27 decided to move Il Duce to an isolated
cottage in Giulino di Mezzegra. At this time, Claretta Petacci
appeared and urged Bellini to surrender Mussolini to the Allies.
He refused—"The Allies have no concern with this and I will
certainly try to prevent Mussolini from falling into their hands."[1]
He did permit her to join Mussolini. By then the news of Mussolini's capture had spread and there were a variety of attempts
to take him into custody—the Allies wanted him as badly as did
the Italians. In Milan there was growing anxiety that the Allies
would succeed. During the night of April 27, two Communist
representatives, Aldo Lampredi ("Guido") and Walter Audisio
("Colonel Valerio"), presented themselves to General Raffaele
Cadorna, head of the *Comando Generale,* with a mandate from
the Liberation Committee. The principal members of the Fascist
Party were to be summarily executed and the two wanted the
appropriate orders cut by Cadorna. The general could not get in
touch directly with the Liberation Committee and had no reason
to doubt the two. He, like others, feared losing Mussolini to the
Allies.

> In no case would I voluntarily have proceeded to bring
> Mussolini into the hands of the allies for him to be tried
> and executed by foreigners.[2]

Discussions dragged on. It turned out that some, but not all, of the
committee had authorized Mussolini's execution. The result, however, was that Colonel Valerio got his papers and left immediately
for Como. He arrived at 8 A.M., but it took much of the day to track
down Mussolini's whereabouts. At last at Dongo, Valerio informed
Bellini that Mussolini was to be shot. Protests were to no avail, and
his papers were in order. Valerio and Guido took two members of
the Garibaldi Brigade as guides, and drove off for the cottage in

a black Fiat 1100 with Rome license plates, commandeered on the spot. All four men and the driver were Communists acting, they felt, not only in the name of the committee but also in the cause of revolution.

An hour later the Fiat 1100 reached the cottage. Valerio threw open the door and announced, "I've come to liberate you."[3] The two prisoners, Mussolini and Claretta Petacci, got into the limousine and were driven a short distance. They got out and walked fifty meters to the iron gate of the Villa Belmonte. It was locked, and Valerio decided to give up the hope of using the garden of the estate. He pushed Mussolini and Petacci up against the wall. "By General Headquarters of the Corps of Volunteers of Liberty, I am charged to render justice for the Italian people."[4] The two seemed stunned, hardly aware of what was about to happen. Valerio raised his submachine gun and pulled the trigger. Nothing happened. He then snatched another gun from one of his men, turned, and fired a burst of shots into Mussolini and Petacci. They collapsed in front of the wall. Valerio fired a second shorter burst into the bodies.

Valerio rushed back to Dongo and drew up a list of fifteen names of prominent Fascist prisoners in the area. Fifteen hostages had been shot in Piazza la Loreto in Milan on August 12, 1944, in retaliation for a partisan bomb attack on a German truck four days before. Even though the partisans over the next several days had carried out their own reprisals at the rate of three for one—fifteen Fascist militia prisoners and thirty German and Italian soldiers— Valerio had not forgotten the fifteen bloody bodies exposed all that summer day in the Piazza la Loreto. In Dongo on April 28, 1945, the fifteen Fascists were lined up on a parapet on the main square facing Lake Como and executed by a partisan firing squad. Valerio had his fifteen—plus Mussolini and Petacci. And on the next day he could savor the last drop of partisan vengeance. At three in the morning of April 29, after a night of creeping down from Dongo, Valerio's yellow truck carrying the corpses arrived at Piazza la Loreto. There were Mussolini, Petacci, the fifteen from Dongo, the former Fascist Party Secretary Achille Starace—and four unidentified victims. Mussolini, Petacci, and three others were suspended upside down from an iron beam on a gasoline station. There were placards for identification. There they remained all day, as huge and almost hysterical crowds flooded through the square to witness the macabre end of an era and the man Mussolini.

The National Liberation Committee took full responsibility for the execution. Fascist apologists called it murder. So did others, including Winston Churchill, who, however, had branded Mussolini a war criminal. The committee was unrepentant. Mussolini had fled Milan, refused to surrender, and become an outlaw. There was no need of a trial, especially for the leader of a regime that had never hesitated to murder its enemies. Besides, there was no time if the Allies were going to be prevented from sweeping him up—and the idea of their own archdemon being brought to justice by foreigners was unpalatable even to those who did not have the singleness of purpose and the brutal efficiency of Valerio. And he had the papers and the authorization to kill. He did.[5]

Tsar Nicholas II and the Romanovs: The Slaughter at Ekaterinburg

If upper Italy had been on the edge of chaos in April 1945, those conditions were stable in contrast to Russia in the summer of 1918. The previous year had been a long and dreadful agony for the country. There had been the March Revolution that on the fifteenth led to the abdication of Tsar Nicholas II and his twelve-year-old son and heir Alexis, a frail hemophiliac, and the Tsar's younger brother, Michael. After three hundred and four years, the Romanov dynasty was swept away and the Tsar and his immediate family—his wife Alexandra, Alexis, and his four daughters, Olga, Marie, Tatiana, and Anastasia—were confined to the palace under house arrest. The new provincial government of Alexander Kerensky staggered from one crisis to another, attempting to stay in the increasingly unpopular war with Germany as the army slipped away in mutiny and the country into anarchy. There were challenges from unrepentant monarchists and eager revolutionaries. The latter organized the failed July uprising and prompted Kerensky to send the Tsar and his family to a safer confinement in Tobolsky in Siberia. There, almost completely isolated from events, they learned that in November the Bolsheviks under V. I. Lenin had taken over. The center under Kerensky had simply melted away. Now with a slogan of "peace, land, and bread," the Bolsheviks rushed to secure their power, though it was frail at best. On March 3, 1918, at Brest-Litovsk, they signed a treaty that gave up vast areas to the German Empire in return for peace. There was no peace, but rather a widening civil war and the intervention of the Tsar's former allies—America, Britain, and Japan—in order to continue the war against Germany and, incidentally, destroy the Bolshevik regime. In April 1918, the Soviet government in Moscow sent Commissar Vasily Vaslevich Yakolev to move the Tsar and his family to more secure quarters, apparently in Moscow. Since Alexis was ill, at first only Nicholas and Alexandra and one daughter, Marie, were transferred—but not to Moscow. Instead, they were transferred to the ultra-Bolshevik city of Ekaterinburg under the control of the Ural Soviet—the Red Urals were the most militantly Bolshevik area in Russia. They were quartered in the house of a prosperous merchant, N. N. Ipatiev, but on May 17 their old guards were replaced with local Red Guards who had no sympathy for the Romanovs. On May 20, Alexis and the three other girls arrived, so that the total of the detained was twelve people, including servants, sharing five rooms, waiting for they knew not what. There were always rumors of escape plots. The family had a fortune in jewels sewn into their clothes and from time to time they could make contact through correspondence with the outside world. But at Ekaterinburg nothing happened.

On July 4, the local Red Guards were replaced by ten "Letts" —the peasant name for most foreigners. The new squad was under the command of Jacob Yurovsky, a photographer from the town and the local contact for the Cheka—the secret police. From the beginning the Ural Soviet had wanted to execute the Romanovs and had sought permission from the key man in Moscow, Jacob Sverdlov, President of the Central Executive Committee of the All-Russian Congress of Soviets. They, like many other Bolsheviks, saw the Romanovs as symbols of oppression, of the Tsarist state that had waged for three years an incredibly incompetent and unbelievably bloody war for narrow personal interests. They were class enemies, and foibles and frailties added insult to the long train of historic injuries: serfdom, pogroms, oppression, executions and exiles, institutionalized murder. Moscow, however, was considering a show trial with Leon Trotsky as prosecutor. In July 1918, matters took a considerable turn for the worse for the fragile Bolshevik regime. British and American troops had landed at Murmansk in the north. In the Ukraine, two monarchist generals, Alexeiev Kornilov and A. I. Deniken, had launched a massive attack from the south with the help of the Don Cossacks. In Siberia, a free Czech legion that had been on the way to the Western front by a round-the-world route on the trans-Siberian railway switched targets and began attacks on the Bolsheviks—now pro-German—units. The Czechs moved swiftly, taking Omsk and then moving on toward Ekaterinburg and the Romanovs. On July 12 Moscow informed the Ural Soviet that the fate of the Romanovs was up to them. Jacob Yurovsky gave orders for the collection of 150 gallons of gasoline and 400 pounds of sulfuric acid. Execution day would be July 16.

At ten-thirty that evening the Romanov family went to bed as usual. At midnight Yurovsky awakened them, and asked them to dress quickly so that they could be moved before the Czechs arrived. Yurovsky placed them in a small semi-basement room, eighteen by sixteen feet with an iron grille over the window, to wait "until the cars arrived." He supplied three chairs for Nicholas, Alexandra, and Alexis. The four girls stood, along with their doctor, the valet, the cook, and the Empress's parlormaid, who was clutching a pillow containing a collection of the Imperial jewels along with stuffing. Even Jimmy the spaniel was there. Yurovsky and his Cheka squad returned to the room: "Your relations have tried to save you. They have failed and we now must shoot you."[6] Nicholas started to speak. Yurovsky pointed his revolver at the Tsar and fired directly into his head. Nicholas died immediately.* The entire squad began firing. The maid survived the first volley but the executioners bayoneted her to death—she

---

*Not surprisingly, given the trends of the times, Nicholas had been the victim of an unsuccessful assassination attempt a quarter of a century before, during a trip to the Far East. In the Japanese city of Otsu a man, for no discernible reason, swiped his head with a sword, leaving a scar that the Tsar still carried in 1918.

was stabbed more than thirty times. On the floor Alexis made a feeble motion. One of the Cheka men kicked him in the head and Yurovsky fired two shots into the boy's ear. Then Anastasia, who had collapsed in a faint, screamed. She was quickly beaten to death with rifle butts. Everyone was dead; even the spaniel's head had been crushed with a rifle butt.

The bodies were wrapped in sheets, placed in a truck, and driven to an abandoned mine shaft near the Four Brothers—four isolated pine trees. There Yurovsky was prepared to erase all evidence of the executions. Each body was hacked to pieces with axes and saws and placed in a bonfire kept burning with gasoline. The large bones that would not burn were dissolved with the sulfuric acid. The whole process took three days before the last of the ash and residue could be dumped down the mine shaft. Then Voikov, the member of the Ural Soviet who had purchased the gasoline, could say, "The world will never know what we did with them."[7] Eight days later, the White armies swept into Ekaterinburg. It was clear from the condition of the Ipatiev house that a massacre had taken place, but who had been killed and the location of the bodies could not be determined until the following January, when a thorough investigation was ordered by Admiral Kolchak, Supreme Ruler of the White government in Siberia. Nicholas Sokolov, a lawyer, ferreted out the story. The Ural Soviet and Yurovsky had not been especially thorough despite the three days of work. There were jewels ground into the earth around the mine shaft, jewels and relics in the ashes—belt buckles, spectacle cases, icons, eyeglasses. There were charred bones and bits and pieces that the fires and acid had missed. And mangled but unburned at the bottom of the pit was the spaniel Jimmy. Along with the dispositions of the killers and other evidence, Sokolov pieced together the story—he had no doubt that Nicholas, Alexandra, Alexis, and the four girls, along with their servants and doctor and Jimmy, had been slaughtered. For the Bolsheviks, the deaths were a necessity —the Romanovs were the lodestones of resistance and symbols of the corrupt empire. Even better would have been for the Romanovs simply to have disappeared, forever lost at the bottom of the mine at the Four Brothers. Still, Moscow and the Ural Soviet had removed that one special piece from the Russian board. There had been no show trial, as there had been for Louis XVI and Charles I, but only the summary and brutal Bolshevik justice in a slaughter authorized by the responsible.

The Logic of Summary "Justice"

At least in the cases of the Romanovs and Mussolini, there had been some minimal vestige of legal procedures. This is not always the case in authorized murder. On June 30, 1934—the Night of the Long Knives—Chancellor Adolf Hitler authorized the SS to wipe out the leadership of the SA Brownshirts of Ernest Roehm. Two weeks after the event, on July 13, during a speech to the Reichstag, Hitler indicated that there had been seventy-seven deaths. There were, however, probably 150 to 200 killed, including not only Roehm but also former Chancellor General von Schleicher—shot seven times in front of his wife, who then was murdered—General von Bredow, Hitler's old friend Gregor Strasser, a former Prime Minister of Bavaria, and Gustav Ritter von Kahr, whose body was hacked to pieces and thrown into a swamp. Killed as well were a variety of potential dissenters—and, of course, the SA leaders. Hitler had felt it more effective to strike without recourse to law: "The nation must know that its existence . . . will be threatened by no one without punishment."[8] Nazi internal terror did not need, did not want "trials" but only to intimidate the many, including their own.

If Hitler acted out of what he perceived as strength, the Italian partisans and Soviet Bolsheviks were for different reasons under the pressure of time; others have resorted to "authorized" murder from weakness, from fear, even from whim. In Uganda President Idi Amin authorized, and reportedly led, waves of murders, slaughtering tribal enemies, suspects, and random victims, the most notorious incident being the murders of the Anglican Archbishop Janani Luwum, Interior Minister Charles Oboth-Ofumbi, and Lieutenant Colonel Erinayo Oryema, the Land Minister, in 1977. Similar "executions" are or have been commonplace: in the Haiti of "Papa Doc" Duvalier, the dark world of Equatorial Guinea, Rafael Trujillo's Dominican Republic, and Cambodia, with its internal genocide. A continuing example of government by murder has been Ethiopia, where in September 1974 Emperor Haile Selassie was deposed by a group of officers. The first chairman of the military council was General Aman Andom. In November, two months after Haile Selassie's abdication, the military committee ordered the murder of fifty leading Ethiopians, all prominent members of the old regime except one, General Aman Andom. He was succeeded on November 28 by General Tafari Banti, although Lieutenant Colonel Mengistu Haile Marriam was considered more powerful. The government remained under extreme pressure. Secessionist movements to the north in Eritrea and to the east in the Ogaden desert grew enormously as the Ethiopian officers squabbled among themselves and tried to hold off challenges in Addis Ababa from the Left and Right—usually by shooting suspects and leaving the bodies in the street. In February 1977, apparently during a meeting of the governing council at the old palace, Colonel Mengistu and his supporters won a shoot-out over the cabinet table. Brigadier General Tafari Banti and six others were killed. Colonel Mengistu formally became number one, with Lieutenant Colonel Atnafu Abate as the second-ranking member of the military council. That is, until November 13, 1977, when Colonel Atnafu was subjected to a "revolutionary measure" —he was executed, joining the long list of arch-reactionaries, imperialist agents, narrow nationalists, and enemies of the state. Again, there was no bother with revolutionary trials—in the council rooms of the old royal palace the fastest gun becomes the authorized instrument of the Ethiopian revolution.

It is clear that summary justice—swift, authorized murder—is more than likely to be the recourse of a regime of uncertain legitimacy under great pressure. The niceties of form can not take precedence over the needs of the moment, even when there may well be internal and international indignation. In some cases such "executions" are no more than whims of despots, as was the case when the Anglican Archbishop of Uganda was shot down on the spur of the moment during a fit of pique by or on the orders of Idi Amin. In Italy the more militant partisans did not want to be cheated of their revenge, and the execution of Mussolini sooner or later by someone or other seemed a sure thing. In Russia, with their government under challenge from a variety of directions and forces, some of which fought in the name of the Tsar, Moscow and the Ural Soviet felt the royal family was a clear and present danger. Their rescue was possible, and a trial and formal execution were of no advantage to a state living from one crisis to the next. At the other end of stability, if not legitimacy, the reigning leader in Nazi Germany could kill with impunity for the specific purpose of terrifying potential opponents, as in the Soviet Russia of the Great Purges. Hitler was sufficiently certain, beyond all reasonable challenge, that during the Night of the Long Knives he could most effectively cleanse his party, threaten any dissent, and display his power by authorizing the murder of his own. By and large, however, authoritarian states, including Mussolini's Fascist Italy and the Empire of Tsar Nicholas II, can eliminate their internal dissenters by conventional procedures. Foreign enemies, however, pose other problems: the alien agitating from exile, the avowed enemy waging an undeclared war, a foolish leader ready to sell a crucial strategic asset to a dreaded rival. Then tempting, indeed, is the option to authorize an operation that will whisk the distant danger off the board.

Mivtzan Elohim, The Wrath of God, "To Murder the Murderers"

Israel was born during a war that had begun before the state was proclaimed in May 1948, a war that seemed to continue endlessly as the Arabs refused to make peace and often could not make conventional war. There were fedayeen raids, a commercial boycott, threats, alarms, constant harassment, no recognition—and then, like giant black exclamation points, the real wars, in Sinai in 1956 and the June War in 1967, and then the October War of 1973. After the great Arab debacle in 1967 with Israeli forces at the Suez Canal in the west and the Golan Heights in the north, with the Arab air forces in ruins, the tanks of Egypt blackened hulks snaking across the desert, and the pretensions of Syria and its armed forces disintegrating, with the West Bank occupied, Gaza lost, and the Zionists everywhere triumphant, there arose a new form of war. With no tanks and no planes, with no regular armies and with all conventional pride gone, there arose a dozen mostly new fedayeen—guerrilla—organizations which insisted that the way to the inevitable Palestinian triumph and the rebirth of the Arab nation lay through a revolutionary struggle based on the guerrilla. And the frustrated and humiliated rushed to join Al Fatah and the Popular Front for the Liberation of Palestine and Saiqua. There arose organizations for every ideological inclination, Iraqi Ba'aths or Nasserists or Communists. The fedayeen became the new Arab heroes, magnets for Western journalists, the trendies of the New Left. They seemed to go—in print at least—from one triumph to another in the two years after 1967. But it became increasingly and painfully clear that the fedayeen had not been able to establish themselves on the Left Bank or the Gaza Strip, and that their operations were not successful but rather an elaborate form of suicide. Some within the shifting, splitting, intensely competitive organizations decided that there must be a better way.

Led by George Habash's Popular Front for the Liberation of Palestine, the fedayeen began to hijack airliners—first El Al, then any vulnerable airline. The practice led to a confrontation with the Jordanian army in September 1970, after a series of coordinated hijackings over Europe and the Middle East. The result was a heavy defeat for the fedayeen, their expulsion from Jordan, and the erosion of almost all guerrilla potential. In response the fedayeen, largely from the largest organization, Al Fatah, founded a secret group—Black September—to carry the war by whatever means to the enemies of Palestine. The first victim was an Arab, Jordanian Prime Minister Wasif Tol, shot down and killed at the door of the Sheraton Hotel in Cairo. There were more hijackings, more assassinations, and then simple massacres of victims chosen because they had taken the wrong airline or were in line to go to Israel—or, in the most spectacular and grotesque operation, were passing through the Israeli air terminal at Lod. There on May 13, 1972, three members of the radical Japanese Red Army, recruited by Habash, sprayed machine-gun fire at their fellow passengers and tossed grenades into the fleeing crowd. When the slaughter was over, two of the Japanese were dead, and the sprawled and bloody

bodies of twenty-five dead passengers lay on the terminal floor—
including eleven Puerto Rican Christians on a pilgrimage to the
Holy Land. In Beirut, Ghasson Kanafani, editor of *Al Hadaf* and
a spokesman for the Popular Front, made no apologies for the
operation. "If we could liberate Palestine by standing on the borders of South Lebanon and throwing roses on the Israelis we
would do it. It is nicer. But I don't think it would work."[9] So they
had sent proxy gunmen to shoot civilians guilty of being in Israel.

Long before Lod, in fact even before the establishment of their
state, Israelis had opted for a policy of retaliation, to punish the
vulnerable if not the guilty, to encourage their own, and to pursue
with vigor the curious no-war-no-peace conflict the Arabs insisted
on waging. Their response to the first hijacking had been an air-
borne commando raid on Beirut airport in December 1968 that
had left the tarmac littered with burnt-out jets. There were regular raids into the guilty Arab host states of Jordan and Lebanon and
into Egyptian-occupied Gaza. And after the Lod massacre, there
was a special operation mounted to get Kanafani. On July 9, six
weeks later, Kanafani and his sixteen-year-old niece Lamis Najem
were killed when a bomb exploded under his sports car.[10]
Kanafani had been carrying Israel-published material picked up
for him in Europe, and fluttering down on the twisted and burned
hulk over the two maimed bodies came a flutter of leaflets. One,
resting on the hood, read, "With the compliments of the Embassy
of Israel in Copenhagen."

Retaliation, however, was not deterrence, and the operations of
Black September, of the Popular Front, and of other almost ad hoc
groups continued. The most traumatic terrorist spectacular, carefully choreographed by Black September, was the Munich massacre at the Olympics on September 5, 1972, that cost the lives of
eleven Israeli hostages, five of the fedayeen, and a German policeman. The murders had a profound effect on most Western governments, now threatened by novel and unsavory terrorists. Although
various security procedures were instigated, new forces organized, and new laws passed, the vulnerabilities remained: in Khartoum in March 1973, Black September seized various diplomats as
hostages and, when Arab demands were not met, killed American
chargé d'affaires Curt Moore, the new American ambassador Cleo

Noel, and Belgian chargé d'affaires Guy Eid, all somehow "guilty" of collaboration with Zionist Israel.

Long before the three men were shot down in a Khartoum basement, Zionist Israel, outraged by Munich and the continued operation of the Arab fedayeen, had decided to respond, meeting violence with violence, as was the country's wont. Unlike the Kanafani operation, the new campaign of retaliation would be directed by a single new organization structured solely to meet the terrorist threat: *Mivtzan Elohim,* The Wrath of God. On October 16, 1972, the month after Munich, the suspected Al Fatah leader in Rome, Wadal Abdel Zwaiter, was shot twelve times with a .22-caliber Beretta and killed, opening up an underground war between the Wrath of God and the Palestinians. Israelis were shot and killed in Brussels and letter-bombed in London, while Arabs were assassinated with radio-controlled bombs or Beretta revolvers.

The most spectacular of all Wrath of God operations came in April 1973. At 1:30 A.M. on April 9, thirty members of Mossad, commandos and paratroops, embarked in rubber dinghies from three Israeli missile boats. Armed frogmen had already secured the landing site on the Beirut beach. There was no alert, and when the Israelis waded ashore they found waiting Buicks, Plymouths, and a Renault, keys in the ignitions, all rented by Israeli agents. The Israelis, armed with grenades, Berettas, and submachine guns, split into three teams: the first, paratroopers, would hit a Black September warehouse-factor to the north; the second, nine commandos, would attack the headquarters of the Democratic Popular Front for the Liberation of Palestine in a refugee camp in south Beirut; the third had three special, personal targets, prominent members of the Palestine Liberation Organization, the umbrella for all the disparate groups dominated by Yasir Arafat's Al Fatah.

The three targets resided in two closely defended apartment buildings at rue de Verdun near the corner of Khaled Ben Al Walid and rue 68. Mohammed Yusif Najjar, "Abu Youssef" in the fedayeen world, was a founder of Al Fatah when he and Arafat were Palestinian refugees in Kuwait in 1965. He rose to prominence after the Black September war in Jordan—according to the

Israelis he was number three in the PLO and the real leader of
Black September. At forty-seven he was a quiet, mild-mannered
man, more the engineer that he had been trained as than a guerrilla leader. After 1970 he had proven a first-rate diplomat in the
shaky world of guerrilla alliances and Lebanese sensitivities. He
was the most effective negotiator Al Fatah possessed, a representative on the PLO executive committee, and in charge of foreign
links, although guerrilla sources denied he had any operational
control of secret terrorist groups. Kamal Adwan, thirty-seven, had
been in charge of the Al Fatah information department and subsequently organized Al Fatah cells on the Israeli-occupied West
Bank—for the Israelis he was Black September's man for Israel.
The third target, Kamal Nasser, was best known to Western journalists as the PLO spokesman, although he did not join the active
resistance until the Israelis expelled him from the West Bank. A
lawyer, a poet, a former left-wing deputy of the Ba'ath Socialist
Party in Jordan, he was an amusing and effective conversationalist
who traveled in intellectual, rather than guerrilla, circles. As
spokesman for the PLO, he was interesting, often witty; he was
also disorganized and imprecise, but always charming. He seemed
an unlikely subject, a delightful man who never carried a gun and
continued to write Arabic poetry.

The Israeli hit team arrived undetected at rue de Verdun. The
three fedayeen guards were killed instantly and silently. Almost
simultaneously the Israelis broke into the three apartments in the
two buildings. Kamal Adwan tried to defend himself with a Ka-
lashnikov assault rifle—the symbol of the Palestinian revolution—
but was shot down and killed in front of his wife. Across the way,
in Mohammed Yusif Najjar's apartment, the door was smashed and
the bedroom sprayed with submachine-gun fire; both "Abu Youssef" and his wife were killed instantly. At that moment, a door in
the corridor popped open and the Israelis quickly shot the curious
neighbor—an old woman—dead before she hit the floor. In the
same building Kamal Nasser was machine-gunned and killed at his
desk where he was writing. The Israeli teams withdrew without
meeting opposition. In fact, only the group that had gone into the
refugee camp took any casualties—two dead and two wounded.
The others moved back to the rocky beach, left the nine cars lined

up with the keys in the ignitions, and embarked in the rubber boats ninety minutes after they had landed. Operationally it appeared a most elegant effort, although it was as much a result of compensating Arab errors and incompetence as proper Israeli planning. Zionist Israel was delighted. Golda Meir announced, "It was marvelous. We killed the murderers who were planning to murder again."[11]

Both the Arab fedayeen and the Wrath of God continued killing in their underground war. In Rome two Arabs were blown up in their Mercedes when the Israelis detonated the Arabs' own bomb. A PLO agent was killed in Paris when a car bomb detonated in his white Renault 16. In Washington the Israeli military attaché was shot and killed between his car and his front door. In the same month, July 1973, a disastrous Israeli operation in Norway persuaded Jerusalem to ease up their campaign—for the time being. On July 21, Ahmed Bouchiki, a Moroccan, had been shot down and killed as he arrived with his young, pregnant Norwegian wife at his residence after seeing a film. It soon became apparent that Bouchiki, a thirty-year-old waiter, was not Ali Hassan Salameh— high on Israel's hit list (who was eventually killed with a car bomb in January 1979)—but just a thirty-year-old waiter. Worse, for the Israelis, the entire bungled operation came apart at the seams; those involved were arrested, and several were tried and convicted. While audacity spiced with contempt for their opponents had regularly paid off for the Israelis, the Wrath of God had apparently run out of luck. But the authorized war of the Wrath of God was far from over, and their Arab enemies were demoralized but far from intimidated.

INTERNATIONAL VIOLENCE AT A DISTANCE

What was unique about the Israeli Wrath of God was that it was a special organization conjured up to deal with authorized assassinations abroad. Most regimes who choose just such an option—and there have been a great many—simply co-opted existing forces or deployed those who could be plausibly denied. As early as 1802, the French, suspecting that they had discovered an English assassination plot against Napoleon, dispatched a special team into a neutral German state to kidnap the suspect, the Duc'd Enghier. He was brought back, tried, convicted, and executed in 1804 in the moat of the Chateau de Vincennes—a precursor of the Adolf Eichmann operation of the Israelis. Certain totalitarian states have been particularly prone to authorize murder at a distance, which is cheaper and quicker than a war.

Mussolini arranged the murder in France of the most active of the exiles opposed to the Fascist regime—the Rosselli brothers, founders of Justice and Liberty. On July 25, 1934, 145 SS of Austrian Standarte 89, led by SS-man Holzweber with the complicity of Major Key, chief of police, mortally wounded Austrian Chancellor Engelbert Dollfus, who lingered on until six in the evening, still refusing to tender the resignation his neighbor Adolf Hitler had hoped for; but then the assassination could be plausibly denied as purely an Austrian matter. And in a similar vein there was a remarkable attrition rate of exiles organizing against the Soviet regime, first White Russians, then Trotskyites, and after World War II Ukrainian exiles. Most recently, Croatians opposed to Tito have been found murdered. Even less authoritarian and more traditional states have become involved in such matters, especially in the Middle East, where the Saudis have been reliably rumored to have put up millions for Nasser to be removed, where Syria and Iraq have argued out the fine points of Ba'athist ideology with authorized assassins, where even ten years after his departure as Syrian strongman, Colonel Adibal Shishakli was assassinated in Brazil in September 1964—vengeance has a long memory. And such vengeance is hardly absent from Latin American politics. Dictator Rafael Trujillo tried to kill Venezuelan President Romulo Betancourt—unsuccessfully—but did manage the disappearance of one of his citizens, Professor Jesus da Galindez, who besides being opposed to Trujillo was involved with a Basque revolutionary group. On March 12, 1956, he disappeared from the campus of Columbia University in New York and, according to rumor, was dropped from a light plane over a convenient ocean. More recently, on September 21, 1976, Orlando Letelier, former Chilean ambassador in Washington and an exile from the military regime in Santiago, was killed when a radio-activated bomb was detonated under the seat of his car while he was driving around Sheridan Circle. A colleague was killed at the same time. Despite general outrage, for some time there were no suspects. Gradually, a pattern emerged that involved the Chilean secret police (DINA), Cuban exiles, and an American, Michael Vernon Townley, who had been involved in Chilean intelligence work. It would appear that DINA had tried to arrange a plausible denial cut-out—but with less than remarkable success. Townley's evidence in court resulted in the conviction of three of the Cubans; two indicted Cubans and three Chilean intelligence officers are still at large. There also had been allegations that Chile had set up a killer squad in Europe headed by Colonel Pedro Ewing, military attaché in Madrid, to track down and dispose of exiled opponents; and there was further evidence of still more DINA agents in other countries as well.

Democratic governments have not denied themselves the assassination option, especially when engaged in an irregular war that seemingly calls for irregular methods. On December 5, 1952, the French secret service directed a successful operation against the Tunisian national leader, Ferhat Hached. In fact, various official, if covert, French agencies and services became increasingly involved in such special operations directed against Arab nationalists in the Magreb. This was particularly true during the Algerian insurrection, when arms purchased by agents in Europe were often funneled to the rebels through Tunisia. A mysterious Red Hand organization operated mainly in Germany and Switzerland against the rebel agents, some of whom died in bombed cars, while one was dispatched with a dart gun. The French intention was not only to interrupt the arms traffic but also to intimidate any replacements—and they did so with some success. Long before the Wrath of God, the Israelis had used letter bombs and threats, often real, to stop work on Egyptian rockets by German scientists. More often than not, however, such campaigns from a distance are not aimed at prominent persons but at dangerous operations previously contained inside a neutral sanctuary.

One of the more remarkable exceptions to a general democratic denial was the series of plots by the American Central Intelligence Agency against Fidel Castro. Once the direction of the Cuban revolution began to become clear, once Cuba seemed likely to become a protégé if not a pawn of the Soviet Union, various individuals in and out of the CIA felt that the Cuban was a clear and present danger to American interests. The country was engaged in a cold war with international Communism, and Castro might well open up both the Caribbean and all of Latin America to the Reds. Within the CIA discussions began in late 1959 about eliminating Castro. Between 1960 and 1965, there would be at least eight plots involving the CIA, almost all bizarre, all unsuccessful, and in retrospect all silly, except for the damage to America's reputation—not to mention that of the CIA.

The first suggestion was peculiarly American—that Castro's "image" be ruined by a variety of absurd technological means: a chemical similar to LSD was to be introduced into the radio studio or through doctored cigars so that his dramatic speeches would be ruined; or thallium salts, a powerful depilatory, would be sprinkled in his shoes so that his beard would fall out. From there the plotting went to more lethal suggestions—a $10,000 reward for an "accident," or cigars infected with botulism toxin so powerful that the smoker would die almost instantly. As had been the case in the Lumumba plot in the Congo, the CIA remained convinced that dirty tricks were best performed by dirty people, and through Robert A. Maheu they recruited John Rosselli as a case officer for further assassination plots. Rosselli and his associates, Momo Salvatore Giacana of Chicago and Santos Trafficante, formerly of Havana, were generally referred to as alleged members of the underworld. They, in turn, recruited secure Cubans, who in turn were horrified by the CIA concept of a shoot-out assassination. *That* was far too dangerous. They wanted the benefits of the agency's lethal technology—poison pills that could be used by a "contact" in a restaurant, not submachine guns. The plots went on, each petering off into vague frustration—agents landed in a small plane with high-powered rifles and disappeared; Castro stopped using the restaurant; arms and pills and explosives were dispatched and never used. After the failure of the Bay of Pigs invasion, the most bizarre of all plots evolved in the CIA labs. Castro would be given a diving suit contaminated with a fungus that would produce a chronic skin disease, Madura foot, and with tubercule bacillus in the breathing apparatus. One of the last efforts came on November 22, 1963, nearly three months after Castro had announced publicly that he knew of the attempts, when a CIA agent offered a poison pen to a Cuban for one more attempt. On the same day in Havana, an emissary from the President was meeting with Castro to investigate means to improve Cuban-American relations. And on the same day in Dallas, John F. Kennedy was shot and killed by the only member of the Fair Play for Cuba Committee.

So there were all the old dirty tricks, inappropriate technology, inept agents, the Mafia and Operation Mongoose, and no real end of it until such discussion was broken off with AM/LASH, the CIA man in Havana—who had sensibly turned down the poison ball-point pen as not very sophisticated. Nor were the plots—Castro claimed twenty-four but the CIA insisted they had no part in fifteen of them—really explicable. They were irrelevant to the reality of international politics—kill Castro and Cuba will be ours —or the importance of Castro's regime as a threat to the West. They were unsavory; they were silly; and perhaps most cruel to the pretensions of the CIA, they were inept, employing "devices which strain the imagination"[12] to no good end—a crime, and worse, a blunder. Of course, the CIA was not alone in having trouble with assassinations, but in some cases the directors were lucky. Certainly their major rival in such matters, Russia, in an earlier effort to dispose of that last great revolutionary who had slipped through Siqueiros' trigger fingers, managed both a success and the ultimate in plausible denial from a captured killer.

The House at Coyoacan, Final Act: The Murder of Leon Trotsky

After the attempt on Trotsky on May 24, 1940, the walls of the house at Coyoacan were raised. A new watchtower was erected. A system of alarm bells was put in, with one pushbutton on Trotsky's desk in his study. The doors and windows were covered with steel. Trotsky said it felt like a prison, with each day courtesy of Stalin. During the summer of 1940, there were fewer visitors. The war in Europe cut off one set of friends and there had been a split in the American Trotskyite movement. One of the Americans, Sylvia Agelof from Brooklyn, who had been staying in the center of the city at the Hotel Montejo, had gone back to America in March. Her husband, Frank Jacson, however, stayed on for a while and although professing no interest in politics, came to see Trotsky on May 28, four days after the assassination attempt. He saw Trotsky some ten times over the next four weeks, and left for New York City during June. No one paid him much attention, a handsome young man, who had no interest in politics.

Frank Jacson was neither Frank Jacson nor Sylvia Agelof's husband. They had met in Paris in 1939. He was introduced by Ruby Weill as Jacques Mornand, a freelance journalist, son of a Belgian diplomat, born in Teheran in 1904. He was a handsome young man with ample funds—and no interest in politics. Sylvia Agelof was very interested in politics, and had served as a translator at the founding conference of the Fourth International in Paris the previous year. She fell madly in love with Mornand and became his mistress, and when she returned to the United States, she was delighted when he followed, using a Canadian passport in the name of Frank Jacson. Jacques Mornand was not Jacques Mornand either; like Ruby Weill, who had arranged the Paris meeting, he was an agent of the Soviet Russian GPU, the State Political Bureau that had replaced the Cheka.

Jacques Mornand, so it would seem, was really Ramon Mercader, born in Barcelona in 1914, son of a Cuban mother, Caridad, and Spanish father, Pablo. His parents separated when Mercader was eleven—it was a difficult family. His mother had artistic pretensions; a woman of powerful character with an interest in politics, she dominated her simple, mild bourgeoise husband. Mercader attended the English Institution and then the school of the Episcopalian Fathers, until his mother moved to Toulouse in 1925. His father followed. No one was happy. Caridad reportedly tried suicide once or twice. Mercader ran away, returned to Barcelona, and became an assistant chef in the Barcelona Ritz. Caridad moved on to Paris and became the mistress of various prominent

Communists. Pablo disappeared from the scene. In Barcelona Mercader became interested in revolutionary politics, and was arrested and imprisoned for three months before being released by the new Popular Front government. When the Spanish Civil War began in July 1936, he joined the Republican army. So did Caridad, who returned from Paris, led an attack and was wounded, and was then dispatched to Mexico to raise funds. Mercader became a political commissar, and when his mother returned he was taken under the wing of her newest political lover, Leonid Eitigon. Leonid Eitigon was also known as Leonid Eitingon and Leonid Eitington (perhaps a difficulty in spelling a cover name), and as Sakhov and Valery and Comrade Pablo and General Kotov. As General Kotov, a high-ranking GPU officer, he sent Mercader to a saboteurs' school in Spain and then on to Moscow. There Mercader disappeared, to surface in Paris as Jacques Mornand, ten years older, a Belgian freelance journalist, soon to be Frank Jacson and then a regular visitor at the house at Coyoacan —visits made necessary by the collapse of the May 24 attempt by Siqueiros.

In June 1940, "Jacson" arrived in New York City to meet the American GPU chief, Gaik Ovakinian, and receive his instructions. He returned to Mexico City and the Montejo Hotel. At Coyoacan Trotsky continued his daily rounds—each day courtesy of Stalin—churning out letters and articles and polemics to a shrinking audience. Frank Jacson continued to visit the Trotsky house. Nearly everyone noticed that he looked ill; his complexion was poor; he was morose. He did express a growing interest in politics. He would write an article. Sylvia Agelof arrived at the Montejo. She, too, noticed he had changed. On August 14, Jacson visited Trotsky. He carried a raincoat that seemed unnecessary and wore a hat for the first time. He still did not look well.

On August 20, he made another trip to the house at Coyoacan, carrying his raincoat and wearing a hat. Sewn into the lining of the coat was a thirteen-inch dagger; in one pocket was a *piolet*, a mountaineer's ice ax with a seven-inch head, one side a sharp point, the other a hammer-claw, with the handle sawn off twelve inches from the head; in the other pocket was a .45-caliber automatic revolver. He talked with Trotsky while the rabbits were being fed in the garden and then the two walked through the French door into the study. The door was closed.

Inside, Trotsky sat down behind his desk. They talked briefly of French statistics. Trotsky picked up Jacson's political article and swiveled his chair toward the window. He must have sensed a movement, because he began turning back toward Jacson, who had taken the ice ax out of his pocket and raised it over his head. A silent kill might make it possible for him to slip away before the body was discovered. He drove the claw-end straight down into Trotsky's head. The *piolet* penetrated two and a half inches into Trotsky's skull and then was wrenched out. It was not a quiet kill. Trotsky let out an incredible, loud, long drawn-out cry, part roar and part scream. And he didn't die. His face covered with blood, his glasses gone, with the incredible gash in his head, he leaned across the desk and began grappling with Jacson, ripping away the ice ax, biting Jacson's finger, staggering across the study after his assailant. When his wife and others had nearly reached the study, the door opened and Trotsky, his face a bloody mask, staggered out, said only "Jacson," and collapsed. Behind him Jacson stood, the .45 automatic dangling from one limp hand, the other hand in his mouth. He seemed in shock, nursing his bitten finger, making no effort to escape. In two ambulances, they were taken to the hospital. Trotsky was still conscious, and although the doctors would operate, there was no hope. He had time to dictate his final statement.

> I am close to death from the blow of a political assassin. I was struck down in my room. I struggled with him. We had entered—talked about French statistics. He struck me. Please say to our friends—I am sure of the victory—of the Fourth International—Go forward.[13]

He soon lost consciousness and died twenty-four hours later, without speaking again.

Sylvia Agelof spent most of the next few days in hysterics, realizing immediately what Jacson had done and who he must be. She visited him in prison, screaming and shouting and finally spitting on him. He—by then recognized as Mornand—seemed disconcerted. He would insist that he really loved her, that he was really Mornand, and that a strange, rambling letter of confession found in his pocket explained everything. It explained nothing. And it was soon discovered that there was no Jacques Mornand—no son of a Belgian diplomat born in Teheran in 1904. On April 17, 1943, as Mornand, he was sentenced to nineteen years and six months for the murder, and six months for illegal possession of arms. He spent the next eighteen years in the Federal Penitentiary on the outskirts of Mexico City; under Mexican prison rules he could and did have girlfriends, and he learned electrical engineering. He was refused parole in 1953—he had shown no remorse—and was moved to a new reformatory, and was finally released in 1960. Despite the accumulating evidence that he was Ramon Mercader, he insisted he was not—that he was actually Jacques Mornand, that he had killed Trotsky, that he had loved Sylvia Agelof. He left Mexico and took up residence in Prague, and then lived for fifteen years in Moscow. He moved on to Cuba and died at the age of sixty-five in October 1978. His story never changed. Sylvia Agelof returned to America and refused to discuss the past. Trotsky was cremated and the ashes buried under a marker incised with a hammer and sickle in the garden at Coyoacan.

After endless months—years, really—of intense interrogation, including nine hundred hours with psychiatrists, and after various independent investigations, Mornand-Mercader remained a mystery. Much of the plot to kill Trotsky is a matter of speculation, the details assumed, the responsibilities guesswork. Almost no one doubts, however, that the unidentifiable man—the perfect example of plausible denial—was programmed to kill Stalin's last, greatest living enemy. All that was necessary was the right man and an ice ax, and a living legend became ashes in a Mexican garden, the victim of an authorized execution. Perhaps, as Trotsky said, "It is the victims that move history forward." Perhaps not.

NOTES

1. Howard McGaw Smyth, *Secrets of the Fascist Era,* Carbondale and Edwardsville (Illinois), Southern Illinois University Press, 1975, p. 193.

2. *Ibid.,* p. 197.

3. *Ibid.,* p. 201.

4. *Ibid.*

5. Colonel Valerio was involved in the disappearance of the treasure of Dongo —assets carried by Mussolini—probably into Communist Party coffers. And for this and other reasons, he was rumored to have been the target of an assassination plot when he was scheduled to speak at Basilica Massenzo on March 30, 1947. In any case, nothing happened on that day, and although two people were killed over the Dongo treasure, Valerio lived on unmolested until 1973.

6. Robert K. Massie, *Nicholas and Alexandra,* New York, Dell, 1972, p. 515.

7. *Ibid.,* pg. 516.

8. Eliot Barculo Wheaton, *The Nazi Revolution 1933–1935, Prelude to Calamity,* Garden City (New York), Doubleday-Anchor, 196, p. 492.

9. *Washington Post,* July 9, 1972.

10. There are reports that the detonation was radio-controlled on a visual sighting despite the presence of the girl.

11. David B. Tinnin (with Dag Christensen), *The Hit Team,* Boston, Little, Brown, 1972, p. 94.

12. United States Senate, Select Committee to Study Government Operations with Respect to Intelligence Activities, *Alleged Assassination Plots Involving Foreign Leaders,* Washington, D.C., Government Printing Office, 1975, p. 71.

13. Nicholas Mosley, *The Assassination of Trotsky,* London, Michael Joseph, 1972, p. 162.

5

Killing as Politics: The Rebels

The revolutionary is a dedicated man. He has
no personal inclinations, no business affairs, no
emotions, no attachments, no property, and no
name. Everything in him is subordinated toward a single thought, and a single passion—the
revolution.
—Serge Nechaev in *Revolutionary Catechism*

For most the classic assassin has not been an authorized agent
of the state, nor a hireling, nor the self-declared defender of the
threatened system, but rather a treacherous rebel, perhaps mad
but always abhorrent. Such murder as a means for political gain
seems immoral, an act against nature, even if a frequent and
catholic act. The toll, even in this century, of famous victims is long
and distinguished: kings, presidents, premiers, peacemakers, and
generals, as well as unsavory tyrants. And the killers were almost
always unknown young men, often members of obscure, elusive
organizations. Some, such as Ravaillac striking down Henry IV,
acted alone in the grip of an obsession; others, such as Gavrilo
Princip, killed within a tradition of nationalism. All sought specific
change, seeking at least to punish if they could not otherwise act
on events.

INDIVIDUALS TO STRIKE THE FIRST BLOW

"I'm going to kill Huey Long."
—Carl Austin Weiss

With a single thrust of a knife, Ravaillac changed history. At the least, even if Henry IV had escaped, as he had so many times before, the tyrant would be warned—at best, he would be dead. That alone was the aim of the classic assassin: to punish the guilty and deter the ambitious, someone must strike the first blow. Often, of course, the punishment of one tyrant had little effect on the conduct of his heir, except perhaps to strengthen security precautions. Just what might flow from the murder was often beyond prediction, except that power would accrue to another. If the lone assassin dreamed of effecting substantive change, other hands would have to do that. The single assassin could only remove a single piece from the board. Almost always the natural and proper heirs, the son or the vice-president or crown prince, took power and the game went on, although not always quite as before. Some princes and presidents seem quite without precedent, controlling the direction of events, as did Henry IV. Some deaths, such as that of Francis Ferdinand, seem to accelerate events irrelevant to the victims' power or position. Rarely, however, can the lone assassin count on more than punishment of the wicked; but again, he may act within a broad strategy of murder for the church or for the cause, as did so many lone anarchist assassins. Mostly, he murders alone. And such treacherous violence is so often perceived as not simply bloody but futile, surely a depraved act not by a desperate man but by a mad murderer. Ravaillac must have been mad to act as he did, either a fanatic driven by visions or a pawn of a conspiracy. Apparently, however, most lone assassins are indeed psychopathic. Ravaillac being on the border of reason, others are quite rational, and perform their murderous deed for explicable political reasons—and are not part of a conspiracy.

The golden age of European monarchy, between the creation

of the German Empire, appropriately in the Hall of Mirrors at Versailles in 1871, and the assassination of Francis Ferdinand in 1914, was also the high tide of revolutionary anarchism, an era of gunmen and bombers who disposed of more royalty and their republican counterparts than inherited disease, the rigors of age, and the field of battle. Many of the assassins acted alone, buoyed up by the belief that others elsewhere would perform similar deeds, that such deeds would release the bottled power of the masses and sweep away in a great cataclysm the imperialist-capitalist system, thus ushering in the millennium of the workers and peasants. It was a vision as luminous as it was narrow, as persistent as it was improbable. The anarchists' butcher's bill grew almost year by year and the millennium drew no nearer, but neither did anarchist hearts grow fainter.

In June 1898, in Paterson, New Jersey, an Italian immigrant, Gaetano Bresci, read that King Humbert had conferred the Grand Officer's Cross of the military order of Savoy on General Bava Beccaris for his rigor in putting down demonstrations—that is, ordering his troops to shoot down innocent civilians—the previous month in Milan. Bresci wept and decided that the responsibility was Humbert's, and he must be punished. Each week for over a hundred weeks, he put aside one dollar and fifty cents from his wages as a textile worker at the Hamil Booth Company silk factory. By May 1900 he had $100, a special third-class excursion ticket to the Paris Exposition, and a gun. He practiced with the gun, and after bidding farewell to his Irish wife and daughter, sailed on May 17. He visited the Exposition and then moved on to Italy. He read that the king would appear at a sporting event in Monza. Neatly dressed, with a gold ring and a watch with an elegant chain, tall, quite dark, Bresci appeared to be a gentleman of some means. At nine-thirty in the evening, the king arrived in a two-horse landau for the gymnastics competition. He was greeted with a roar. Humbert took his place in the stands. An hour later the contest was over. The king again boarded his carriage. The athletes gathered around to send him off with a cheer. The spectators also began moving down around the carriage. Everyone was crying, "Long live the King!" Bresci broke out of the crowd, lifted his short-barreled, five-chamber pistol, and fired three times directly at the king. The horses lurched. The king slumped down. When asked if he had been hit, he replied, "I don't think so."[1] But he was mortally wounded: one bullet had entered just above his collarbone and lodged behind his shoulder blade; a second had penetrated between his third and fourth ribs and rested in his breastbone; the third had gone through the center of his heart. King Humbert the Good was dead before the carriage could reach his villa. In Italy there was no praise for Bresci. The Left disassociated themselves from the deed. His family disowned him. The jury found him guilty in nine minutes. There was no death penalty; he was given life, and ten months later it was announced that he had committed suicide. By then he was forgotten. In fact, his deed had been generally condemned except by American anarchists, most of whom Bresci had felt were insufficiently revolutionary. Emma Goldman—queen of the anarchists—said that the assassin had her sympathy.

A year after Bresci's death, Emma Goldman was deeply involved in an American assassination and an anarchist crisis. In 1890, at twenty-one, Goldman, a recent Russian Jewish immigrant, became deeply involved with a German exile, Johann Most, editor of the anarchist weekly *Freiheit* in New York. With a deformed body and a twisted face, he glowed with a barely suppressed rage—Most radiated hatred and love. He wrote of dynamite and nitroglycerine, and published an explicit guide to the world of bombs. His charisma was insufficient for Goldman, who simultaneously began an affair with Alexander Berkman, a handsome, bull-necked Russian Jewish immigrant, who had become a confirmed anarchist despite a bourgeoise upbringing in Russia. For all three, the crucial political moment came in July 1892— there had already been a not unexpected series of personal crises as a result of their triangular relationship. In June 1892, the workers of the Carnegie Steel Company's Homestead plant struck in protest over a wage reduction. The company had decided to confront the union and ordered a provocation wage cut. Barbed wire was put around the plant and three hundred strikebreakers were recruited by the Pinkerton Agency. The grand old man, benefactor and philanthropist, Andrew Carnegie, quietly withdrew from the scene to fish for salmon in Scotland, leaving matters to his manager, Henry Clay Frick. A quiet, determined man, handsome with a dark mustache and short beard, contained and confident, Frick had every intention of winning. On July 5, the strikebreakers were ferried in, setting off a day-long battle that left ten dead and seventy wounded. To the amazement of all, the strikebreakers had been repulsed. The Governor immediately sent in eight thousand militia. Frick announced that he would use only non-union labor and evict from company houses workers who refused to return to work. "Homestead, I must go to Homestead,"² Berkman shouted to Emma Goldman.

On July 23, Berkman was admitted to Frick's office as an agent of a New York employment fund. Frick was consulting with his vice-chairman, John Leishman, and looked up to see a strange man firing a revolver directly at him. The first bullet hit him on the left side of the neck, the second hit him on the right side, the third went wild as Leishman knocked Berkman's arm up. Frick was bleeding profusely, and Leishman began struggling with Berkman. The three fell to the floor. Berkman managed to free one hand and pulled out a dagger. He stabbed Frick in the side and legs seven times before he was dragged away. Shaken, bleeding, and still on the floor, Frick whispered, "Let me see his face."³ Frick lived. The strike was broken. Berkman could not commit suicide after his trial—where he wanted to make a statement— and spent sixteen years in prison. Back in New York, the anarchist movement was shattered when, in the *Freiheit* of August 27, Johann Most denounced Berkman's deed. When he repeated his contemptuous attack on Berkman in a public meeting, Emma Goldman leaped from the audience, rushed to the platform, and flayed her old lover with a horsewhip. American anarchism never recovered.

Although revolutionary anarchism seemed to breed individual assassins as well as the demented who would mimic their deeds, there have always been others determined to punish even at the cost of their own lives. In 1935 one of the rare American political, rather than pathological, assassinations occurred in Louisiana, when one of the most charismatic of all the politicians of his day was shot and killed. Senator Huey Long had transformed himself from a traveling salesman to a dominant figure in American politics. Shrewd, cunning, without scruple, a spellbinding orator who espoused the radical, populist causes in a state long dominated by the big corporations, the old families, and the Regulars, Huey Long built a political dynasty that many thought was to be the base for a drive for national power. In Louisiana, he left his trail littered with electoral victories and destroyed opponents. He would not compromise with the old guard; once in office he crushed any dissent—he owned and operated the state of Louisiana. In Washington, with his Share the Wealth Program, he took on President Franklin Roosevelt—just one more patrician, an apple planter, another old regular. And there were those who felt that with America in the depths of the Depression the Kingfish might go all the way, turn the whole country into Louisiana, soak the rich, pay the poor, take a cut and smash the old regulars, and incidently the American political system. Others felt that much of the criticism of Long's latent "fascism" arose from political jealousy, a deep hatred of the man who took away the privileges from the proper people.

By the summer of 1935, there were rumors of a real conspiracy against Long in Louisiana. The old Square Dealers, forty bitter men, were ready to draw straws to get Long, and there was a strange Minute Men organization with similar ideas. It might have been mostly talk, but the atmosphere in the summer of 1935 was certainly tense. Long had returned from Washington interested in pushing a couple of pieces of state legislation—one would limit federal employees' activities in the state and was probably unconstitutional but would work until the litigation was finished; the other would gerrymander away the base of one of his most vocal opponents, Judge Benjamin Pavy. The judge's son-in-law was a brilliant, intense young doctor, Carl Austin Weiss, who had studied in Vienna and Paris. In Louisiana, married, with a son born in June 1935, he took no part in politics. But he was deeply idealistic and felt Huey Long was an evil man—"I'm going to kill Huey Long."[4] No one paid any attention, certainly not on Sunday, September 8, when Weiss spent much of the day quietly with his family. He then left and made his way to the state capitol.

At 9:20 P.M., Senator Long walked across the capitol rotunda, turned right down the corridor to the Governor's office, and stopped, turning back the way he had come, waiting for his aides to catch up. Then, from behind a pillar, a man in a white suit, Dr. Carl Weiss, appeared; he brushed past the little group of politicians and raised his right hand. A Long aide standing beside him, John Fournet, suddenly saw the pistol and grabbed at Weiss' arm. There was a bang. Long screamed, "I'm shot." Fournet and Murphy Roden grappled with Weiss, who fired again, shooting off Roden's watch. He began to back away from the two, crouching, holding out his pistol. Roden had his pistol out, as did a policeman, Elliot Coleman. Both fired at once and Weiss began to crumple. The other guards opened up, some continuing to fire after Weiss lay sprawled on the marble floor, his white suit soaked in blood— he had been hit twice in the head, and there were thirty bullet wounds in his back. He had been dead before the guards began to fire. Long was still conscious—and curious as to why he would be shot. He was rushed to the nearby Lady of the Lake Hospital, where an examination showed his pulse was up and his blood pressure down, indications of internal hemorrhaging. Although Dr. Arthur Vidrine would have preferred to wait for more experienced surgeons, he began to operate at 11:30 P.M., two hours after the shooting, in a room crowded with aides and friends and politicians who had flocked to the hospital at the news. There did not seem to be any serious damage—merely a perforated colon— and little bleeding. Vidrine was finished in an hour, and the senator seemed in no great danger. When the experienced surgeons arrived, however, it was discovered that Vidrine had missed a damaged renal duct to the kidney. The internal bleeding continued, and Long was too weak to stand a second operation. All day Monday, September 9, he weakened. Four blood transfusions did not turn the tide. He drifted in and out of consciousness, rambling and incoherent. The next day, September 10, it was clear he was not going to make it. In the afternoon, with his family at his side, he began to sink very rapidly. At four he said, "God, don't let me die. I have so much to do."[5] Six minutes later he was dead. There was little public outcry or outrage except among his own. A great many prominent people attended the funeral of Weiss— "a sincere and idealistic young man."[6]

CONSPIRACIES: THE SEARCH FOR POWER

"Kill him!"
—Lieutenant-Colonel Klaus Philipp Schenk, Count
von Stauffenberg, at the end of 1942 in answer to
what should be done about Hitler

Sincere and idealistic young men may punish, perhaps even may deter, but into any violent vacuum others rush for power. There was, of course, no one to replace each of the previously mentioned three victims, but history seemed little changed. Huey Long's family and friends remained dominant factors in state politics for years. Frick returned to his office and the ultimately unsuccessful struggle against the unions. King Humbert was entombed in the Pantheon and Victor Emmanuel III, the Little King, came to the throne—matters continued, often as before. Of course, certain conspiracies have been so severely restricted by the security forces, by their own lack of talents and resources, that they cannot hope for power. The reverse is to be so blessed with resources that an immediate seizure of power is possible and any accompanying assassinations are a convenience rather than a necessity.

The optimum asset is to possess a substantial portion of the armed forces, a prospect ordinarily open only to members of the officer corps, who, unlike revolutionaries, are most often solely ambitious for the fruits of power and quite unconcerned with previous injustice or future reform. In some states the coup has become almost an institutionalized means of transferring power from one elite to its mirror image: a *pronunciamento* is announced, and the threatened leaders poll the barracks, add up their chances, and decide to resist or join their assets in foreign parts. Where such a system is not so formal, the chances of violence increase—in Ethiopia the dissident officers ran a coup on the installment plan that so absorbed the interest of the military that the country collapsed into anarchy. At other times, the strategists of the war-coup intend from the first to seize power and the palace, and in the process intentionally, rather than incidentally, kill the incumbent and, perhaps, his friends and family.

A recent example is that of the Afghanistan coup of April 1978. A leading leftist ideologist of the Parach (Flag) Party, Mir Akbar Khaiber, was assassinated. No one claimed responsibility. The funeral drew a huge crowd; there was a demonstration in front of the United States Embassy, and government panicked and began arresting leftists. On April 27, the cabinet met to consider purging the armed forces of unreliables. The frightened "unreliables" swiftly mounted a coup the same night that led to the bitter fighting, the murder of most of the government, and the new pro-Soviet regime of Noor Mohammed Tarakki and an influx of Russians to aid the revolution.

On July 14, 1958, dissident Iraqi army officers and units under their command seized Baghdad, rounded up the inhabitants of the royal palace, and machine-gunned their radical republic into power—killing King Faisal II, Crown Prince Abdul Ilah, and, two days later, Prime Minister Nuri al-Said, long-time strongman of the monarchy. A more technologically sophisticated war-coup occurred on August 16, 1972, when Moroccan Air Force jets fired on the Boeing 727 bringing King Hassan II back to Rabat. Three American-built F-5s swept in to escort the King's Boeing over Tetuán in northern Morocco. They opened fire on the royal plane, with rockets and machine guns chopping up the fuselage and cockpit, wounding several persons—but not the king. One F-5 peeled off and machine-gunned the reception committee at the Rabat airport while other jets hit the palace. And despite all this, the pilot of the Boeing managed to take evasive action and land successfully. Hassan returned to the palace and loyal troops surrounded the military air field at Kenitra, where the fighter pilots were based. The war-coup based on assassination by F-5s had failed.

An equally remarkable failure by what might be called overkill occurred on Cyprus on July 15, 1974. Over the previous years relations between Archbishop Makarios and the Greek colonels in Athens had deteriorated. There was ample evidence that the underground activities of the old guerrilla leader General George Grivas, with his new EOKA-B organization, was subversion encouraged by if not directed from Athens. There had been assassination attempts against Makarios. The most spectacular and most public had occurred over the Archbishporic Palace, when his helicopter had been machine-gunned from the roof of a neighboring building. The pilot managed to crash-land and Makarios was unhurt; soon thereafter, one of Grivas' old fighters, Antonis Georgiades, who was "thought to be involved," was himself assassinated. Although by July 1974 Grivas had died, the situation was even more tense because it was clear that EOKA-B was now without doubt controlled by the colonels—not even the colonels had been able to completely control Grivas. Makarios decided to take matters into his own hands and dispatch a public letter to Athens that could only be seen as a direct challenge to the junta. Caught by surprise, the junta hurriedly put together their response—a war-coup directed by regular Greek officers stationed on the island. On Monday morning, July 15, just after eight o'clock, the tanks of the Cypriot National Guard began deploying in front of the Presidential Palace, rumbling about, turrets swirling. Makarios, traveling from the Archbishopric Palace, arrived slightly before the fifteen tanks maneuvered into final position. They were hard to miss, and, when they opened fire into the palace, so was their intent. By then, with seconds to spare, Makarios had simply run out the back door, through a gap in the wall, and down to the road, where he hailed a car and escaped to Paphos, and ultimately off the island. Back at the palace, the tanks were still pumping in shells while the archbishop's death was announced at the Cypriot Broadcasting Center. Since they *had* tanks, the Greek officers were determined to use them, and as a result a chain reaction of disaster began for Greek Cypriots, the first step in the collapse of the junta.

Most coups, however, are not war-coups but elite-coups, where one ambitious group seizes power and its privileges. At times the assassination of the power center—president, premier, or monarch—does not produce the desired results. On September 21, 1956, President Anastasio Somoza of Nicaragua was shot and mortally wounded. Nicaragua had for twenty years been a wholly owned Somoza corporation, but his death changed nothing. His son, Anastasio Somoza, Jr., commander of the national guard, and the President's older son, Luis, took command of the family business. The conspirators were rounded up, tried, convicted, and punished. Luis became the new president and Nicaraguan matters went on much as much as before. Across the Caribbean, the Dominican Republic of Rafael Trujillo, an even more closely held family concern, having been defended over thirty years with frequent recourse to brutality, torture, and murder, experienced a quite different experience when the dictator was murdered. On May 30, 1961, a group of assassins shot and killed Trujillo, but made no effective effort to seize control of the country. Their plans miscarried, and Rafael Trujillo, Jr., flew home and rooted out the conspirators with the aid of President Joaquín Balaguer. Some were killed immediately, others were captured and killed later, and two escaped. But there the Nicaraguan scenario ended. Rafael, Jr., seemed interested mainly in saving the family fortune or getting it out of the country, and Balaguer had no interest in being a dictator—and had no support either. The exiles returned, open politics returned, Rafael, Jr., ultimately left the country, and in early 1962 Balaguer stepped down. The republic entered upon interesting and violent times that involved civil strife, American intervention, and new institutions and personalities. Except as an unpleasant and unsavory memory, the Trujillo years had passed.

The Classic Coup—Conspiracy: Germany, 20 July 1944

Count von Stauffenberg was from an old devout South German Catholic family, graduate of the War Academy in Berlin, a promising officer who had served with distinction in Poland, France, and Russia. From 1938 and the beginning of the anti-Jewish pogroms, he had grown increasingly more alienated from the Hitler regime. During the winter of 1942–1943, the momentum of the war had changed; everywhere the Axis' great offenses had ground to a halt. In Russia the Sixth Army was trapped inside Stalingrad, doomed. In Africa Field Marshal Erwin Rommel had lost half of his army in the fighting at El Alamein, and within two weeks the British Army had advanced seven hundred miles; while to the west, on

November 8, Anglo-American troops under General Dwight
David Eisenhower landed at several places in French North
Africa. While this was the beginning of the end for Germany, it
certainly did not seem so in Berlin. Africa was still not lost. There
were ample troops to regain the offensive in Russia, and Fortress
Europe still existed. For months it would not even be apparent
that Germany had lost the initiative. But 1943 brought one catas-
trophic defeat after another—the loss of all Africa, the loss of Sicily,
the Allied invasion of Italy, the collapse of Mussolini, the mounting
loss of U-boats, the strategic air raids into the German heartland,
and most of all the frightening and irreplaceable losses in men and
equipment on the Eastern Front and after the brutal defeat at
Kursk—"The Tigers are Burning"—the long retreat out of Russia.
And with each disaster the number of von Stauffenberg's colleagues who focused on Hitler as the prime architect of German
disaster grew, coalesced, and debated what should be done. Yet,
somehow, "Kill him!" still seemed both too simple and too complex a solution, one that caused more problems than it proposed
to solve.

The secret opposition to Hitler was at once many conspiracies
and none. Ultimately thousands were involved, if only marginally,
and yet no one ever seemed responsible despite the most detailed
and Teutonic preparations, plans, and prior provisions. There
were basically three groups with all sorts of ties to other elusive
individuals and organizations. All three main groups, however,
were composed of alternative elites—any radical opposition from
below, from the Left, had been shattered, driven into the camps,
co-opted into the army, silenced, or intimidated. Only the elite
had been left to conspire. The first was the Kreisau Circle, really
no more than a discussion group of mild social reformers and
devout Christians under Count Helmuth James von Moltke. The
second was a who-might-be-who of opposition leaders: General
Ludwig Beck, who had resigned as Chief of the General Staff in
1938 over Hitler's Czechoslovakian policy; Carl Goerdeler, former
mayor of Leipzig; Ulrich von Hassell, former Ambassador in
Rome; Admiral Wilhelm Canaris, director of the Abwehr intelligence unit; Count Wolff von Helldorff, chief of the Berlin Police;
ultimately even Field Marshal Rommel—and as time passed, more

and more old-line senior officers. With few exceptions, this opposition was deeply conservative and anti-democratic, foreseeing, perhaps, the return of the Hohenzollerns and an arranged armistice in the West and continued resistance to the Communists in the East. They were a mix of the Prussian officers, high civil servants, important academics, and clerics—the proper people that had been shoved aside or used by the crude and violent men of the Nazi regime. The third group had no time for Hohenzollerns, seeing the advantages of an accommodation with the Russians, not the Western allies, once the Nazi regime had been swept from the board—and they increasingly lost patience with the involved and convoluted questions of moral values that obsessed Beck and the generals. Although most of them were officers—von Stauffenberg, Colonel Freiherr von Gersdorff, even General Henning von Tresckow—they tended to be younger, more determined, and increasingly impatient with their elders.

For nearly two years the conspirators drifted in an atmosphere of uncertainty, anxiety, and hesitation. As was later pointed out, the German army did not foster in the regular officer corps those traits that are advantageous to conspiracy. The Prussian nobility, locked into a lifetime of dedicated and unquestioning service to the state, honed on old and tried values, loyal to their commitments, their class, and their country, had serious problems being devious, in understanding the motives of others, in dissembling, in employing consciously or unconsciously hypocrisy, in accepting the need for patience, tact, and guile—and most curious of all for military men, they lacked the sense for the jugular. Facing a brutal and unscrupulous band of cutthroats who were without mercy or morals, capable of manipulating the old loyalties of the simple soldiers, capable of killing without compunction, with an acute understanding of the nature of power, the aristocrats were quite outmatched in their hesitant and uncertain determination to do something about Hitler. Few had Count von Stauffenberg's singleness of purpose—"Kill him!"—for had they not taken an oath? Was an oath to a perjurer valid? Was assassination a proper means? Could a coup be legal? Would history understand? Would their own understand? Did they themselves understand?

Despite the doubts and uncertainties, by March 1943 Beck and the others were ready to act. Hitler would be killed, and Operation Valkyrie to seize Berlin and hence the country in a "legal coup" would begin. General von Tresckow acquired a British-made bomb from Admiral Canaris. Disguised as a bottle of brandy, the bomb was placed in Hitler's plane flying back to his headquarters from Smolensk. At the last minute, a button was pressed. A small bottle inside broke and released a corrosive acid, which began eating away a wire that held back a spring which released the detonator. As the plane swept westward, the acid ate through the wire, the spring released. And nothing happened. The bottle of brandy was delivered.

On March 21, Colonel Freiherr von Gersdorff undertook a suicide mission. When Hitler visited the Berlin Arsenal, he would set the fuses in his pockets and then grab the Führer. The Führer at the last minute changed his plans and stayed only ten minutes, and von Gersdorff could not set his fuses and get close to him.

Matters did not improve. General Helmuth Stieff first failed to plant a bomb in Hitler's headquarters at Rastenburg, and then his bomb supply detonated; fortunately, the plotters were not discovered. Captain Alex von dem Bussche, who was to model a new military uniform for Hitler, had *his* bombs arranged so that they would go off in seconds—while Der Führer was next to him. Then the RAF bombed the warehouse and destroyed the uniforms. Attempts to use a briefcase bomb at Berchtesgarden failed twice in December. On February 11, the uniform ploy was attempted again; this time Heinrich von Kleist replaced Bussche, who had been wounded. Hitler did not show up at all. Cavalry Captain von Breitenbuch tried to shoot Hitler at a conference at the Berghot, but SS guards refused him entry. Nothing worked. The key man had been lost early: on April 7, 1943, Count von Stauffenberg was badly wounded in Tunisia when a mine exploded under his vehicle—he lost his left eye, left hand, and two fingers on his right hand.

There were divisions and squabbles, attempts to set one Nazi clique against another, that outraged many of the conspirators. The Anglo-Americans showed no interest in the various and usually inept feelers about an armistice in the West. And the plotters were running out of time. In February 1944, the Kreisau Circle had been broken and Count von Moltke arrested. During February and March, the Abwehr was under intensive investigation. Hitler, especially after Mussolini's arrest and imprisonment, had become increasingly cautious. The only good news was that Count von Stauffenberg, who had returned to Berlin in October 1943, had been promoted to colonel and as the deputy to General Friedrich Fromm, Commander of the Home Army, would have access to Hitler's military conferences at the Wolf's Lair at Rastenburg in East Prussia. On June 6, 1944, the Allies landed in Normandy, poured men and supplies ashore and began battering to break out of the beachhead, chewing up German divisions. On July 4, the Russians crossed the Polish border and began a drive on East Prussia. The Germans' war was well and truly lost. The hope of an Anglo-American armistice was gone. The conspirators decided that the attempt *must* be made even if Operation Valkyrie did not work; even if they were all caught and Hitler destroyed Germany, the deed would be witness of the opposition to the Nazis.

On July 6, von Stauffenberg flew with his bomb to the Wolf's Lair. He did not push the button; Goering and Himmler were not present. On July 11, he flew with his bomb again to the Wolf's Lair. Goering and Himmler were not present; he did not push the button. On July 15, at the Wolf's Lair, he could not press the button with his maimed hand. He flew back to Berlin. Time was really running out. Goerdeler had been arrested and there was fear he would talk. Two other members of the conspiracy had been arrested. It would not take very long before the Gestapo discovered enough to move. On July 20, von Stauffenberg set out once more with the bomb in his briefcase. He arrived at the Wolf's Lair at 10 A.M. It was announced that the conference would begin at 12:30 P.M. and would be short. Just before 12:30 P.M., outside the conference room, von Stauffenberg reached down into his briefcase and pushed the button. The acid began eating at the wire. He had ten minutes. He walked into the room, sat down, and slipped his briefcase almost directly beneath Hitler, who was listening to an unusually gloomy report on the Eastern Front. Four minutes later, without anyone noticing, von Stauffenberg got up and quietly walked out—a violation of custom and etiquette. At the table Colonel Heinz Brandt leaned over to see the positions on the map better and felt von Stauffenberg's briefcase. He moved it to the far side of the heavy table support, away from Hitler. No one noticed. Outside, at a distance, von Stauffenberg waited as the ten minutes ticked past. Then another minute. Then another. And at 12:42 P.M., there was a huge explosion. The building seemed to bulge. Windows were smashed outward, bodies tossed about, and a great cloud of black smoke began to rise. Von Stauffenberg rushed away, eager to bring the first-hand news back to Berlin, where Operation Valkyrie should be about to start. He bluffed his way past three checkpoints, arrived at his plane, and took off undetected for the three-hour flight to Berlin. His colleague inside Rastenburg would see that communications with the capital were cut off after the conspirators had been told the news.

There had been twenty-four people inside the conference room. One man was dead and three were mortally wounded, including Colonel Brandt, who at the expense of his own life had saved that of Der Führer. Hitler staggered out of the building clinging to Field Marshal Wilhelm Keitel. His singed hair was still smoking, his face blackened, and his trousers in shreds. His legs had been slightly burned and peppered with wood splinters. Both eardrums were ruptured and his back had been lacerated by a fallen beam. His right arm was bruised. Shaken and stunned, he was in fact quite all right, quite able to meet Mussolini, who arrived at four in the afternoon. By then, the nature of the conspiracy was unfolding and the swift response of the regime was proving effective.

When von Stauffenberg arrived in Berlin—the order to arrest him at the airport was delayed—he found to his horror that nothing had happened. No one had activated Valkyrie. The precious hours had been lost, and continued to be lost, as his fellow conspirators had had a real plot only on paper. No one wanted violence. No one had shot anyone—all the plotters were officers and gentlemen, the men with guns had not been involved. General Erich Hoepner refused to take command of the army reserves without a specific written order; such was the stuff of a Prussian coup. As the realization came that Hitler was alive and well and vindictive, the end had come. Beck tried to commit suicide and failed. He tried again and failed. The Gestapo moved in; those actively involved were rounded up and shot that night. The arrests and murders continued for weeks, for months. Everyone remotely involved was gathered in—a few, such as Rommel, were allowed to commit suicide. The more important were strangled, hanged on meat hooks, twisting and turning before the whirr of movie film taken especially for Der Führer. The families of the conspirators were arrested and shipped to concentration camps. Thousands died, most of them brutally. The killing continued until April 1945. Hitler had no need of written orders, legal procedures, or second thoughts about *them*. "This time we shall settle accounts with them in the manner to which we National Socialists are accustomed." And they did.

CAMPAIGNS: STRATEGIES OF MURDER

History moves terribly slowly, we must give it a push.
—Andrei Zhelyabov,
Executive Committee, *Narodnaya Volya*

A conspiracy founded on assassination, for high purpose or low, almost always anticipates that to strike the effective blow will be a matter of import. There are conspirators that recognize from the first that the target regime is far too strong to be swept away by a single violent act, effective or not: the imperial center will dispatch another governor general or the monarch's son will ascend the throne. In such a case to undertake a revolt to begin a revolutionary national liberation movement the conspirators must plan on an extended campaign. Given varying assets, this may mean a rural guerrilla struggle, perhaps initiated by widespread peasant revolts, or, more simply, a single small *foco*. On the other hand it may mean a long-prepared internal war, with gunmen in the capital, columns in the hills, and self-proclaimed cabinet ministers hiding in attics. Such campaigns have long been an almost conventional form of unconventional warfare—guerrilla campaigns, insurrection, colonial revolt, urban terror. One technique regularly associated with such internal campaigns has been assassination; in fact, contemporary social scientists find that one of the few factors concurrent with a high incidence of assassination has been guerrilla war. In this situation assassination is simply a facet of internal war, at most a tactic. Some guerrilla campaigns present few such incidents; either the targets are too elusive in a rural struggle or else the rebel leaders prefer to avoid the illegitimacy that assassination might bring, preferring respectability to a dead opponent. Most guerrilla leaders, however, are quite willing to use assassination of their prominent opponents as a practical technique—and almost all undertake the murder of entire groups: soldiers, police, enemy sympathizers, and at times the rich, the educated, Catholics, or this tribe or that tribe. In a few cases in internal war, the capacity of the rebel severely limits all tactical options—so much so that the organization opts for a campaign of assassination directed almost entirely at specific leader-targets. The single great example in modern experience has been that archetype of all terrorist organizations, The People's Will, in nineteenth-century Russia.

The Classical Campaign: Russia and People's Will (Narodnaya Volya)

Imperial Russia has been called a despotism tempered by assassination. Certainly murder, rebellion, regicide, pogroms, and mass repression had long been integral parts of the Russian system, and formed the context in which nineteenth-century radicals operated. With an autocratic absolute despot, a huge, deprived serf population, an arrogant, often alien nobility, miserable workers, and a brutal system of repression, Tsarist Russia was hardly rushing into the future imagined by the men of reason, much less the classless society of Marx or Bakunin. Yet the massive lethargy, innate conservatism, and outright suspicion of the serfs and the emerging proletariat, who preferred to hold their factory bench rather than to seize the factory, frustrated generation after generation of radicals. The serfs loved the Tsar. In desperation, some radicals circulated false Tsarist proclamations, urging the serfs to rise against the nobility and snatch the land that was rightfully theirs. For the Russian radicals the great question remained: what could be done? The Tsarist system seemed evil incarnate; somehow the potential revolutionary fervor of the masses, especially the serfs, had to be released. Somehow the endless discussions, the plots and cabals, the latest theories smuggled in from abroad, the risings and treks into the country, produced nothing. Serfdom was abolished from the top, but the new "peasant" was as miserable as before. The industrial proletariat grew enormously but the benefits flowed to the bourgeoisie, not the workers. Radical prophets came, preached, and failed, driven into exile, transported to Siberia, or frustrated by the intractable reality of Russia.

Some radicals despaired and began to argue that change could be achieved only through terror, perhaps even regicide. Some of these clandestine circles, talk of terror aside, remained little more than debating societies for the young. The discussions of one—*Hell*—did have a profound impact on a sickly young student, Dmitry Karakozov, who in 1866 decided that he would kill the Tsar. He had been consumed with a new passion while listening to the endless late-night discussions. He was always unwell; he could not have long to live; and he had done nothing. "I have decided to destroy the wicked Tsar and die for my beloved people."[8] His radical colleagues tried to dissuade him—he had confused the thought and the deed. Karakozov paid no attention. He acquired a cheap pistol and traveled to St. Petersburg, to Moscow, and back to St. Petersburg. On the afternoon of April 4, he fired a single shot at Alexander II after the Tsar had left the Summer Garden and was walking toward the royal carriage. A bystander—a cap-maker of peasant stock—knocked his arm aside, or so the authorities reported. Karakozov was tried, convicted, and sentenced to die with another conspirator. On September 3, thirty-three co-conspirators were imprisoned. Karakozov's colleagues had his death sentence commuted to life at hard labor as he stood hooded, waiting for the trap to spring. For Karakozov the trap sprang. His single wild shot unleashed new and further repression—the White Terror. The liberals were disillusioned. The unorthodox were justly fearful. The radicals crept deep underground, leading precarious lives. Revolution was far from dead, however, although no closer to the magic means to power.

Over the next decade the various amorphous clandestine organizations avoided such violence, and kept their faith in the power of the peasant—despite a discouraging lack of evidence. The movement to go to the people, children's crusades endowed with a religious fervor, showed how little the radicals knew of those people. Once again disillusionment settled over the radicals. The peasants would not rise, would not listen. Worker agitation was largely futile. And there were always splits and schisms. In 1876 the major secret society was Land and Liberty *(Zemlya i Volya)*, one of the first named after a program instead of a leader. The program still was based on arousing peasant disturbances, but it also advocated, first, armed resistance to arrest, and second, striking down too-zealous security officials. There were still all kinds of problems. Communication and central control, especially between groups in the south and St. Petersburg, proved difficult; and increasingly for some there was a drift away from the goal of a peasant revolt and a concentration on efforts to free prisoners, to establish a printing press, and to execute spies. In fact, in the winter of 1877–1878, many were weighing various tactical alternatives, discarding one after the other, until only terrorism remained as a valid option.

At the best of times, the Russian revolutionary underground was in a state of constant flux. Conspiratorial circles came together and flourished briefly, nurtured by a charismatic figure or a novel idea or new hope, and then disappeared or merged or were uncovered. All the underground knew the enemy; but there was no consensus on means, on the inevitable and proper direction of history, on first steps or the ultimate Russia. Ideas seeped in from the theorists of Europe and were adapted or discarded. A constant, unending activity of revolutionaries everywhere is the fashioning of appropriate ideological positions, the search for right thinking, the shaping of theory to perceived reality—writing and talking, writing and talking. The establishment of a printing press, the issuing of a journal, the distribution of proclamations—these often become the central task, rather than the armed struggle. In the winter of 1877, for some there was the almost unrecognizable shift away from the old Land and Liberty priorities toward rebellion. Most revolutionary attention, however, was focused on the great Tsarist show trial, Trial of the 193, that ran from October 1877 until January 1878. On January 23, the trial ended. Many of the charged were actually released—the regime continued to dither between indulgence and repression. By then the pressure toward a strategy of personal terrorism had become considerable. There was as yet no effective form of organization. Conspiracies were limited to two or three. But there was a sense that the time of the assassin had come.

On January 24, 1878, the day after the Trial of the 193 ended, a young woman, Vera Ivanovna Zasulich, entered the office of General Trepov, the governor of St. Petersburg. She stood there quietly among a milling crowd of those who had petitions or requests. Trepov was the *bête noire* of the underground; the previous July he had visited the House of Preliminary Detention and ordered, illegally, one of the political prisoners flogged. Radical circles were deeply indignant, but getting to Trepov posed problems and would endanger the defendants in the Trial of the 193. There were those who were simply waiting for the trial to end. They were forestalled by Vera Zasulich, who drew her pistol, stepped forward, and at point-blank range shot the general. He was gravely wounded, but survived. So did Zasulich, who was tried as a common, not political, prisoner and thus had an open court to turn the proceedings against the state. To the amazement of all, on March 31, she was found not guilty and in the confusion slipped away before she could be rearrested. She found her way abroad, the heroine of the hour. Her single shot had begun the time of the assassins for Russia.

In February 1878, a spy was killed and an attempt was made on the assistant public prosecutor in Kiev. In May the chief of the Gendarmeris in Kiev was killed. Then, on August 4, Serge Kravchinsky, editor of the *Land and Liberty* journal, stabbed to death General Mezentsov, director of the counterrevolutionary Third Section. His companion shot but missed Mezentsov's aide. The attack had taken place in broad daylight in the center of St. Petersburg, and both men escaped in a fast carriage driven by a third conspirator and drawn by the same racehorse that had carried the famous anarchist Prince Kropotkin to liberty. Excitement was intense. There was a feeling that it was now or never, the system was at last vulnerable, a feeling that had intensified both in the underground and in revolutionary circles abroad because of the events following the Trepov shooting. But the government did not collapse. It simply instituted more severe repressive measures—the drift between indulgence and coercion had ended. In February 1879, Prince Dimitri Kropotkin, governor-general of Kharkov and a cousin of the anarchist prince, was fatally wounded. The next month there was an unsuccessful attempt on Mezentsov's successor, General Drenteln. Two spies were killed. Then Alexander Konstantinovich Solovev announced to his terrorist colleagues within Land and Liberty—the Executive Committee—that he intended to kill the Tsar alone. On the morning of April 2, 1879, Solovev fired at Alexander II five times in the garden of the Winter Palace. He missed. The Tsar stumbled off while the accompanying police grappled with Solovev, who managed to wound one and swallow poison. He lived, was tried and convicted and, on May 28, hanged. Before the end of the year, eleven men had been put to death—and from the ruins of Land and Liberty arose *Narodnaya Volya*, the People's Will, led by an Executive Committee dedicated to personal terror and the death of the Tsar.

Even before Solovev's attempt in April, the strains within Land and Liberty had become acute. The terrorists wanted an end to anarchist chimeras and utopias—typeface should be melted down for bullets and shots substituted for sermons. Others absolutely opposed conspirators who would seize power as a cabal, who relied solely on murder, who advocated the dagger and the pistol. Yet considerable effort was made to hold Land and Liberty together. Finally, in August, the two main groups went their own ways—*Chornyi Peredel*, Black Repartition, the orthodox populist group, struggled on for a while and then dissolved, irrelevant to Russian reality. Those of the gun and dagger, the People's Will, sentenced the Tsar to death on August 26, 1879. The party took upon itself the responsibility to act at once, to begin an armed struggle, even and especially accepting that any mass rising or general support would be distant. They could not see very far ahead, only that they must attempt to destroy the existing system through terrorist deeds—through the propaganda after the deed, more might be possible. Actually, beyond the deed little was possible, for these momentous revolutionary issues were being parsed by a tiny handful of radicals. Over the next six years, at different times, some fifty individuals served on the Executive Committee, and five hundred in the People's Will. By 1896, when the organization had been moribund for ten years, only two thousand, at most, had been involved in some manner. Mostly there was only a tiny core of activists, scattered in cells and centers; but they, unlike the orthodox populists, had found a role—a means to act upon history, a clearly defined responsibility.

Almost the entire resources of the People's Will had to be focused on the assassination of the Tsar. And the government was all too aware of their goal. Following Solovev's attempt in April and two weeks before the Executive Committee condemned Alexander II to death, Solomon Wittenberg had been hanged for planning to lay a mine in Odessa harbor where the Tsar was to land. Murder was in the air. The Executive Committee had a hundred kilograms of dynamite manufactured by their own explosives expert, Nikolai Kibalchick, who on his release from prison in 1878 had devoted himself to the study of explosives. The first plan was to tunnel under the Tsar's rail route north of Odessa, but in November the Tsar changed his plans and the operation was abandoned. A second mining operation was begun under the rails near Alexandrovsk, on his new route. In miserably cold weather, digging in the mud, a small team managed to plant two cylinders filled with explosives brought from Kharkov. On November 18, the conspirators moved out to the embankment with an electric battery and an induction coil. The train roared down the line. The circuit was closed when the cars were directly over the mine. Nothing happened. When the cylinders were examined, no one could detect anything wrong. The mine was left in place. There was still a chance to get the Tsar, because a second mine waited in a tunnel under the tracks two miles south of the Moscow station. This mine had been even more difficult to site. The conspirators had tunneled for 150 feet under increasingly difficult conditions: the air was so bad that it put out the lamps, the earth crumbled every time a train passed overhead, and then water seeped in, turning the floor to a muddy ooze. Only at the last minute did they get the brass cylinders containing eighty pounds of dynamite into place. The next day, November 19, the Tsar's train, along with a separate imperial retinue train, sped north. A little after nine, the retinue train sped over the mine and on into Moscow. An hour later the lights of the second train appeared. When the cars were directly over the mine, the circuit was connected. There was a huge roar. The two locomotives and the first car were derailed, dragging others after them. No one on board was hurt. And the Tsar had already arrived in Moscow on the nine o'clock train. At the last minute, the imperial train had been sent ahead. On November 22, the Executive Committee issued a proclamation: "He deserves the death penalty for all the blood he has shed, for all the pain he has caused. . . . war, implacable war, to the last drop of our blood."[9] On January 1, 1880, an epigraph in the party paper quoted Edouard Vaillant of the Paris Commune: "Society has only one obligation toward monarchs: to put them to death."[10] For over a year this was to be the prime preoccupation of the Executive Committee, the tiny band of zealots and fanatics who had challenged an empire.

The next plan was, if nothing else, bold. Stepan Khalturin, a cabinetmaker employed in the maintenance force of the Winter Palace, approached the Executive Committee with a request for dynamite. He, alone, would smuggle the explosive into the Winter Palace, construct a mine, and blow up the emperor. The Executive Committee agreed, and bit by bit the dynamite filtered into the palace. No one suspected Khalturin, who at times wandered about the palace quite freely. One day, hammer in hand, he opened a door and found himself standing almost directly behind the Tsar. There was no one else about. All he needed to do was step forward and swing his hammer. He could not do the deed, and backed out of the room. He went on smuggling in dynamite until he had accumulated a hundred pounds. On February 5, he fired a fuse connected to the detonator of fuminate of mercury buried in his chestful of dynamite placed in a basement room just under the Yellow Hall. The Tsar and his family were to dine in the Yellow Hall in a few minutes, at six-thirty. Khalturin quickly left the palace and was a short distance away when the huge explosion occurred. Eleven people were killed and fifty-six wounded. The dining hall was only slightly damaged. And the Tsar had not arrived. Still, the impact was tremendous. The ground under the monarchy seemed to be shaking. To observers the Tsar seemed pale, shaken, and aged.

A special body to cope with subversion was set up under Count Mikhail Loris-Melikov. A week later, an attempt was made on his life by a young man acting independently of the Executive Committee. His shot missed. He was captured and hanged two days later, on February 22. In March two men were hanged in Kiev for distributing leaflets. But there were also a few liberal concessions. The balance seemed to work. Loris-Melikov seemed to have broken the terrorists' spirit—a mistaken assumption, since there had been two more failed attempts on the Tsar that had not been discovered by the authorities. Another mine was placed under a street in Odessa, and remained in place even after the Tsar had changed his plans. He might pass that way again. Another bomb was installed under the Kamenny Bridge to be detonated when Alexander II arrived in the capital from Tsarkoe Selo on August 17. The effort aborted for no clear reason, and there was a lull until winter, when the Executive Committee decided on their seventh attempt since the Odessa project. Work was to begin in St. Petersburg on another mine tunnel, under the Tsar's route to the trooping of the colors in the Mikhailovsky Manege. In December it was decided to combine the mine with a bomb attack on the Tsar's carriage. And if *that* failed, Andrei Zhelyabov was to assault the Tsar with a pistol and a dagger.

There was a growing sense of urgency. There had been an unwitting informer, who committed suicide when he realized he had been tricked into revealing the organization. There were regular arrests and irreplaceable people were lost. The faithful few at the center of the conspiracy became fewer. While the regime believed in a great conspiracy, the Executive Committee began to suspect that their time was running out. There were too few activists left. Work on the tunnel was pushed. Four bomb-throwers were selected: Ignaty Grinevitsky, a twenty-six-year-old engineering student; Timofey Mikhailov, twenty-one, a boilermaker; Ivan Yemelyanov, twenty, a cabinetmaker; and Nikolai Rysakov, nineteen, a student. The bomb, made by Kibalchick from a kerosene can, would hold five pounds of nitroglycerine and pyroxilin—and might detonate. Two were tried. One exploded.[11] The arrests continued. On February 27, Zhelyabov was taken. The Executive Committee felt the time to act had come, before the police closed in. The wires were laid for the tunnel-bomb. The four bomb-throwers were told to report on the following morning, March 1. Sofya Perovskaya took control. Blonde, slim, at twenty-six she was an absolutely dedicated revolutionary, eager for the most difficult task, severe, disciplined, the obvious successor to Zhelyabov. The organization was ready. There were four finished bombs. M. F. Frolenko was ready to set the electric switch that would detonate the street mine. The only question left was whether the Tsar would appear on the Malaya Sadovaya, or even leave the palace.

On Sunday, March 1, Alexander II was in good spirits. The news that Zhelyabov had been arrested the previous day buoyed the entire royal household. He dismissed Loris-Melikov's plea that he not leave the palace. He did agree to change his route and follow the road that went along the Catherine Canal. He left the palace in his two-seater sleigh just before one o'clock. There was no attempt by the bomb-throwers on the Tsar's journey out to the Manege. He might still come back by Malaya Sadovaya; but Sofya Perovskaya hurriedly put her bomb-throwers along his route back from the maneuvers. They arrived in time because the Tsar paid a brief visit to his cousin, Grand Duchess Catherine. Timofey Mikhailov lost his nerve and went home. The other three, grasping their oddly wrapped "packages," stood and waited. The royal party, moving swiftly, suddenly turned into the quay. First came the Tsar's two-horse sleigh. Alexander II sat alone. An orderly sat next to the driver. Behind came three more sleighs filled with security officials. There was a small screen of six mounted Cossacks. A hundred and fifty yards down the quay, Rysakov stepped forward and tossed his bomb under the legs of the Tsar's horses. It was two-fifteen.

The bomb went off, sending up a cloud of snow, earth, and splinters. A cloud of blue smoke twisted up. One Cossack was mortally wounded, as was a passing delivery boy. The windows of the royal sleigh were shattered, the floor and back smashed, and

the Tsar dazed, but with only a small cut on his hand. Colonel
Dvorzhitsky, district chief of police, rushed up and urged the Tsar
to get into his sleigh. Alexander agreed, but wandered over to look
at the site of the explosion. Several policemen had Rysakov pinned
against an iron railing. The Cossack and the boy still lay on the
ground. The delay had been only five minutes. Alexander turned
and began walking toward Dvorzhitsky's carriage. He passed near
a man leaning on an iron railing holding a parcel—Grinevitzky.
The second bomb-thrower turned and hurled his parcel at the
Tsar's feet. There was a second roar, another cloud of blue smoke;
this time the street was littered with the wounded and dying.
There were long splashes of blood on the snow, torn and burned
clothes strewn in the street. Grinevitzky lay unconscious, mortally
wounded. The Tsar crouched in a pool of his own blood. His
uniform was torn and burnt, his legs shattered, blood gouting from
his wounds. Dvorzhitsky struggled back to consciousness and
grappled with Alexander, trying to get him into a carriage and
back to the palace. Several people rushed to help him. One was
Yemelyanov, with his bomb still under his arm, who then made his
way back to headquarters. The Tsar was driven swiftly to the
palace, his sleigh leaving a trail of blood behind. By the time
medical aid could be summoned, it was too late. He rallied briefly,
was given Holy Communion, and then, at three-forty in the afternoon, he died. "The nightmares that had weighted down on
Young Russia for ten years had vanished. . . ."[12]

The police swiftly closed in on the remaining conspirators. Six
were put on public trial: Rysakov, who informed on his colleagues;
Kibalchick, the technician who was now engrossed only in design-
ing a flying machine; Zhelyabov, the core of the Executive Committee; Timofey Mikhailov, who had brought his bomb back; and
two women, Sofya Perovskaya, who had directed the deed, and
Gesya Helfman, who was pregnant and escaped the death penal-
ties awarded to the others. On April 3, 1881, the informer Rysakov, Zhelyabov, Mikhailov, Kibalchick—disappointed only that he
had not finished his flying machine—and Sofya Perovskaya were
taken out of prison in two tumbrils. Each wore a placard containing the word "Regicide." They were driven to Semenovsky
Square between two rows of spectators. At the gallows there was

a crowd of one hundred thousand. The four condemned kissed each other goodbye. Rysakov was ignored. The hangman and his helpers slipped hoods over their heads. A little after nine, the executions began. Kibalchick was first, and then Mikhailov. The rope broke twice before the executioner added another reinforced noose. The other hangings went more smoothly. Rysakov was last. It was all over before ten. The bodies were cut down and placed in wooden coffins.

The Executive Committee and the People's Will did not die with the five; but March 1, 1881, was the epitome of personal terror in Tsarist Russia. There would be other assassinations, but the fortunes of the Executive Committee were waning. There were arrests, feuds, splits, more arrests, withdrawals into exile, and a growing uncertainty. Finally, there was little left but the name and the dwindling dream. In 1886 a small independent group of conspirators assumed the name Terrorist Section of the People's Will and prepared to assassinate Tsar Alexander III. On March 1, 1887—six years later to the day—they appeared on the street with their bombs. The police were waiting. All the conspirators were rounded up, and five that would not plead for mercy were hanged on May 8.[13] One, Alexander Ulyanov, shouted from the scaffold, "Long live the People's Will." His brother, seventeen-year-old Vladimir, read of the execution in a newspaper. "I swear I will revenge myself on them!"[14] Under the name V. I. Lenin, he dedicated his life to the revolution.

The militants of the People's Will, especially up to March 1, 1881, were a pristine example of terrorists dedicated to a campaign of assassination and very little else. This, however, was a tactical option. Unlike some revolutionaries, they did not attempt to erect an ideology of terror—a strategy of murder that would explain everything. In a search for revolution after 1877–1878, they felt that as Socialists and populists, assassination, especially of the Tsar, was the appropriate revolutionary road. The Executive Committee, for example, strongly disapproved of the murder of President Garfield in a country where the free popular will determined the law and its administrators.[15] In Russia they felt that their only remaining weapon was assassination, the only way to give history a push. Perhaps they were right.

NOTES

1. Robert Katz, *The Fall of the House of Savoy,* New York, Macmillan, 1971, p. 148.

2. Barbara W. Tuchman, *The Proud Tower,* New York, Bantam, 1972, p. 95.

3. *Ibid.,* p. 96.

4. T. Harry Williams, *Huey Long, A Biography,* New York, Knopf, 1969, p. 872.

5. *Ibid.,* p. 876.

6. *Ibid.,* p. 872.

7. Joachim C. Fest, *Hitler,* New York, Harcourt Brace Jovanovich, 1974, p. 739.

8. Avrahm Yarmolinsky, *Road to Revolution,* New York, Collier, 1971, p. 139.

9. *Ibid.,* p. 249.

10. *Ibid.*

11. In theory, as a result of the nitroglycerine in two twisted glass tubes, the device would detonate at whatever point it struck a hard surface.

12. Yarmolinsky, *op. cit.,* p. 271.

13. A further abortive attempt on Alexander III was reported that autumn, of interest primarily because it was to employ a silent revolver—over a decade before patents were issued for such a device elsewhere—firing poison-filled bullets, when the Tsar visited the Black Sea shipyards.

14. Yarmolinsky, *op. cit.,* p. 320.

15. "The Executive Committee, expressing its profoundest sympathy with the American people on account of the death of James Abram Garfield, feels it to be its duty to protest in the name of Russian revolutionaries against all such deeds of violence as that which has just taken place in America. In a land where the citizens are free to express their ideas, and where the will of the people does not merely make the law but appoints the person who is to carry the law into effect, in such a country political assassination is the manifestation of a despotic tendency identical with that to whose destruction in Russia we have devoted ourselves" (Thomas G. Masaryk, *The Spirit of Russia,* London, Allen and Unwin, 1919, p. 545).

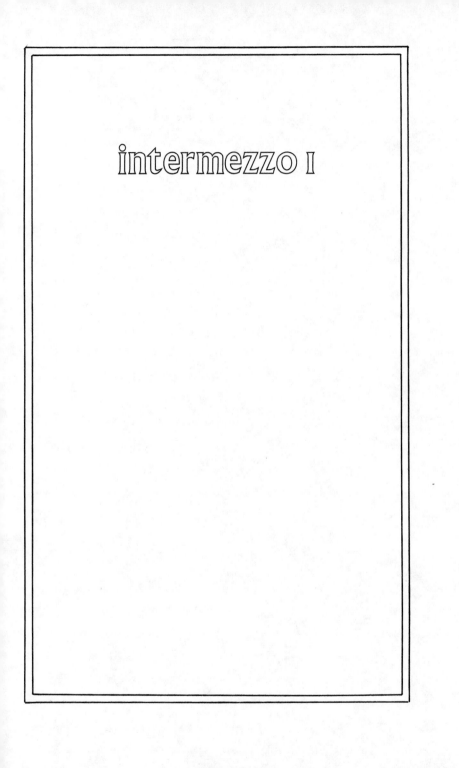

intermezzo I

In 1974 Nicos Sampson was nearing forty, and in Cyprus he was an undeniable success. His newspaper *I Machi* had the highest circulation on the island. He was a member of the Cypriot House of Representatives, and had an expensive ranch house on the outskirts of Nicosia, a lovely wife, and handsome children. He owned a string of racehorses. For many, he was the recognized leader of the militant Greek nationalists who wanted union with Greece, and he had delivered the oration at the funeral of their old hero General George Grivas. He was also, according to his former associates in the EOKA organization, a psychopathic killer. His EOKA assassination squad shot and killed twenty people in Nicosia between August 1956 and January 1957, mostly in the narrow main shopping street, Ledra Street, in the old city: murder mile. Sampson admitted publicly to four of the killings, and privately to more. In 1963, his private army was involved in murderous attacks on Turkish villages. And yet, in private he remains charming, shortish by American standards, dark, handsome, stocky and solid with carefully styled hair; he resembles a former boxer not yet out of shape. His office is cool, with the steady hum of air conditioning in the summer, paneled in wood, the wall dotted with family pictures. In accented English he is delighted to go over the old glory days of EOKA and propound on the possibilties of the future. There is no easy way to tell that he did in fact enjoy killing, and was given to strange claims in *I Machi*—God visited him in visions. For his critics the most damaging criticism of all was that he enjoyed killing. In 1974, after the coup, he became a seven-day wonder, President of Cyprus. Today he is in a Nicosia prison, convicted of treason. He has been in prison before—forty days under sentence of death by the British, followed by nineteen months in Britain until 1959. He does not look much like an assassin, and there are others, salesmen or tailors, who are more likely to exaggerate their importance or their military careers. But Sampson is, perhaps, the most notorious of all Cypriot gunmen. And charming, handsome, delightful, enthusiastic in conversation, still proud of his past and his presidency, he's not unmindful of the future.

ii

"Doros" is the other side of the Nicos Sampson coin. Of a like age, he is taller, his English more elegant; his wife is even more attractive, his young daughter a delight. Although without racehorses, he holds and has held for some time a senior position in the Cypriot Foreign Service—is in fact almost the ideal popular conception of the perfect diplomat, serious, sincere but with a wry sense of humor, considerate, compassionate, committed but without rancor. He too was in EOKA in Nicosia, and he too was involved in killing operations. The most famous and flawed attempt was an effort to detonate a bomb in a culvert as the limousine of Governor-General Sir John Harding passed over it. That morning a breeze blew away the signaling handkerchief, so the timing was slightly off. The bomb detonated but missed Harding's car. "Doros" was a failed assassin. However, once the EOKA campaign was over, he left war and killing behind. Like many of his former colleagues, he went into the government, delighted to have survived and to have found a career.

iii

The idea of this is it's anti-personnel, to be placed in the right provocation to an explosion which will take place with a direct target. The system is simple. It will go off even if it isn't touched. It is pre-set by one turn. Your main mechanism runs through here back to the lid to this wire which comes through there and into the lock, which has a wire here. The det which will connect to the timer itself which is set at intervals of four hours. One end of that wire is connected here to turn off the batteries. The other det wire is connected to one terminal on the timer itself. It is completely safe till the lid's closed which activates this and is made alive.

Now—are you clear on this? Doubtful of anything at all? Your det is the last thing to connect to the timer pre-set. Connect one end to the battery terminal and the other det wire to the terminal on your time. You know where your target is—you know what to do.

> Taped, April 1972, Belfast Brigade,
> operations center, Provisional Irish
> Republican Army, Northern Ireland

iv

Seamus Costello, leader of the extreme militant Irish Republican Socialist and Republican Party, said that the strangest sensation during a 1975 attempt on his life, while driving down a road in Waterford, was the ten submachine gun slugs smashing through his car but, somehow, with no sound of firing. Two years later the second attempt was made off Dublin's North Circular Road on Northbrook Avenue. A man, perhaps two, suddenly appeared. One was tall, with long hair and a gun. The other, smaller, nondescript, had stayed back. Perhaps he wasn't involved. There was a flat hard crack. Costello was shot once, then again more slowly. He died almost instantly. The gunman stepped back. He trotted off. The other followed. Some said the two got into a grayish car and drove off. They left Costello's body and vague, frightened witnesses.

v

From November 1965 almost until the British withdrawal at the end of 1969, the commando-assassination units in Aden

were commanded by Saleh Abdullah Bakaris, "Hag Saleh."
Along the Ma'alla road, with its ugly pastel concrete apartments, he re-created the Murder Mile of Ledra Street in
Nicosia. Once again, assassins walked free, crowds looked the
other way, and women swiftly hid revolvers after the NLF killers left the sprawled and bloody bodies of British victims behind on the street. After the National Liberation Front took
power, there was some problem with Hag Saleh. Slender and
wary, from the up-country, with none of the veneer of Aden
and no education, he was a perfect gunman, but of little use in
building a Marxist-Leninist state. For a time he was placed in
charge of security—*that is,* he kept on killing. Eventually, he
showed no signs of revolutionary fervor and a growing interest
in private pleasure. He, too, was killed. There is always a problem with old gunmen.

vi

An explosion is a conversion of a solid substance into
a gas. We have gelignite and quarags. Now explosives
are mainly in three different categories. You have the
lifting, the shattering and the cutting. They are determined by the rate of expansion of gases. Now there are
explosives that we manufacture ourselves which are a
low type of lifting explosive because they have a lower
rate of expansion in gases. Now these commercial ones
—they've a higher rate of expansion in gases and the
cutting explosive has the highest rate of expansion of
gases. Now then in the lifting explosives—there's a rate
of expansion that is lower and when it detonates that it
tends to lift and push an object rather than to burst it.
With the shattering ones, which we have here with us
tonight. . . .

Taped, March 1972, Provisional Irish
Republican Army training session in
engineering, Ireland

vii

Can an individual of [deleted nationality] descent be made to perform an act of attempted assassination involuntarily under the influence of Artichoke? . . . It was proposed that an individual of [deleted] descent, approximately thirty-five years old, well educated, proficient in English and well established socially and politically in the [deleted] government, be induced under Artichoke to perform an act, involuntarily, against a prominent [deleted] politician or, if necessary, against an American official. . . . After the act of attempted assassination was performed, it was assumed that the subject would be taken into custody by the [deleted] government and thereby "disposed of."

1954 Central Intelligence Agency documents,
publicly revealed February 1978

viii

Not all book bombs are well made. The package messily wrapped in brown paper and tied with dirty twine arrived at the office in the morning mail. It was about the size of a quality paperback. When the string was removed and the paper loosened, a spring would be released, detonating the contents. From across the room, there was simply a sudden, intense flash. Five feet away, there was hardly any feel of heat. Closer up, above the parcel, Tony's face was burned; it looked like a nasty sunburn. Opening his package at home, Séan received a similar burn and a slight eye injury. Across town, Cathal opened his in the backyard with a stick. Each parcel consisted of a small wooden box, the flash powder, and the crude detonator—they looked like the work of a not especially talented child.

Some are more cunningly constructed. In March 1971, a parcel arrived at the FRELIMO headquarters in the Liberation

Centre compound in Lusaka, Zambia. It had been mailed from Japan and contained a book by the president of North Korea, Kim Il Sung. Twenty-five-year-old Matteus Childende flipped open the cover and disappeared in a heavy blast that shook the tiny wooden office.

ix

King Hussein Ibn Talah of the Hashmite Kingdom of Jordan rose early. He is a short, sturdy man with fading hair, sure movements, and an uncertain future. Almost since he ascended the throne in 1952 as a seventeen-year-old schoolboy, he has been the target of assassination plots, conspiracies of domestic rivals, embittered Palestinians, and rival Arab leaders. This morning he opened the medicine cabinet and took out his nose drops. He pushed in the small rubber bulb and sucked up the proper dosage. Just before he put the glass tube to his nose, a single viscous drop trembled at the tip and then fell into the basin. There was a faint, almost inaudible hiss, the slightest hint of smoke as the acid burned through the enamel and steel and dropped down into the bathroom tiles, burning another neat round hole. The king replaced the dropper in the bottle, lucky once again.

x

To operate the Skorpion, the magazine must first be loaded. Place a cartridge on the magazine platform and press down until the cartridge rolls sideways under the magazine lips. Repeat until the magazine is full. Insure that the selector is not in its mid(0) position (safe); then insert a loaded magazine into the recess ahead of the trigger guard until the magazine catch (fig 25) engages the magazine. Using the thumb and forefinger, grasp the cocking knobs (fig 25), pull them full to the rear, and release them. The bolt will return forward.

CAUTION: The pistol is now loaded and ready to fire!

Instruction for the Czechoslovak Vz61
"Skorpion" machine pistol with folding
stock used by the Japanese Red Army at
the Lod Airport massacre

part II

TO STRIKE AT THE STATE: PATTERNS OF POLITICAL MURDER

L'arbe de la liberté ne croit qu' arrosé par le sang dei tyrans.

Betrand Barère, 1792

Rationally planned political assassination has become almost endemic to Western society as a means to strike at the state, not to mention murder for other, including nonpolitical, motives. Over the last century or so there have been sufficient specific examples of assassination conspiracies (well over a thousand), enough explanations and memoirs, studies and records, to permit the beginning of an anatomy of assassination—or, more important, a tentative physiology. First there is the *milieu* for assassination. Some societies have been relatively immune, while in others political murder has practically become an accepted means. On an apolitical level, some societies have institutionalized murder, the clan feud being one of the more notorious examples and Sicilian cases often the most unappetizing. At Godrano, a small township near Palermo, the Barbaccia and Lorello families have been killing each other for half a century. The end came recently when, after a total of sixty killings, ten-year-old Antonio Pecoraro was his family's only surviving male. The Lorello hired three Mafia killers who found the boy on a hillside at Ficuzza and murdered him. The vendetta accounts were balanced. The shoot-outs between the American Hatfields and McCoys seem practically healthy in contrast. Obviously open societies permit, if they do not encourage, variously motivated assassinations, just as closed, effective, authoritarian regimes are far more secure, certainly in matters of access and control. Some ineffective tyrannies—Tsarist Russia and Ottoman Turkey—proved ideal arenas for assassins, and even Hitler was not safe.

Second, no matter what the objective socio-political conditions that might encourage recourse to assassination, there must be those who plan and carry out the deed. Is there then an archetypical assassin? It is possible to speak of the mind of the sergeant-major or the poet—but what of the mind of the assassin? How does an assassin structure his deed? What is the internal *logic*—the theory of murder, the rationalization, the ideological basis, the analysis of the assassin? And what of the *victim?* Some victims seem especially appropriate, ideal candidates for political murder. Who is chosen? And once the victim-target is selected, what kind of impact does the conspirator anticipate that the *deed* will have on history or the masses, on friends or enemies? In the assassination continuum the deed—the murder—is, to all except the victim, usually the least important aspect, and the perceived impact is the most crucial. And it is thus vital to consider from a distance the aims of assassins' aspirations as they perceived them. Was the deed a success? Were the historical processes changed to effect? Was history given a push? And not just a push, but the specific push intended, even if in retrospect the deed appears self-defeating, counterproductive, or futile to others.

THE MILIEU: AN OCEAN FOR VIOLENT FISH

> The revolutionary group is immortal because its way of struggle becomes a tradition and part of people's lives. The secret assassination becomes a terrible weapon in the hands of such a group of people.
>
> —Nikolai Morozov

At certain times there have been no incidents of assassination in a society or nation—or even an entire civilization. From 1368 to 1620 in China there was no evidence of assassination, and up to 1912 only two murders: in 1620 Ming Tas-chang was poisoned in a court plot, and Manchu Kuang-hsü was killed apparently on the orders of the Dowager Empress, who died naturally the next day. The same situation, as previously noted, existed in Western Europe before the Renaissance. In both cases the rulers appeared absolutely legitimate—possessed of the Mandate of Heaven or Divine Right. In the Christian West, the absolute certainty of eternal damnation for regicide may have been a factor. With the slow unfolding of the new learning and the ensuing discussion of tyrannicide, a clash of ultimate loyalties arose. First, a ruler might *be* a tyrant—and then what?

What happened in Italy during the "renaissance" was the end of absolute legitimacy for a monarch, the rise of an era of assassins, and then, with the Reformation, the spread of the Italian technique. The conflicts between the evolving national states and religiously divided populations produced an era of murder, an era that ebbed as the new national absolute monarchies arose as legitimate ruling forms. Yet almost simultaneously the ideas of the Age of Reason ensured that there would be disputes about the appropriate forms and institutions. When those ideas began to be put into effect after 1789, there would never again be a consensus in the West on the appropriate legitimate government structure. Within a generation there arose a dispute about the very structure of society that determined the government. Socialists of all varieties, and the anarchists and syndicalists, denied the legitimacy of all existing regimes—from feudal Russia to republican America—except as stages in the inevitable triumph of the proletariat and final classless society. Europe became an arena for clashing ideologies, each absolutely determined on the one true vision, and whose advocates were often capable at one time or another of creating an appropriate regime. After Bourbon absolutism collapsed, France alone experimented with a bewildering variety of forms—four republics, various monarchies, committees, forms as diverse as the Parisian workers' commune and the neofascism of Lavaol-Petain. Still, amid the chaos and clash of exclusive ideologies, if no nation or regime became absolutely legitimate, some were clearly more legitimate than others.

Since 1789 the obvious triumph has been that of nationalism; and presently one of the most potent forces for violent change remains a submerged nationalism. But with over 160 nation-states, many demonstrably artificial, and the patent impossibility of every proclaimed nation achieving absolute independence, much of the revolutionary potential for disorder has eased. Most existing nations have been accepted, for the foreseeable future, as legitimate geopolitical structures. Since 1945 there have been very few border changes, and while many new states have appeared, few have disappeared. Tiny islands are independent, and desert enclaves and huge squares of bush filled with disparate tribes live under a national flag. All, sitting in the United Nations, are considered legitimate. There are only a few exceptions. Most Arabs still deny the legitimacy of Israel. Guatemala refuses to accept the transformation of British Honduras into Belize. And a few states profess aspirations to dissolve into a larger, unified entity, as Syria and Egypt attempted with the United Arab Republic. The present nation-map is, however, largely taken as legitimate.

Opposition to the frozen "legitimate" boundaries can be found worldwide in the advocates of a submerged nationality—separatists who seek or dream of additional states. The Basques don't want to destroy Spain but to establish a free *Euskadi,* as was the case with the Ibo in Nigeria, and now with the Eritreans in Ethiopia. Some of the separatists have accepted less than the nation; the rebels in the South Sudan, and the Germans in the South Tyrol of Italy, have negotiated compromises. Others have no power to alter reality—the Estonians of Russia and the Tibetans of China. In some cases the existing legitimate "nation" simply could not cope with the centrifugal forces: Cyprus is effectively partitioned between Greek and Turk, and Lebanon between Christians and Moslems, but even then there is reluctance to redraw the map. This general recognition of the status quo, of the legitimacy of the map, has greatly reduced the number of rebels who might employ assassination in a campaign to liberate a submerged nation. But scattered about are many separatists who deny the legitimacy of the frozen map.

In large parts of the world, the institutions of government, imposed by force or created by choice, have become legitimate in that few rebels can be found to oppose them by force. Very few existing governments have long, uninterrupted roots. Imperial Japan has existed for a millennium, but in the last century the legitimacy of the regime that governs has been under repeated challenge. And a great many nations are creations of the last decades. However, there have been institutions that have acquired a legitimacy, reluctant or enthusiastic acceptance, that dissuades the rebel. However cruel and brutal the roots of the Russian system, however uncertain succession at the top, Soviet Communism is perceived as legitimate. This is quite obviously not the case in Eastern Europe, where the system is perceived as inevitable and unavoidable. Thus, with some imposed institutions there is no serious challenge to the only viable system, as in China, while in other cases there is no rational possibility of challenge—for example, Poland.

Although the old open democratic societies, once the models of the future, have proven fragile when exported to the new nations, they are legitimate institutions by selection. The most divisive issues of the past have been resolved by compromise or force: the bounds of the nation, the division of wealth, the forms of the government. Sweden and the United States and Australia appear capable of responding to most foreseeable radical demands for change, for the existing institutions reflect agreement. Thus, while there have been riot and turmoil during this century in America, the political assassin has been rare and revolutionary conspiracy missing entirely. The People's Will stated the ideological position that no people had the right to kill the leader they selected, reflecting a reality—hardly anyone does.

Thus, serious revolutionary violence and hence the concomitant possibility of political assassination is unlikely—though not impossible—in efficient democratic states without a nationality problem. There is no need for an armed challenge to the form of the nation or the means of rule. Yet democratic societies are not immune. Some become inefficient and vulnerable, such as Uruguay. Some open, efficient democratic states do have a nationality problem: Canada with Quebec, the United States with Puerto Rico, the United Kingdom with the Irish nationalists. The weight of legitimacy—the frozen map—may be on the side of the center, but "legitimacy" means little unless the present is accepted without question, really without consideration. Then, indigenous national separatists aside, all open societies—simply because they *are* open —are tempting arenas for alien rebels to carry out operations, and assassination is a peculiarly effective means. There have been international campaigns of assassination against Turkish diplomats and Yugoslavian diplomats, and between those involved in the semi-war between the Palestinians and Israelis. Assassinations take place in Paris or Washington or Stockholm which have nothing to do with France or the United States or Sweden. Finally, open societies permit, if not encourage, the deeds of the psychopaths. Important people appear in public, security is often lax, weapons are available, and previous examples tempt the prepared mind. In Great Britain between 1840 and 1882, there were six "attempts" on the life of Queen Victoria. Five men fired revolvers, one with a blank cartridge, and an army officer struck her with a stick. None had anything to do with politics, any more than the man who threw a pistol at King Edward VIII in 1936 or the more recent displays before the royal family. In March 1978, a shabbily dressed woman shouted at Queen Elizabeth II and Prince Philip outside Westminster and raised her purse. Later in the year, an unemployed joiner impulsively threw a rock at Prince Charles' Rolls-Royce. Of course, even in a closed, authoritarian society the odd lunatic can slip through security with his cherished revolver, as occurred in January 1969 when a man shot at the Soviet cosmonauts outside the Kremlin under the impression that they were members of the Politburo. And when authoritarian rulers travel abroad they become more vulnerable to both the psychopath and the political assassin, as Soviet Prime Minister Kosygin discovered in Canada in October 1971 when the police arrested two members of the right-wing Edmund Burke Society for preparing an assassination attempt.

Generally, then, revolutionary violence is unlikely in efficient, open, democratic societies without nationality problems, simply because it is unnecessary, and it is improbable in efficient, closed, authoritarian societies because it is both futile and difficult. Much of the world, however, is ruled by uncertain and often unsavory regimes. Many refuse to accept the frozen map and a few will kill to change it. Consequently, in this century, a combination of factors have produced at certain times and places a climate, a milieu, congenial to political violence. Rebels professing a different and higher legitimacy are encouraged to strike at the state—an illicit institution, an illegitimate regime, the legacy of an evil past or an alien imposition of the present.

There has been a bewildering variety of reasons given to explain why men rebel: to liberate or fashion nations, to strike at institutions perceived as illegitimate, to right old wrongs, or to make a new people. Those are the reasons rebels proffer, but social scientists and historians and even the threatened find other and often deeper causal factors. The elite has been alienated by the regime.

The people feel a sense of relative deprivation, appetites whetted and hopes thwarted. Individuals and groups are frustrated and turn to aggression. Classes suddenly recognize their destiny and rise in the name of workers and peasants. Some see the gunmen of redemption as psychopaths who kill at random for mad motives. Historians have pointed to the impact of the frontier mentality, order imposed by violence without recourse to law. Sociologists note the relation between weapons and male pride, the macho violence of the American West or Latin America. All the models do indeed explain more, offering a special if often limited insight into the nature of the rebel. As for assassins, clearly some fit the appropriate pigeonhole, being psychopaths or having been frustrated or alienated or seeing themselves deprived; but so are some of their contemporaries who find satisfaction or relief in conventional lives, holy orders, or simple rancor. At best the description of the contemporary milieu congenial to assassination only indicates conditions that appear to encourage revolutionary violence that often entails assassination of the powerful. Politics, especially revolutionary politics, is not an exact science, nor is the investigation of such matters. Still, certain contemporary conditions have demonstrably encouraged rebellion.

The most basic contemporary foundation for revolutionary violence remains a disagreement on nationality, and the most obvious violation of the concept of national legitimacy has been traditional imperialism. The modern archetypal struggle of national liberation was that of Ireland between 1916 and 1921, but most of the revolts have come in the generation after World War II. Although in a few cases the rebels denied themselves the tactical option of assassination—FRELIMO in Mozambique, for example—most did not, especially if the struggle came into the cities from the bush and countryside. The urban guerrilla is by necessity going to use the methods of the nineteenth-century terrorists. Thus the killing of categories—the police or the army or collaborators—has been heightened by the selection of specific and distinguished targets, the governor-general or the chief of staff. Consequently, there have been clusters of assassinations during modern colonial wars in Algeria and Cyprus and Indochina.

A continuing variant of the wars of national liberation has been the persistence of separatism. In some cases, the rebels can wage a conventional irregular war, as the Kurds did in Iraq or the Eritreans in Ethiopia, with assassination selected or rejected for tactical reasons. When the separatists challenge an advanced state in Quebec or Ulster or Corsica, and the campaign goes beyond symbolic bombing, murder is likely—and murder of the very important is an appealing option. Some separatists (such as the Croatians) have so few assets that spectaculars abroad are their only means to gain prominence, if not power. Finally, the disappearance of the old empires, except for the odd isle or rock, has revealed new, post-colonial targets for the revolutionary world, alien regimes, albeit with national flags. There are the minority regimes in Rhodesia and South Africa and the imposed state of Israel in the Arabic Middle East, all defined as illegitimate. There are as well old nations ruled by unrepresentative regimes—such as the military dictatorships in Latin America—or by proxy from imperial centers in Paris or Washington. So once again there are campaigns of national liberation in Southern Africa or Latin America to free the people from an imposed and illegitimate despotism—and again an opportunity to employ the assassin.

Especially in the post-colonial struggles, the line between a national liberation struggle and an ideological one is blurred, for the second basis for irregular war has been a call to overthrow institutions that appear to reflect elite or alien interests rather than those of the nation and the people. The ideological rebels of both the Left and Right in Italy seek to transform not the bounds of the nation but the nature of the nation and state. This has been especially true with the various Latin American revolutionary movements, and Argentina, for example, has produced a decade of assassination and group murder. Finally, some institutions of government, whether legitimate or not, cannot provide for an effective, tranquil transfer of power. If the Russians are not quite sure how to go about it—the leadership stakes are not really determined by the constitution—it is no wonder that in South Arabia, two premiers in San'a and the president in Aden have been killed in less than a year.

In October 1977, North Yemen President Ibrahim al-Hamdi, his brother, and two Parisian models were killed in "mysterious circumstances" during a party at a rest house outside San'a. The assassins were not discovered. In June 1978, a successor, Ahmed Hussein al-Ghashmi, was killed when the briefcase of a South Yemeni envoy exploded. The envoy was killed as well. The South Yemen had been in office for only two months and had survived a previous attempt. In Aden, it was reported that President Salem Robaya Ali, on learning of the plot, had tried to put through a telephone call to San'a but was unsuccessful. Two days later, on June 26, President Robaya was put to death by his colleagues of the National Front for "individualistic attitudes" after a day of heavy fighting in Aden.

There is also little escape through retirement for South Arabian prime ministers. The first South Yemeni prime minister was arrested and killed "while trying to escape," and his successor in exile in Cairo was shot and wounded on the street. On the other hand, former North Yemeni Prime Minister Qadi Abdullah Ahmed Al-Hajiri, along with his wife and a Yemeni diplomat, was shot and killed outside the Royal Lancaster Hotel in London in April 1977.

Basically, then, the milieu most congenial for revolutionary violence and hence assassination is that where a regime is illegitimate, alien to the real nation, and vulnerable to assault. The weaker the assaulters, the more likely the recourse to assassination, as long as the rebels are beyond compromise. For example, in 1944, LEHI, the Stern Group, began a campaign of personal terror based on Eastern European experience because they could not undertake a guerrilla campaign. And LEHI wanted everything—a Zionist state. On the other hand Breton nationalists have detonated over 200 bombs since 1966, including one in June 1978 in the Palace of Versailles; but they have killed no one, even by mistake. In any conspiracy to murder the level of existing capacity and consequently violence is important as well. In a conspiracy that kills for power, the removal of the incumbent is vital. In a conspiracy that seeks to liberate a nation it is equally vital, a tactical opportunity seldom overlooked. Often, as in the case of LEHI, it appears the only way to begin—and especially to punish. And there is always the possibility that assassinations for punishment will produce conditions advantageous to the murderers. In Egypt immediately after World War II, the venal king and court had lost all respect, as had most of the ruling elite. New men, some with old orthodox religious ideas and some committed to new ideologies, conspired to punish the corrupt to spark chaos, and perhaps ultimately seize power. One of the new nationalists, a young air force officer named Anwar Sadat, supposedly trained Hussein Tewfik in grenade throwing, but not to great effect, for Tewfik missed Prime Minister Nahas Pasha by several yards. The second attempt, with Sadat reputedly as chief accomplice, went better and Amin Osman, Nahas' finance minister, was killed by Tewfik. After that—with Sadat in prison for eighteen months—the murders of punishment escalated into a campaign of assassination by the Moslem Brothers that ended only when their Supreme Guide, Hasan al-Banna, was assassinated on February 12, 1949, by "unidentified supporters" of the government. It is possible in the midst of such "promising" conditions for political murder—the illicit regime under pressure—that one individual will suddenly be encouraged spontaneously by the perception of the need for murder. This was the case when Vera Zasulich shot at General Trepov in January 1878, even before the founding of the People's Will, with her spontaneous response to Russian conditions.

And as Zasulich's shot led to years of assassination, it is likely that one attempt will lead to repetition even if the first shot is an individual effort. LEHI began the campaign for a Zionist state in 1944 with the murder of Lord Moyne, and ended it with the murder of Count Bernadotte in Jerusalem in September 1948. During the revolt the organization was constantly plotting other assassinations, even when deeply involved in an urban guerrilla war. In Egypt there had been other significant political murders: Prime Minister Butros Ghali Pasha in 1910 and Sir Lee Stack, British commander-in-chief of the Egyptian army, in 1924; but these remained singular events, the revenge of the ultranationalists. In 1945 the court and the regime were utterly discredited, the forces of nationalism unleashed, and ambitions whetted, but the years of assassination began with punishment: Premier Ahmed Maher Pasha was killed in Parliament in 1945 while announcing Egypt's entry into the war against Germany, a last-minute gesture that other nationalists felt was a betrayal. After that came the men with guns, or, in Sadat's case, grenades. But there are some political benefits to be garnered by the repeated targets of assassins, evidence added to a reputation for invincibility or demonstrable grace under pressure. In June 1978, Colonel Mengistu, chairman of the Ethiopian Dergue, permitted the state news agency to announce that he had survived nine murder attempts—"meticulously prepared." This is hardly evidence of political stability, but permits intense security measures, and one assumes that Mengistu feels that it burnished his image. To the south, Idi Amin regularly used to announce plots against his regime and his life by practically everyone in his bad graces. Some of the plots were real enough, for in most ways the Life President was an ideal target-victim.

If the milieu remains much the same, after the killing begins, the regime being no more legitimate, efficient, or brutal, the rebels no more powerful, still beyond compromise, then it is likely that the assassinations—or at least the attempts—will continue as well. In Russia after 1878, the People's Will and its successors embarked on revolution by assassination. And although the specific campaign dwindled away after the 1887 attempt on the Tsar, assassination remained a facet of Russian politics even after the 1917 revolution. If the People's Will sought to make a revolution by assassination, then between 1920 and 1936, Japan appeared to have government by assassination; in fact, from the Meiji Restoration of 1868 until World War II, Japan was plagued with assassins. Without exception, the assassins were traditionalists, ultranationalists suspicious of the rapid changes in Japanese society, suspicious of party politics, and who, citing historical examples, killed for emperor and country. Still, on January 8, 1932, an attempt was made on the life of God-Emperor Hirohito. Between 1920 and 1930, they killed two prime ministers, a high financier, and two socialist leaders. From 1932 and 1936, a prime minister, a former prime minister, two finance ministers, and four other officials were killed. Two of the prime ministers killed, Hara in 1921 and Hamaguchi in 1930, both strong men, could not be adequately replaced. Party politics grew more divisive. Successive ministers reflected on the fate of the slain and failed to oppose the army's expansionist ambitions abroad. The assassins were treated leniently, as the army delighted to reap the benefits of murder.

Although the coup attempt of February 1936 was crushed and the conspirators executed, there was no longer need for a coup or for further murders, since the Imperial Army dominated Japanese politics through the Control Faction.*

A striking example of both revolution and government by assassination was the situation in Mexico between 1910 and 1944, when political murder seemingly became institutionalized. In November 1910, President Porfirio Díaz, who had been in power since 1876, was deposed and sent into exile. The Mexican revolution had begun, directed by the moderate Francisco Madero, who unwittingly released forces beyond easy control. Until 1910, there had been two Mexicos. One was the elite, fragmented pseudo-European society, deeply devout, innately conservative, looking to Paris and Madrid for style and substance. It was a minority regime unconcerned with and often unaware of the other Mexico —poor illiterate Indians, exploited, superstitious, indigenous. The latter were the wretched of the Mexican earth, and before 1910 beyond politics, out of sight, on the land. After 1910 the struggle was to fashion a "real" Mexico—a society at once just, benevolent, stable, reflecting all its complex roots. It took over thirty years, transformed the structure of society, created new forms and institutions and altered old ones, engendered that unexpected Mexican school of muralists, and, in the midst of this swirling change and violence and revolution, not a single significant political figure failed to be a target of the assassins.

The Mexican revolution produced a fascinating pantheon of heroes and villians. Madero himself, a kind and gentle man of limited ambitions, was betrayed and killed by Victorian Huerta, a cold and calculating man of vast personal ambition. In February 1913, he directed a revolt, had Madero seized, forced his resignation, and, on February 22, had him and Vice President José Maria

---

*The attempted coup took place during the trial of Lieutenant-Colonel Sabura Aizawa, who was charged with the murder of Major General Nagata, Chief of the Military Affairs Bureau of the War Office, the previous August. The conspirators killed Viscount Saito and General Watanake; Finance Minister Takashi, then eighty, was wounded, as was the Imperial Chamberlain Admiral Suzuki and Count Makino. Prime Minister Admiral Okada was killed.

Pino Suarez killed. He then had to defend what he had stolen from colleagues less trusting than Madero: Emiliano Zapata, the charismatic peasant leader from Morelos who knew revolution was about land and not ideas; Plutarcho Eliás Calles, a schoolteacher who had worn his first shoes at sixteen; Álvaro Obregón, a peasant rancher; Lázaro Cárdenas, who had had three years of schooling and joined the revolution at sixteen; and Pancho Villa, a man of panache and élan. Villa was warm, cheerful, and brutal, a partisan horseman who kept "Major" Fierro as a personal killer. Huerta began his defense with the assassination of Senator Belisario Domínquez, and a shifting and fluid civil war followed that deposed Huerta and led to the Constitution of 1917 with Venustiano Carranza as president. Carranza proved to have no interest in revolutionary matters and considerable concern with his personal fortunes. Zapata revolted, but was trapped and killed in April 1919. Only his great white horse escaped to roam free in the hills of Morelos, the symbol of a revolution made by men in white pajamas carrying machetes and possessed by the dream of land. Carranza did not last long. He tried to impose his own candidate as the next president. His support evaporated and he was forced to flee the capital, with twenty railway cars of loot. On the night of May 21, 1920, he was killed as he lay asleep in the village of Tlaxcalantongo. Obregón became president and the revolution continued. The rebels were co-opted into the army, schools were built, trade unions were encouraged—and the painters Rivera, Siquieros, and Orozco appeared. No one, of course, could co-opt Pancho Villa who, after several aborted attempts, was murdered on July 20, 1923, by those who felt his bandit ways endangered the revolutionary state.

The progress of the revolutionary state often proved halting; every four years, at the approach of the presidential election, there was a rebellion. In 1924 Calles was elected after the fighting. On November 13, 1927, there was an unsuccessful attempt on Obregón. In 1928 Generals Gómez and Serrano revolted. They, along with eleven friends, were taken from a banquet in Cuernavaca and killed, and their bodies exposed in Mexico City. The revolt continued for a while and flickered out when Obregón was elected president. But before he took office, on July

17, 1928, while sitting in a restaurant, he was assassinated by a young religious fanatic belonging to a sect led by the nun Madre Conchita. Calles, who escaped, managed to prevent a civil war and dominated politics from the background, a domination that did not prevent an army revolt during the 1930 presidential elections. An attempt on the life of President Pascual Ortiz-Rubio failed on February 5, 1930. Repudiating the corruption of the Calles system, Lázaro Cárdenas was elected president in 1934 for six years. Calles went into exile in the United States, where an attempt was made on his life on January 1, 1937. Under Cárdenas the revolution continued; however, there was a rebellion in 1938 and extensive violence, although not a rising, during the presidential election in 1940, including an attempt on the life of the unsuccessful presidential candidate, General Juán Almazán, on February 7, 1940. (Not only were there other attempts against these major Mexican leaders, but also numerous political murders and deaths during the various aborted coups and failed risings.) The era of the assassins came to an end with an attempt on the life of President Manuel Camacho on April 10, 1944. During the 1946 presidential elections there was no rebellion, no rising, no violence, and the election of Miguel Alemán, the first civilian president since Madero. The Mexican revolution had been institutionalized; the time of Pancho Villa with his crossed bandolieros and huge pistols, of Zapata on his great white horse, was long gone, to be found only in the huge murals and the history books. Mexico had been transformed and although vast and serious problems remained—too many people, too many poor, uneven development, urban sprawl, and rural misery—they did not appear amenable to solution by murder.

Mexico 1910–1946 was hardly alone in providing an encouraging milieu for assassination. In some cases the killing becomes increasingly random, everyone or anyone is vulnerable, the "regime" irrelevant to the killing. In Colombia la violencia killed thousands upon thousands for, at best, marginal political purpose. The civil war in Lebanon put everyone at risk, often for little reason. It is no longer simply a milieu that permits or encourages murder as an acceptable means to affect events, but rather a time of endemic murder, personal feuds, greed, arbitrary executions, random bombing of big houses—anarchy, so that what impresses is not that so many important figures are killed but rather that so few die. The defining line between this endemic slaughter and rational campaigns of murder is a narrow one. In Guatemala for two decades the number of political killings has been appalling; whole classes and groups, members, and representatives—students, the rich, the poor, labor leaders, bureaucrats, professors—become and remain targets. The most recent prominent victim was Senator Fuentes Mohr, former Foreign Minister and leader of the moderate Leftist Authentic Revolutionary Party, shot, according to the government, by the Guerrilla Army of the Poor. And no government seems able or willing to impose order or operate under the law or achieve a satisfactory degree of legitimacy.

At times, the murder milieu has specific and recognizable bounds: those who kill know what they are doing, what impact they anticipate, and when to stop. In Germany from 1918 until 1924, perhaps as many as sixty ultra-Right organizations *(Vehme)* killed at least 354 "enemies." They operated under a principle— self-declared—of *Ubergesetzlicher Notstand,* super-legal urgency: to punish those who betrayed the nation, to undermine the corrupt and illicit Weimar government, and to pave the way for the real Reich to emerge. When it became clear that the road into the future could be more easily paved through the electorial triumphs of the National Socialist Party than with the bodies of politicians, they not so much gave up violence but rather joined up with Hitler. Behind them they left a trail of victims, notably Kurt Eiser, the Republican Premier of Bavaria, killed in 1919 by Count Arco-Vally, an anti-Semitic nationalist. Matthias Erzburger, former finance minister, was killed in 1921 by two members of a secret nationalist organization, and Walter Rathenau, a Jew and a foreign minister seeking to fulfill reparations, was killed the following year, again by anti-Semitic members of a nationalist organization. But after 1924 murder was no longer endemic in Weimar politics, although turmoil and street violence continued. The special point is that because of German conditions between 1918 and 1924, when the nature, even the bounds, of the nation and the legitimacy of the regime and the Weimar institutions were a matter of deadly dispute, the ultra-nationalists felt that they had a legitimate right to pursue politics by murder—and when such means were no longer necessary or effective, they stopped.

Elsewhere, assassination too is at times a normal means of political action, so normal that the less political adopt it. Thus in both Syria and Iraq governments have tended to be changed by gunmen, and the quarrels between Baghdad Ba'athists and Damascus Ba'athists have been pursued by assassins. Then, beginning in 1976–1977, at least thirteen members of the Alawite Islamic sect of President Hafez Assad were killed. Other Alawites escaped, and explosions and fire-bombings hit newspapers and army officer clubs. Perhaps the first attempt was made on Foreign Minister and Deputy Prime Minister Abdel Halim Khaddam, on December 1, 1976. He and his wife were being driven along the Beirut road in western Damascus when two men on a motorcycle pulled alongside. One fired five shots at Khaddam from a submachine gun at point-blank range. One bullet struck Khaddam in the right shoulder and another in his left hand; a third and potentially fatal bullet was stopped by the headrest. The motorcycle sped off. The limousine slowed to a stop. Khaddam's wife leaped out to hail a passing car and was run down. Both ended in the Mouasat Hospital in satisfactory condition. The assassins were not found, despite a number of arrests.

Although the government would have preferred the campaign to have been an attack by the Iraqi enemy, it became apparent that the victims, Shia Moslems representing only eleven percent of the Syrian population, who had taken power through their control of the army, were being killed because of their presumptions and prominence. They were murdered because they were despised Alawites.

In a time of international terrorism, however defined, with massacres and murders on the television screen, it is not unexpected that some individuals, a long way from the traditional blood feuds of the Middle East, may see killing as an accepted means. Thus members of the Indian religious sect Ananda Marga (Path of Bliss), to protest the arrest of their leader, P. R. Srakar,* have attacked Indian officials in various foreign capitals as well as murdered the Indian Railways Minister, L. N. Mishra, in a bomb attack in January 1975. Iraqi and Syrian politics by assassination tend to seep over into the international arena with attempts on those in exile who might be a future threat. Targets are shot down in Beirut or, more recently, London—Adib al-Shishakli was shot in Brazil long after he had been president of Syria. Iraq is no different—Abdul Razzak Al-Nayif, briefly prime minister in Baghdad in 1968, escaped one attempt in 1972 in London when his wife Lamya stopped the bullets, but was mortally wounded in front of the Intercontinental Hotel on Hyde Park on July 9, 1978. If television has made this world a global village, it has also been responsible for encouraging a time of terror—a general milieu for murderous fanatics: Croatians, South Moluccans, Palestinians, and Armenians.

The new milieu for revolutionary violence has two strands, international and transnational. In the first case, the victims, random or specific, are selected because away from home they are vulnerable: the Yugoslavian ambassador in Stockholm, or the Arab exiles in Beirut or London. In the second case, it appears that for a few tiny militant groups the entire global system is the target, so that squads of mixed nationalities strike at what they define as institutions of oppression—kidnapping, for example, the entire international organization called OPEC. What is clear is that these spectaculars, when broadcast worldwide, have been adapted and adjusted by others for local conditions—and, as in the case of the Anand Murthi sect, with only marginal political conditions. A similar situation arose with the rise of violent, revolutionary anarchism in the nineteenth century that created a milieu encouraging to all who would strike at the guilty—rulers—in the name of the future. As with the contemporary terrorists, some copied the murders for other, often pathological, purposes. In both cases there was a compellingly attractive international model for murder, an assassin's milieu.

---

*Sarkar, or Anand Murthi, had his life sentence for murder quashed by the high court at Patna Bihar on July 4, 1978, which might end the two-year terror campaign—unless the government takes the case to the Supreme Court.

THE MIND: THE DEDICATION TO DEATH

We are the men without names, without kin, who forever
face terror and death. . . . in the days that are red with
carnage and blood, in the nights that are black with despair.

—Avrahan Stern

The milieu for murder is as difficult for the rebel to perceive as
it is for the advocates of order to avoid. Madera did not *plan* to
unleash all the forces that led to three decades of murder, any
more than Díaz in 1910 foresaw the end not of just his power but
of his Mexico. Suddenly, however, those elusive "object conditions" exist, and often concomitantly the rebels recognize that the
way to strike at the heart of the state is through murder. Often
such a means is not considered most desirable, the proper ideological approach being a massed rising or a guerrilla campaign or a
general strike, but it is accepted as the only and obvious alternative to the continuance of the intolerable. And so Vera Zasulich
shot General Trepov. Afterward there could be detailed ideological contemplation, moral exegesis, and consideration of the cost
benefits. Sometimes, in fact often, the plotters recognize that the
conditions encourage murder as a pragmatic deed, but still agoniz-
ingly analyze the nature and necessity of the killing beforehand.
Thus there is a strategic and tactical level of the mind of murder
as well as an emotional—and individual—aspect.
    Like the theologians of the People's Will after 1878, the High
Command of LEHI—the Stern Group—spent considerable time
on the logic of murdering Lord Moyne in 1944, pondering the
strategic benefits and probable tactical losses. If Zasulich seemed
to act spontaneously, LEHI most certainly did not, although to a
considerable degree the logic of personal terror—given the milieu
in Palestine, the Middle East, and the world in that year—had
suddenly become obvious even as the analysis went on. First, for
LEHI, there appeared no other way for a few score badly armed
people, isolated in an obscure backwater, in the midst of a world
war, to act on events. They had no resources to effect a rising, or
to undertake guerrilla war, no real organization that might act

"politically," no friends in court, no powerful allies, no other means to give history a push but the propaganda of the deed. Second, the ideological background of the leadership—Eastern European Zionists quite familiar with the theory and practice of terrorism—considered assassination a normal and legitimate revolutionary tool, ethical as well as practical. Thus, it was relatively easy to move from the ethical to the practical: Would the deed change history? What the High Command wanted was to transform the world's perception of the Palestine "problem." Moyne was a symbol, a replaceable symbol, whose violent removal from the board would have several effects. The British could no longer treat the future of Palestine as an internal imperial matter. The death of Moyne would internationalize the future, pose not only for the British but for the Allies the simple question: Why did this man die? Other Zionists might supply the answer, but the question would have been asked. Also, the British would be forced to realize that an imposed "solution" would provoke further violence, that the Zionists were serious, to be ignored only at British peril. This was then propaganda by deed on the broadest scale. Certainly there were other aspects: the excruciating need to act after 1943 as the news of the holocaust began to seep into the Palestinian Mandate, and the real need to give LEHI a mission and to compete with their rival organization, the Irgun Zvai Leumi of Menachem Begin. Obviously, the killing of Moyne would create all kinds of tactical problems for LEHI because of the anticipated increased security pressure in Palestine—one of the reasons that Begin was not informed beforehand; but the High Command felt LEHI could hardly undertake a revolt by avoiding provocation. So the deed was authorized, one of the classic assassinations of the century; and the plotters selected the players, the two young gunmen who would shoot Moyne.

The first, Eliahu Hakim, a twenty-year-old Sephardic Jew, was born in Beirut. His family immigrated to Palestine, and he was brought up in comfortable circumstances in Haifa. His interest in politics was abruptly awakened when, during a demonstration, a British policeman lashed him on the back with a riot whip—a psychic scar that he carried with him to Cairo. "A British policeman made me decide to join LEHI." In 1942, while still in school, he joined LEHI, and later underwent training under Joshua Cohen. His family was appalled, and pressured him to quit. Instead he drifted. He worked briefly at a military camp at Bat Galim, but was restless and unsettled, and soon was fired. Family pressure to change his ways increased. They knew all too well the fate of many of Eliahu's older colleagues. At last they persuaded him to accept conscription into the British Army. He was shipped off by the army to Cairo where, unknown to his parents, he continued his LEHI activities, mainly acquiring arms and aiding in smuggling them into Palestine. It was a small-time operation, but at least he was doing something. When he was ordered back to Palestine, he deserted and went underground full time. He became one of the small group of activists involved in a long string of abortive attacks on British General MacMichael, including a final ambush on the Jaffa Road. The High Command recognized that Eliahu Hakim, with his dedication, military training, and Cairo experience, was an ideal candidate.

The other volunteer was less obvious. In fact, Eliahu Bet-Zouri was really self-selected, having convinced the High Command that he *must* undertake the mission. At twenty-three he was three years older than Hakim and, too, had long been involved in politics. Born in Tel Aviv, a sabra, he attended Balfour High School until expelled for political activity. He and two friends even planned a private attack on the high commissioner. When that misfired, he joined the Am Lochem movement. When that collapsed, although he remained in his position in the government survey department, he came to LEHI. Seething with indignation, he wanted action. His dedication and determination, it was felt, would compensate for his lack of operational experience.

Autumn 1944 was golden in Cairo. The searing heat of the summer had faded. The Nile, still red with the topsoil of the Ethiopian highlands, ebbed swiftly. The nights were cool, the breezes no longer filled with desert grit. The ever-present crowds would thicken at sundown. The narrow lanes and dilapidated squares of the old city became a mass of swirling jellabas, turbans, sheep, and lost camels, even the odd clerk in a three-piece suit and red fez. The more affluent, in summer suits and dinner frocks, sat on restaurant boats moored along the river, or in garden cafés, and ate grilled pigeon and tahini salads late into the night. The poor had to make do with *ful* sandwiches and black tea at the edge of the Azbakiya Gardens. The rich filled Shepheard's Hotel and the French restaurants; the clubs were always full. All through the night people were buying and selling—orange juice from the tiny carts, American cigarettes from British soldiers, or each other. The city never slept, teemed with life—camels to one side, Land Rovers to the other, goats at the traffic crossing. The taxis circled endlessly about the Place de l'Opéra, honking and hooting at the old lorries held together with baling wire and the Bren gun carriers filled with cheerful drunks.

In many ways, despite the wartime shortages and problems, 1944 was for Cairo a special moment, a brief year of respite. The politics of violence, the endless wars, Nasser, Palestine, the coups and the conspiracies, lay ahead: the exciting days of the desert war with Rommel at the gate were in the past. Cairo enjoyed the pause. The bars, clubs, and bordellos were full of people celebrating their distance from the wars or their triumph over the bureaucracy. There were all sorts and conditions of clerks and soldiers and authorized personnel. Out of sight, the pashas and the court, fully corrupt, venal without charm, lived in their own lush Carine society, far beyond the economics of clerks or the ken of drunken Anzacs, staggering through the dim streets. Theirs was a vastly international city of Greek merchants, Coptic importers, Albanian planters, Italian bankers, Armenians, Turks, Jews, all floating on the misery of the Egyptian poor. The rich were largely ignorant of the dreams of the newly ambitious bank tellers and officer cadets—the heirs to the future. The British ruled all this with arrogance and few qualms, manipulating the politicians when necessary, dismissing them if need be, largely uninterested in the muttering of Egyptian nationalists—"little men," mustached, whispering on the sly in French. For the British generals and administrators, Cairo, even wartime Cairo, remained simply an imperial bastion. Most of them loathed the vacuous and venal froth of Farouk's Cairo, knew little of its wretchedness, and found their pleasures and friends among their own. In the autumn of 1944, this huge sprawling city, filthy and various, absorbed one more exotic, Eliahu Hakim, a prospective assassin.

For Hakim that Cairo autumn was a strange, unreal time, stretched between his Palestine past, his friends in the dingy rooms of the underground, and the awesome, looming deed that would change history. On arrival, he began the traditional rituals of the assassin. The misleadingly aimless wandering about on the victim's trail, seeking patterns and rumors. Where does he eat? When does he leave the office? Where does his limousine park? Who is always at home? Who guards him? Who visits him? There was the strange, erie dislocation of moving among a crowd of real people, rushing about their business. They dash past with their vital briefcase or their tray of black tea or their blank mind. All the while, a thin young man with a dark mustache in a blue shirt, walking beside a pretty, dark-haired girl called Yaffa, loiters near the Nile Cornice, not far from the British Embassy. He is aware that he and she, unlike the others, are not real people, but instruments of fate.

From his previous visit Hakim was familiar with the world of LEHI in the city, the strange aliases, the safe rooms, the tiny circle of the trusted, the double and triple life of the underground; but in the autumn of 1944, the British did not even know he was in the city. Palestine and its troubles were a long way off; one deserter more or less did not matter. Hakim could wander freely. He went dancing, ate in restaurants, walked with Yaffa along the river, and each night returned to his small room at 4 Sharia Gheit el-Noubi in the Mouski district, far from the elegant embassies and gardens along the Nile. He could have been anyone. He certainly attracted little attention. And by the end of October, he knew Moyne's patterns, and chose his moment. Bet-Zouri arrived. Hakim's drifting was over. On November 2, Hakim walked past Moyne's residence once more. The bicycles were hired, the pistols loaded. The deed that had seemed so unreal when the two young men accepted the mission had come down to a matter of timing and distance.

Monday, November 6, 1944, was pleasant as usual for the time of year. The warm, clear skies and bright sun of Cairo were a far cry from the fogs and drizzles of wartime Britain. The trimmed lawns and gardens of the diplomatic quarter in Garden City, the elaborate Italianate palaces, the long, black limousines of generals and ambassadors, created an oasis along the Nile. This quarter de luxe was as isolated from the great winter battles along the Rhine as it was from the teeming, chaotic bazaars of central Cairo—except perhaps for the Bren gun carriers in the streets. The aura was of quiet and confident elegance, in an imperial world of ease and deserved comfort. In his office at 10 Sharia Tolumbat, at 12:50 in the afternoon, the Right Honorable Walter Edward Guiness, first Baron Moyne, had all but finished his morning's work as British minister of state in Cairo. Beyond his window, the steady din of the city reached faintly into the cool and shaded lawns. Down further, on the Nile Cornice, great lateen-rigged boats drifted past date palms. It looked like a picture-postcard world; but Moyne, at the center of the web, ran a real world of British Mideast imperial matters. The war might have moved on but Moyne, and Churchill, remained acutely aware of future British influence in the area. For Moyne it was a splendid posting, a serious responsibility, a sign of esteem. He was competent, ambitious, and talented, and Cairo had so far been good for him.

At 1:00, accompanied by his personal secretary, Dorothy S. Osmond, and his ADC, Captain A. G. Hughes-Onslow, Moyne left the building to be driven across Cairo for lunch. It was a quick ten-minute run and a welcome break from the office routine. His black Packard Saloon, driven by Lance Corporal A. Fuller, soon edged through the impossible traffic and crossed over the Nile bridge into Gezira. At 4 Sharia Gabaliya, Fuller turned the car into the walled yard, drove on past the underground garage, and pulled up before the three steps leading to the front door. Hughes-Onslow popped out of the right front seat and ran up the steps, reaching into his pocket for the key. Fuller opened his door and got out. There was a single moment of quiet just as Hughes-Onslow stopped before the door. Fuller snapped shut the front door of the Packard and started around the back to open the door for Moyne. From over the walls drifted the faint sound of traffic and the endless din of Cairo. There was the slight crinkle of cooling metal from the Packard. The garden was bright with the full afternoon light; a mass of color nodded in the flower pots at Hughes-Onslow's feet. It was 1:10, lunch would be on time.

Hughes-Onslow was about to take the key out of his pocket

when he heard someone say in English, "Don't move. Stay where you are. Don't move." Hakim and Bet-Zouri were on time as well. Fuller had reached the rear of the Packard. He stopped. Bet-Zouri raised his revolver and fired directly into Fuller's chest. The slugs tore through his body, severing his right internal iliac artery, then smashed against the far garden wall. Fuller collapsed in the driveway, sprawled on his back. With massive intra-abdominal hemorrhages, he bled to death within minutes. Inside the car, Dorothy Osmond leaned forward at the sound of the shots. She heard Fuller groan but could not understand what was happening. There was a young man of medium height, about thirty, wearing gray trousers and a lighter jacket and tie. He was standing back from the car, holding a revolver. Another man, taller and darker, moved away from Hughes-Onslow on the stoop and up to the Packard's rear window next to Moyne. He looked once at Dorothy Osmond and said again in English, "Don't move." Moyne started to open the door and began to turn toward the young man. Hakim, pulling open the door, thrust his revolver toward Moyne, and began firing into him, slowly and deliberately. The first slug hit Moyne in the neck on the right side, just above the clavicle, jerking his head around. The second ripped into his abdomen near the twelfth rib, becoming embedded to the right of the second lumbar vertebra. Before Hakim fired again, Moyne raised his right hand to ward off the shots. The third slug only ripped across his four fingers and tore in and out of his chest in a superficial wound. Hakim stepped back. Moyne managed to cry, "Oh, they've shot us!" Blood was spurting out of his neck. Hakim drew further back and moved away from the car. Moyne slumped forward, unconscious. By the time Dorothy Osmond, sitting stunned next to Moyne, and Hughes-Onslow, still standing on the stoop, could grasp what had happened, Hakim and Bet-Zouri had run out of the yard.

Once out of the grounds, both jumped on their rented bicycles and began pedaling madly down Sharia Gabaliya toward the Zamalek Bridge. Once across and into the traffic, they could simply disappear in the mob. Chasing after them, Hughes-Onslow was only forty yards back, because he had cut through the back of the house. He rushed out the gate and stopped at the sentry box— Hakim and Bet-Zouri might have a forty-yard lead, but the alarm was given. Hearing the hue and cry behind them, the two men turned off into a side road, Sharia Bahres Amer, and then turned again by the residence of King George of Greece—they were very nearly away. Suddenly, just at the bridge, El-Amin Mahomed Abdullah, a member of the Ministerial Protection Squad, appeared on his motorcycle. He ignored a volley of warning shots fired into the air—Hakim and Bet-Zouri were determined not to injure any Egyptians in their operation—and pushed on. Others rushed up. There were more shots and no place for the two men to go. They were captured.

In the meantime Dorothy Osmond ran into the house and telephoned for help. She asked the duty clerk to send for the police. As soon as Hughes-Onslow gave the alarm, he ran into the nearby Gezira police station and phoned to the Fifteenth Scottish Hospital, to arrange for a doctor and ambulance. By the time he returned to the yard, Major H. W. Forester, alerted by Osmond's telephone call, had already arrived from the ministerial resident's office. It was just 1:15. Air Vice-Marshal Nutting and Major Woodford appeared. Forester walked over to Fuller, who was lying on his back in a pool of blood, obviously dead. The rear door of the Packard was open, the window down, and Moyne, hunched over in the seat, was covered with blood, apparently dead. It was very quiet. Three or four Egyptians huddled, terrified, at the gate. Two house suffragii stood in front of the steps gaping. No one said anything. The three British officers stood appalled, until suddenly Major Woodford noticed that Moyne's hand had moved.

When they rushed over to him, he regained consciousness but seemed confused. He asked Forester if he could be moved to his room, since he was feeling rather uncomfortable. Soothing him, Forester suggested that they wait until the doctor arrived. Moyne asked several times in a low voice when the doctor would come. In a very few minutes the doctor and an ambulance appeared. Moyne was driven straight to the hospital and admitted at 1:40, just forty minutes after he had left his office. At the hospital it was at once clear that his condition was critical. He had lost a great deal of blood through gross hemorrhaging, and was still bleeding. His pulse was imperceptible; he was in shock. At 1:45 he had the first of three transfusions. His condition improved markedly; his pulse was 120 and his color was better. He could talk and began to complain of a burning pain down his right leg and an inability to move the leg. X-rays revealed an injury to the right side of his first dorsal vertebra. Later in the afternoon, his right arm became paralyzed as a result of the severe trauma around the neck wound. The doctors were reluctant to operate until his condition improved. At 5:30 a lumbar puncture revealed a blood stain. The time had come to operate. He was given another transfusion while the bullet was removed from beside the second lumbar vertebra. It was discovered that the bullet had punctured both the colon and large intestine, causing gross internal bleeding. The doctors cleaned the neck wound and the minor damage to his fingers and chest: all told, there were eight wounds. The prognosis remained poor. Despite the quick treatment and the surgeons' skill, there was little hope that Moyne would weather the shock and the loss of blood. Soon after he was wheeled out of the operating room, his condition began to deteriorate. His vital signs steadily weakened. The doctors could not reverse the decline. At 8:40 that evening, he died.

Even before his death British security forces and Egyptian political circles had been thrown into chaos. No one had expected assassins in Cairo. No one knew who the two men were, who had sent them, or what they represented. All that was known were the names they gave: Saltzman and Cohen. The authorities remained confused: was it Saltzman or Zalzman? Anyway, the British did not believe these were their real names. During the afternoon and evening of November 6, the authorities continued to interrogate the two men.

The Egyptian government reacted to the news of the assassination with deep horror and immediate panic. In 1926, when an Egyptian assassinated Sir Lee Stack Pasha, British governor of the Sudan and commander in chief of the Egyptian Army, the reaction by London had been swift and far-reaching—the Egyptians were expelled from the Sudan and Britian took sole control there, and demanded a large Egyptian indemnity as well. One mad moment in 1926 had lost the Egyptian monarchy an empire to the south that might never be regained. Neither King Farouk nor his premier, Ahmed Mahir Pasha, wanted another such disaster in

1944. Farouk hurriedly sent his own physicians to the hospital. The premier, accompanied by the foreign minister, rushed first to the Gezira police station to get a detailed account, and then to the British Embassy to offer their condolences. Farouk personally sent Hassanein Pasha to Moyne's residence to express his dismay. Amid the confusion of the moment, the Egyptians finally learned the only good news of the day—the assassins were not Arabs. Beyond that, no one knew anything. The next day the newspapers were filled with horror and outrage.

The British soon decided that one of the young men, first identified as Moshe Cohen Itzak, might actually be Private Eliahu Hakim, who had deserted on February 9. The other, Saltzman or Zalzman, remained an unknown. Although both suspects admitted the deed, Saltzman to shooting Lance Corporal Fuller and Hakim to shooting Moyne, they were forthcoming with very little else. They wanted to give the LEHI people in Cairo time to go underground. On Tuesday, November 7, after nearly twenty-four hours of questions, the two finally announced they were members of LEHI: "What we have done, we have done on the instructions of this organization." The British then discovered that Saltzman had used the name Hanan Michael while at a Cairo hotel on October 20–21, and that Cohen had been in Cairo for two months as Private Samuel Bernstein. Even later, when the two told as much of their story as they intended, British security never quite managed to completely fill out the Cairo picture. For weeks the security forces continued an intensive investigation of the trail left by the two. A vast search and sweep operation checked out all Palestinians in Egypt. Eventually, several LEHI suspects were arrested, including four LEHI women. Hakim's "girlfriend" Yaffa ended up in the women's prison in Bethlehem.

The two men, however, did not act like terrorists or fit into comfortable categories. They had not even killed to save their own lives. It was apparent that they realized the risks they had taken in not shooting El-Amin off his motorbike. They explained why: it would have been the death of a potential ally, and would have alienated Arab opinion. Moyne was guilty; El-Amin was not. So El-Amin was alive, and on January 10 the two men were in an Egyptian dock, charged with murder. Those in the crowded courtroom saw two rather conventional-appearing young men, the taller Hakim in a jacket, Bet-Zouri in an open-necked shirt. Both stood calmly manacled among a group of Egyptian guards with red fezzes. They were placed behind an iron grille overlooking the courtroom. Both were, and had been since their capture, self-possessed, almost serene. They had, of course, no defense, only an explanation.

> Our deed stemmed from our motives, and our motives stemmed from our ideals, and if we prove our ideals were right and just, then our deed was right and just. . . . If we have turned to the gun, it is because we were forced to the gun.

The court was not impressed. On January 11, both were condemned to death. Despite the almost universal horror in Cairo at Moyne's assassination, the bearing and presence of the men produced among many Egyptians a grudging respect. There was no doubt that both were idealists as well as fanatics; neither had hesitated to take responsibility for the deed; neither seemed to fear death.

Both retained their composure to the end. In his last letter, Hakim insisted he was prepared for anything. "I am absolutely calm and my conscience settled because I have the feeling I have done my duty." The British had little sympathy with such idealists, or with the validity of such a duty. Lord Killean decided not to forward the final letters to the men's families. "I do not feel any consideration is due to these two self-confessed murderers." Such men were beyond reason, compassion, or mercy. On February 24, Churchill, a personal friend of Moyne, said in Parliament that the execution of justice upon men should be swift and exemplary. Prime Minister Ahmed Mahir took the point.

On March 22, the eve of their execution, the Chief Rabbi of Egypt, Nissim Ochana, spent the last night with Hakim and Bet-Zouri. They remained calm. On March 23, they were dressed in the traditional ill-fitting red-burlap suits of condemned men, marched barefoot to the gallows, blindfolded at the scaffold, and hanged. They never anticipated any less. Hakim said just before he died, looking down at the red burlap, "This is the finest suit of clothes I have ever worn in my life." For Hakim and Bet-Zouri it was a uniform of martyrdom and patriotism, not of shame. By the time the two put on the red suits, their deed had become part of the past, part of history.

There are, then, usually two variants of the mind of the assassin in any assassination conspiracy: the plotter and the player. The lone political assassin involves both in varying degrees, but in the Moyne murder the separation was absolute. In the murder of Tsar Alexander II the blend was perfect, directors as actors. In some cases, the distance between the plotter and the player is very hard to define. In the plot against Hitler, most played at plotting and the plotters in the end had no one to play their leader.

One of the more striking examples of the mind of political murder—on various levels, from strategic to technical—can be found in the assassination of Mahatma Gandhi on January 30, 1948. The key to the conspiracy was Vinnayak Dannodar Veer "The Brave" Savarkar, sixty-five, a Hindu ascetic, slender, intense, with steel-rim spectacles and a dedication to the concept of a greater Hindu India. He opposed the British raj, the concept of partition, the idea of Pakistan and, in 1947, the emerging reality of all those things. Trained in the Inns of Court, he had been imprisoned on the Andaman Islands with a double life sentence for the murder of a British bureaucrat, then freed by a postwar amnesty. He had been involved at a distance in previous attempts on the lives of the governors of Punjab and Bombay. His organization, Rashtriya Swayam Sewak Sangh (RSSS), had an inner and violent core, Hindu Rashtra Dal, established on May 15, 1942, made up of Chitpawan Brahmans fanatically dedicated to the Greater Hindu State. Savarkar, not actually so ascetic, was a secret homosexual and an opium addict, facts unknown to most of his followers and irrelevant to his influence. By January 1948, he and his followers had grown increasingly frustrated by the direction of events: India had been partitioned, Pakistan existed, and Moslems and Hindus had indulged in a long orgy of massacre that had finally largely ended because of mutual exhaustion, the flight of the vulnerable, and the last fast of Gandhi. On January 18, 1948, after fasting for

121 hours and 30 minutes, Gandhi had forced the government to agree to a series of accommodations and concessions—including turning over 550 million rupees to Pakistan as promised. For the RSSS this was treason, a betrayal of Hindu India, not simply a maneuver to end mass murder but an open recognition of Pakistan by India's most renowned figure—the moral blessing of treachery. Savarkar, of course, knew what should be done; but after his time on the Andaman Islands, he also knew how dangerous such a deed could be. He would wait. Others surely would not. He would not even need to plot.

As soon as he heard of the results of Gandhi's last fast, Gopal Godse, twenty-nine, announced, "We must kill Gandhi."[1] He was "just a shrunken old man" but "he was a bad influence on the people." Almost at once the conspiracy was born. All Savarkar need do, and did do, was listen. The two key men in the plot were Gopal Godse's older brother, Nathuram Godse, and Narayan Apte, the "brains." Nathuram Godse, thirty-nine, had failed in twelve different trades from tailoring to retreading tires. He was a rigid moralist who hated women and at twenty-eight had taken a vow of abstinence; in fact, his only known sexual encounter was a homosexual one with Savarkar. Narayan Apte, at thirty-four, was quite the reverse, although he had been raised by a strict Hindu father, a mailman making fifteen rupees a month. Apte loved food, whiskey, and women. He was a devotee of palmistry and mysticism, a manipulator and entrepreneur, flexible and flashy. The others were an equally mixed lot: Vishnu Karkare, thirty-four, who ran a sordid travelers' hotel; Madanlal Pahwa, twenty, who quite simply wanted to revenge his father, mutilated by Moslems; Digamber Badge, thirty-seven, an arms peddler disguised as a holy man, who had been arrested thirty-seven times for bank robbery, murder, aggravated assault, and arms violations; and Badge's servant Shanker Kistaya. Others were involved but this was the core, all marginal men but each with a special motive—idealism, profit, revenge, excitement.

The conspiracy succeeded, as is often the case, as much from compensating errors and official incompetence as from the skill and proper planning. There was difficulty with the pistols—one would not work and the other hit nothing; with the planning—

Nathuram was incapacitated at a crucial moment with a migraine headache; with one blundered attempt and the ever-so-slow unwinding of the plot by the police. Eventually the conspirators tracked down a black Beretta automatic pistol and twenty rounds of ammunition from a RSSS homeopathic physician, Dattatraya Parchure. On January 30, 1948, with the Beretta in his pocket, Nathuram waited with the crowd at Birla House for Gandhi to arrive to lead prayers. Ten minutes late, Gandhi emerged with his nineteen-year-old grandniece, Manu, and walked across the lawn toward the prayer ground. Manu carried his spittoon, eyeglasses, and notebook. She noticed a stout young man in khaki stepping toward Gandhi and tried to explain that "Bapu" was already ten minutes late. Nathuram pushed her aside and while she groped for the spittoon and eyeglasses raised the Beretta and shot Gandhi in the chest three times. He collapsed on the ground, his white *khadi* covered with blood, and gasped, *"He Ram"* ("Oh God.") He died almost immediately. Nathuram Godse was taken into custody with his pistol still in his hand. The rest were soon arrested; Apte was the last, on February 14. The trial of the eight major conspirators took place on May 27 with the arms dealer Digamber Badge as the state's witness. He was released; his servant was acquitted on appeal. Dr. Parchure's conviction was reversed in Appellate Court. Vishnu Karkare, Gopal Godse, and Madanlal Pahwa received life sentences, and Narayan Apte and Nathuram Godse were condemned to death. Apte, who from reading his palm knew that he would receive a last-minute reprieve, had no worries. On November 15, 1949, at the foot of the gallows, he collapsed and had to be carried to the noose when he realized that palmistry had let him down. Nathuram Godse arranged that his ashes would not be put in the Ganges but rather handed down until the subcontinent was Hindu. Vinayak Damodar Veer "The Brave" Savarkar died peacefully in 1966 at the age of eighty-three.

Savarkar, the twisted fanatic, fits the most popular romantic ideal of the plotter—politically pure, personally corrupt, a manipulator of idealists, an evil genius dedicated to an impossible cause, a man without scruple. And in his way Nathuram Godse is the perfect assassin—a failure at every trade but murder, a fanatic in his sex life as well as his political commitments, narrow-minded, without toleration or vision, an instrument of fate in Savarkar's hands. And what of the charming and delightful Narayan Apte with his whiskey and women, engaged in the politics of excitement? He, too, has a mind thought typical, just as the criminal badge fits a different stereotype. Actually, simple Madanlal Pahwa, who merely wanted to avenge his father, may be most typical. At twenty he was a soldier of revenge who put on a rumpled blue suit—the first time in his life that he had worn a collar and tie—and went forth with his bomb. But vengeance is a poor motive for revolutionaries, and he collapsed immediately and told nearly all. Few assassins possess the curious and not especially attractive compound of the Gandhi assassins. Certainly most plotters would avoid the criminals, the dilettantes, the aging fanatics, even the simple-minded Madanlal Pahwa, for effective planners seek the ideal revolutionary soldier, not a self-selected killer.

Most of the ideal assassins, ideal for revolutionary purpose, have remarkably similar characteristics. As rebels performing violent deeds, they must seek a higher authority than the recognized state. They kill in the name of the nation or the masses, without, of course, polling their constituents; there is no need. Eamon De Valera once said that he need only look into his own heart to know the wishes of the Irish people. Those who kill the king or the premier can do so with untroubled conscience and great dedication because they know that the deed is legitimate—it is their duty, their obligation, their historical responsibility to kill for a cause that can offer no pensions or medals, no fringe benefits or uniforms. They, the chosen, ride with the winds of history and the angel of death. Young, deeply dedicated to the dream, eager to please, desperate to serve, not unmindful of martyrdom and avid to belong to the band of brothers, touched by limited ambition, they are possessed of a self-righteous indignation. And they can kill with a ruthless brutality, without regret; even at the foot of the gallows, they regret only that they failed.

On 12 December 1960 Charles de Gaulle inspected the Air Force parachute commandos on the airbase at Réghaïa before boarding his aircraft. I and certain others were due

to shoot down the head of this police state. Owing to inde-
cision we let slip this opportunity of putting an end to the
machiavellian activities of the tyrant and probably of saving Algeria. . . . In the autumn of 1960, having equipped
a party destined to shoot Charles de Gaulle during his visit
to the South-East, I showed lack of courage in failing to
take part myself. As a result, although fully prepared, the
operation was never attempted. So having failed in my
duty in the face of the infamous conduct of those upon
whom the fate of French Algeria, my native country, de-
pended, I deserved the death penalty, not once but twice.
I rely upon the justice of God.
> —Pierre Delhomme before the Military Tribunal on
> September 2, 1963, after the prosecutor demanded
> the death penalty[2]

These men rely not upon the state's justice but that of God or
history. They serve not the recognized state and the visible banner
but their own nation and their own device. They live with a fierce
intensity, all the more so because they often do not fear death but
await it. The two young men who shot and killed Lord Moyne
refused to shoot and kill a pursuing Egyptian policeman because
he was innocent. And so captured, they hanged. The pure assassins
take unimaginable risks, throw the bomb at their own feet, wait
for capture with the smoking pistol or the dripping knife. Death
at the supreme moment is a matter of indifference. Alexander
Mikhailov of the People's Will wrote, "Who does not fear death is
almost omnipotent."[3] And at the end he could thus feel that
"From my earliest youth a lucky star has shone over my head."[4]
These, the endowed gunmen, the righteous bombers, could grasp
only stark alternatives—Liberty or Death; they were possessed of
tunnel vision, gripped by an ideal that encouraged audacity, sacrifice, and violence. For the planners, who often shared the same
characteristics but had other responsibilities, such players were
invaluable revolutionary weapons. Some of the assassins, obviously, have been less than ideal, such as the mixed bag that killed
Gandhi; those who enjoy their vocation, who kill for pleasure and
not the cause, are the most dangerous and unsavory of all. These
have been rare, for no revolutionary organization wants those who

can be hired by blood or money, and few are tolerated for long. The plotters want instead the pure in heart, who at vast personal risk will perform as scheduled, as logic demands.

THE LOGIC: THE METHOD BEHIND THE DEED

> We have said a hundred times or more that when modern revolutionaries carry out actions, what is important is not solely their actions themselves but also the propagandist effect they are able to achieve . . . action as propaganda.
> —John Most

If there is an internal logical process in the mind of the assassin, from a distance there is also, for the uninvolved, a logic in the deed no matter what the killers intended, no matter how they arrived at their decision. At times the analysis would be identical. Clearly the attempt to kill Hitler in July 1944 was a logical analysis of the existing conditions and the aspirations of the planners. They knew *why* they were killing Hitler, and so do we. What was not so obvious from afar was the conspirators' refusal to follow where the logic of assassination indicated—a ruthless, brutal seizure of power. The generals were not revolutionaries but soldiers. Any one of them could have acted as the ideal assassin, and many sought to, but almost no one wanted to be responsible for "illicit" insurrection even against monsters. The single righteous assassin who kills the tyrant or punishes the wicked is in the grip of an easily understood obsession complete with internal logic. We can understand the anguish and frustration that possessed Vera Zasulich to shoot General Trepov, and the deed did punish if not intimidate. There is a self-contained logic to such discrete events —the tyrant is at least dead—that tends to erode when a revolutionary campaign begins. Despite the almost continuous ideological disputation of the People's Will on the necessity of assassination, from afar their audacity could more logically be seen as criminal optimism. Some provocative deeds, however, despite the subsequent denial by the threatened, do appear to have a logical consistency—the results reflect the intention; the murder option was quite rational and quite effective.

In the summer of 1948, for example, with the state of Israel established and a United Nations truce in force, LEHI was running out of a mission. The campaign that had begun with the assassination of Lord Moyne in Cairo in 1944 had ended for the High Command not in triumph but despair. There was no greater Israel but only a tiny remnant. Their Zionist enemy David Ben-Gurion was in power. There was no move to seize more of the promised land, to unite Jerusalem, to act on events. Their own LEHI volunteers were going into the new armed forces of the state. And even that "state," they felt, was a clear and present danger to the Zionist dream, too cautious, too likely to accept a *diktat* peace at the hands of the great powers or the United Nations. They trusted no one, neither the United Nations nor the great powers nor Ben-Gurion. And yet they could do nothing. LEHI was once again a small band of fanatics, operating only in Jerusalem, a city still with an uncertain future. Increasingly over the summer the LEHI High Command concentrated on the greatest threat to the Zionist future—an imposed United Nations "solution" drafted by the old enemy, Great Britain. The new United Nations Mediator, Count Folke Bernadotte, whom they felt had a dubious background of dealing with Nazi Germany, was a tool, wittingly or unwittingly, of the enemies of Israel. Frustrated by their own impotence, by the direction of events, by the decay of the organization, fearful that time had passed them by, the LEHI High Command decided that their target would be Bernadotte—symbol of an imposed peace, author of a plan that only he could effect, tool of Britain.

In the summer of 1948, to others such an analysis would appear skewed; but there was a certain logic in many of the assumptions. Everyone foresaw a "solution," for not even the most pessimistic could imagine three decades of no-peace punctuated with war. Most assumed that, having authorized the establishment of Israel, the United Nations would oversee such a solution. The United Nations Mediator Bernadotte would, therefore, play the crucial role. And Bernadotte felt that the most important factor was not the desires of the Arabs and Jews but those of the great powers—

and the great power with the most interest in the Middle East was Britain. His plan, then, was not quite evenhanded, and, most important, ignored the intense determination of every Israeli to see that Jerusalem, the golden city, was *not* internationalized. His plan then would be unacceptable to Ben-Gurion as well as LEHI, but what was to be done?

On September 17, 1948, in Jerusalem, a LEHI squad killed Bernadotte. The world was horrified. The Israeli government was stunned, fearful of international retaliation. LEHI members were rounded up, the leadership taken off to prison. And then, nothing. Bernadotte was dead and so was the Bernadotte Plan. The United Nations did nothing—and never again would Israel assume that the UN was a benign organization or, more important, an effective one. No one, in fact, did anything. That autumn the boundaries of Israel were rounded out by force and the neighboring Arab states driven to the truce table when Israeli armor moved into the Sinai. The 1948 boundaries would be defended by force and extended by force by "cautious" Ben-Gurion and his successors. LEHI had made their point, pushed history. And what if they had not? Perhaps, almost probably, the same events would have occurred at a slower speed. No one was going to impose the Bernadotte Plan— a fact not as obvious in September 1948 as it was later. No Israeli government was going to give up Jerusalem or take for the state less land than had been allotted. The concern and anguish over international opinion and United Nations pressure might have worried the cabinet without the Bernadotte experience; but again no Israeli government was going to compromise the security of the state except as a result of unbearable pressure. Inside LEHI the murder of Bernadotte seemed logical—ignoring the quite personal anxiety to act upon events before it was too late; from a distance it was also a logical deed, not completely unexpected and not without consequences foreseen by those who ordered it.

The assassination of Bernadotte is amenable to analysis partly because it was a single deed ordered by men who have subsequently explained their intentions, and partly because those intentions can be adjusted to subsequent events. When murder becomes less discrete, a chain of deaths in a campaign of assassination haltingly directed by those who are less introspective, producing an effect too contemporary to parse exactly, the logic of the process seems vague. It is possible to analyze the logic of assassination by the People's Will with some rigor, although often with differing conclusions; but the deeds of Black September, for example, often seem, especially to the West, inherently illogical—self-defeating brutality by hysterical, irrational fanatics. Yet this is not really the case. There is a clearly definable logic in the campaign of Black September and the other Palestinian fedayeen.

Of all contemporary revolutionary movements, the Palestinians have been the most spectacular, the most inventive, and the most ruthless. This has not been by choice but by necessity. Until the mid-sixties, Palestinian leaders, largely in exile, had counted on conventional Arab regimes and armies to win back their homeland. Seemingly they had no other options, despite past betrayals —King Hussein ruled over the annexed West Bank—and past incompetence: the Egyptian debacle of 1956, military disaster, political triumph. A few lost patience, and, encouraged by the growing revolutionary prestige of guerrilla war, founded Al Fatah. Between 1965 and 1967 a series of small, not especially effective commando-guerrilla raids were launched from the West Bank and Syria into Israel. It was a logical, if ineffectual, revolutionary strategy criticized by the Arab Left as ideological posturing and by Arab governments as unnecessarily provocative. Then, after the sweeping Israeli victories of June 1967, the Left appeared to be posturing, and the Arab governments and their conventional armies had provoked their own destruction. The only way was the way of the guerrilla, and the various fedayeen organizations became the new Arab heroes. By 1968–1969, the fedayeen were a media sensation, a new political force in the Arab world, but operationally a disaster. There were no effective organizations in the occupied territories, much less Israel; guerrilla operations had become commando raids into almost certain ambush; and the various fedayeen groups splintered, quarreled, and issued grandiose competing communiqués about triumphs invisible to the alien eye. With limited forces on the ground, one of the more militant splinters, the Popular Front for the Liberation of Palestine, inaugurated airplane hijacking in July 1968. It was the first tactical step away from the fashionable, but futile guerrilla strategy into spectacular revolutionary deeds against soft targets.

In September 1970, the Popular Front simultaneously hijacked a Pan Am 747, a Swissair DC-8, and a TWA 707, and missed capturing an El Al flight. The Pan Am 747 was destroyed on the runway at Cairo and the other two planes, joined three days later by a BOAC VC-10, were held on an old, unused British airfield outside Amman, Jordan. Hussein and his government, long concerned about their provocative role as host to the guerrillas who had set up a state-within-a-state, ordered the Arab Legion to clear out the fedayeen. The airliners were blown up, the hostages were taken into refugee camps and later freed, and the Arab Legion wiped out the fedayeen. The Syrians dithered and then did not intervene. For the fedayeen these days of September meant that operations out of Jordan into the occupied zone were finished, that their patron Syria would keep them on still tighter rein, and that the prospect of Lebanon as a base was possible but not pleasing. The one, true, inevitable revolutionary strategy of guerrilla war was no longer possible, and no longer possible because of the intervention of Jordan.

The more militant military and intelligence leaders in Al Fatah, in conjunction with members of other groups, formed a new and shadowy organization—Black September. They adopted the tactics of spectacular violence and re-ordered revolutionary priorities. Clearly *something* had to be done. The way of the guerrilla had been closed off, had actually failed well before September 1970, although no one wanted to admit this. The prime architects of this disaster had been Arabs, and they would be the prime targets. The first to be punished was the Jordanian Premier Wasfid Tal, shot down and killed in the lobby of the Sheraton Hotel in Cairo. One of the assassins stooped down to lick the dying man's blood. The West was horrified, and the horrors had barely begun: the Lod massacre, the Munich massacre, the Khartoum massacre. If there was no justice for Palestine, there would be no peace in the world. It was a simple message dispatched by the brutal means of leaving the sprawled and bloody bodies of innocent tourists scattered on airport floors. A campaign was waged against the allies of Zionism—TWA or Pan Am—and against those who betrayed the cause of Palestine—Jordanian Ambassador Zaid al-

Rifai, shot and wounded in Kensington, and never-ending plots and attempts focused on King Hussein. A few of the targets, the Jordanians especially, were chosen as individuals to be punished for past errors, a logical and congenial policy hardly novel to Arab assassins. Most of the "targets," however, were groups, anyone boarding a flight to Israeli, or Israeli agents. These category-victims (the target was always world opinion, Arab leaders, and their own militants) could be slotted more easily into an international terrorist campaign than a special assassination campaign, such as that of the People's Will. Even at Khartoum, where the three senior diplomats were killed, the victims were chosen because they were vulnerable, because of their nationality, and because of the location of the operation, rather than because of their specific identity. The primary focus of fedayeen operations for the years after Black September was on spectaculars of horror rather than specific, discrete murder. They felt that they had no option if Palestine were not to be forgotten. They had little chance of striking often or directly at Israel or killing specific enemies, but they could horrify the world to Palestinian advantage. This was a perfectly logical conclusion, given their eroded assets in 1970, their continuing determination, and their opponents' strength. Thus, before 1970, no fedayeen leader was interested in assassinating Moshe Dayan, because this would be terrorism, not revolutionary guerrilla war. After 1970 the technicalities of assassinating Moshe Dayan were insurmountable, so the only option was spectacular terrorism, intensified from time to time with assassinations of the specifically guilty.

THE VICTIM-TARGET: THE ROLE AT THE END OF A GUN BARREL

I'm me.
—Malcolm X, on why anyone would want to kill him

For most assassins in or out of a conspiracy, the chosen victim appears obviously guilty, obviously a revolutionary target. Some few victims are truly symbolic, without political pretensions: the Spanish poet Federico Garcia Lorca, a people's artist, or actress-singer Thanh Nga, murdered recently in Ho Chi Minh City by "reactionaries." Anyone familiar with the recent Mideast could have made out a target list for the fedayeen by factoring in accessibility. The Jordanian victims of Black September, however, were hardly the *ideal* victims; rather, they were officials who could be punished for past acts, personally replaceable, whose death would be unlikely to intimidate Jordanian policy. Certainly regular attempts against Hussein had wrought no policy shifts. Most victims, then, are easily replaceable—history is changed only insofar as another member of the elite sits in the president's chair, the triumphant gunman or El Supremo's son. But certain victim-targets are not easily replaceable and/or their death guarantees a transformation of the existing political structure. In 1944 Lord Moyne could be and was replaced, but his death had let the Palestinian genie out of the lamp and Britain could no longer act with impunity. In 1939 or 1944 the assassination of Hitler, quite irreplaceable, would have most assuredly given history a push and transformed the German scene, although perhaps ultimately only accelerating events. So if history is to be changed—the ultimate aim of an assassination conspiracy—the victim must be irreplaceable or his position endowed with a symbolic significance that, once damaged, is equally irreplaceable.

There have always been many targets who cannot be replaced, charismatic leaders who become the embodiment of national or world aspirations: Nkrumah in Africa, Nasser in the Middle East, Gandhi in India, Mao and Stalin and Hitler and Perón. These were special people, the source of authority, messiahs in political roles crafted through their own sense of destiny, their own magnified image, their own cult of personality. While the leader is alive almost all is tolerated, almost to the end: Nkrumah, corrupt and arrogant, was deposed only after years of misrule; Nasser was forgiven for the debacle of 1967, engendering a frenzy of grief by the millions on his death in 1970; Gandhi's personal foibles and convoluted nonviolence were easily ignored in India's conscience. The massacres and murders, purges, battlefield defeats, and chaotic domestic policies of Mao and Stalin and Hitler, the corruption and incompetence of Perón, were evaded, forgiven, excused. No one could really replace them—no one really wants to, after their hectic and intense period of domination. Even Perón, on his return to Argentina, found he could not go home again with charisma intact; time had eroded his special quality and he was simply another politician, still corrupt, still incompetent, but no longer the embodiment of the future. Each, as the steady patina of awe builds up around his person, increasingly becomes a prospective target for murder, an irreplaceable victim. Mao did not rule China but became China. Recognizing the process and evading the implications of vulnerability, lesser men seek such a role—Mobutu in the Congo and Amin in Uganda and Duvalier in Haiti—but they represent absolute power, not the nation or the cause incarnate. In time, of course, the nation or the cause may move on organically without the great leader, may move on more effectively with the charisma entombed—Maoist China without Mao—or, in fact, the system no longer depends solely on the leader, has been institutionalized to the point that the murder of the target would change as little as would a natural death. The special target allure erodes. Murder will not hurry history, only benefit the career of a successor.

Some of the great victims in recent times have seemingly possessed all the ideal target characteristics, charismatic, irreplaceable, maximum leaders in the process of transforming the nation and the world. In this century one of the great magnets for a variety of assassins was Mussolini, often a target but not a victim until the last days of the war. In keeping with his flamboyant and bombastic character, which masked brutal political cunning, the attempts tended to reflect the man. On November 4, 1925, in the second plot that year, the prospective assassin, the former Socialist deputy Tito Zaniboni, was lured into position. Mussolini's valet, Quinto Navarra, was instructed to appear on the balcony of Piazzo Chigi just as Il Duce was scheduled to appear. Zaniboni was immediately arrested across the way in the Hotel Dragoni with a rifle mounted with a telescopic sight. A series of laws regulating potential opposition were swiftly promulgated: advantage Mussolini's.

On April 7, 1926, when Mussolini opened the International Convention of Surgeons, he was approached by the Honorable Violet Gibson, a sixty-two-year-old half-mad Irish mystic, who fired at him. The pistol shot clipped his nose. The lady was hustled away, Mussolini's nose was repaired, and he appeared bandaged to give his scheduled speech, "If I advance, follow me, if I retreat, kill me, if I die, avenge me."[5] High drama laced with a touch of gallantry —the lady was expelled: advantage Mussolini's. On September 11, 1926, his limousine passed the Porta Pia in Rome at ten in the morning, seconds before the bomb of Gino Lucetti, an anarchist marble worker, exploded, wounding four people. A month later, on October 11, there was a closer call in Bologna while he was riding in an open car. A single pistol bullet cut through his Order of S.S. Maurice-et-Lazare, tearing his uniform across the chest. Fascist squadristis threw themselves on a fifteen-year-old boy, stabbed him, and threw him to the mob to dispatch. Not only was the boy—whose name was Zamtoni—probably not the assassin, but the affair was also either a put-up job or an intra-Fascist plot. As usual, Mussolini seized on a good thing, and the attempt was the pretext for the establishment of the Laws for the Defense of the State, including OVRA, Organization of Volunteers for the Repression of Anti-Fascism—the internal security police: advantage Mussolini's. Italy was rapidly becoming an authoritarian, closed society. Fascism was in the process of institutionalization— and at the very least assassination had become technically difficult even for the lone gunman. On May 29, 1931, Michele Schirru, an anarchist who had sailed from America to kill the tyrant, was arrested and swiftly executed without ever seeing Mussolini. On June 17, a young man named Angelo Shardellotto was arrested in Piazza Venezia, questioned until he admitted he intended to kill Mussolini, and shot.

The years of vulnerability then ended. Physically Mussolini was more secure; politically neither he nor the Fascist regime was as vulnerable—and his murder would no longer change everything. Italy had a brutal, efficient, authoritarian regime, a milieu that inhibited most potential assassins.

Some great victims do not have the advantages of the full repressive machinery of a totalitarian government, nor the benefits of an effective democratic system without a nationality problem. Perhaps the one great victim-target of the twentieth century was Charles de Gaulle, focus of at least thirty-one fully realized assassination attempts and dozens of aborted plots. Like Mussolini, he had luck.

The first attempt against his life was in Dakar in 1944, a typical punishment assassination by a lone gunman who blamed de Gaulle for the destruction of the French fleet at Mers-el-Kébir by the British. A fellow petty officer on the *Air France III* interrupted the attempt but did not reveal the fact until much later. Fourteen years later, in 1958, the Fourth Republic was on the edge of collapse and President René Coty turned to de Gaulle— "the most illustrious Frenchman"—accepting his terms of plenary powers without parliamentary control, suspension of parliament for a year, and his preparation of a new constitution. It was a mandate to create a system in his own image—the Fifth Republic—and to solve the single great crisis—Algeria. It was also the beginning of an era of French assassins who sought first to eliminate de Gaulle from the board and save French Algeria. Later, when the dream faded, they sought to punish him for his betrayal, and finally, at the end, they simply wanted to kill the target because such attempts had become almost institutionalized. From 1958 until 1964, France was an ideal milieu for the assassin. The Fifth Republic, the France of de Gaulle, had not been fully erected and certainly not fully accepted as legitimate, and the bounds of the nation had not been determined. Thousands would die futilely for a French Algeria. For those six years the plotting was almost constant, as one attempt after another was aborted, postponed, or discovered—or failed. Some of the plots were bizarre—to poison the Host at the village church in Colombey-les-Deux-Eglises; others were daring if inept—to crash a small plane into de Gaulle's helicopter, but without discovering which helicopter would be the right one.

The most famous attempt was an attack on de Gaulle's Citroën DS 19 limousine on August 22, 1962. An ambush site with a squad of gunmen had been set at the Paris suburb of Petit-

Clamart. When de Gaulle left the Elysee Palace, word was telephoned ahead. There were two motorcycle outriders and then de Gaulle's black Citroën. He and his wife were in the back seat; his son-in-law and *aide-de-camp* Colonel Alain de Boissieu was in the front, next to the military chauffeur, Marroux. A second Citroën followed with two security agents, Puissant and Djouher, the military doctor, Degas, and a driver. At 8:10 P.M., the convoy suddenly appeared out of the gray drizzle. There was barely time to open fire with the submachine guns as the limousine drove straight through without wavering. Inside there were the roar of the barrage and the clank of bullets tearing into the Citroën. From the front seat Boissieu shouted, "Father, get down!" De Gaulle wouldn't budge. Boissieu shouted again and reluctantly de Gaulle leaned forward a bit just as a stream of bullets scythed through behind his head. The firing stopped. The car kept on going. De Gaulle flicked away the glass fragments scattered on his coat. "What, again?"

And there would be others again and again, but none such a near thing until the last flicker in 1964 by a group of young people who mounted an attack on de Gaulle as much from a desire for adventure as from idealism. The attempt ended in farce with a mad, cinematic chase through the streets of Paris after a bungled robbery—they had explosives but no getaway money. Six years later, on November 9, 1970, de Gaulle would die quietly, sitting in an armchair watching a segment of the television serial "Nanou." By then the Fifth Republic was a reality, its founder retired, French Algeria a matter for historians, and the great target and almost-victim no longer personally acting on events. But during the crucial years between 1958 and 1964, in an ideal milieu for the assassins of redemption out of Africa, he was the Great Target whose elimination surely would have changed history, whose death had a compelling logic for his enemies. Then French Algeria was irrevocably lost and only revenge was left, a revenge with declining importance, a revenge cherished by fewer and fewer zealots—and in 1964 left to children mimicking their violent elders. Politically the time for murder had passed, and personally other priorities attracted. De Gaulle was safe to retire to Colombey-les-Deux-Eglises and watch television.

THE DEED: THE STRUCTURE OF MURDER

> What matter the victims provided the gesture is beautiful.
> —Lourent Tailhade

The actual attempt to kill the powerful is usually of only technical interest. Technically, of course, certain assassinations have a morbid fascination, from the plot to kill Oliver Cromwell with an early repeating pistol to the murder of the Bulgarian exile George Murkov in London in September 1978 with a poisoned pellet shot into his leg from a "cane-gun." Victims have been killed with darts, complex poisons, mysterious gases, all manner of exotic and bizarre weapons, more often to disguise the deed than to induce awe and horror. For the technicians, there is a search for a vulnerability and a means of access and escape, and some concern with the form of murder. Sometimes there is a deep concern that no one innocent will be killed, the actual attempt aborted because of the presence of a wife or a crowd of children; at other times there is no interest but murder—a bomb attack at Sofia Cathedral in Bulgaria killed 173 people. There are some idealistically pure, almost surgical assassinations. On February 2, 1905, the Social Revolutionary terrorist Ivan Kalayev postponed his attempt on the life of Grand Duke Sergei because the prince's wife and children were in the carriage. Two days later he repeated his attempt, threw his bomb, killed the prince—and then, although he believed assassination necessary, he immediately surrendered, for he also believed he should suffer the penalty of paying for the deed with his own life. Other Russian attempts, the bomb in the palace or the mine on the railway, were not as surgical, if not as bloody, as Sofia Cathedral.

The most effective deed is one that relates the techniques of murder to the strategy of the operation, not only killing the victim but doing so in such a way as to maximize the effect on the target.*

---

*Perhaps the most spectacular of recent assassinations in South Arabia occurred while the new National Front Government was trying to secure control of the

Most assassins, especially lone assassins, must focus only on being successful, getting close enough to act. Then, perhaps, there will be an opportunity for drama. John Wilkes Booth, leaping to the stage from the box containing the slumped and dying Lincoln, shouting *"Sic transit gloria!"* produced for once in his life real theater, if of the macabre. Yet the farcical machine-gun attack on Trotsky followed by the brutal ice ax wielded by an unappetizing automaton mattered little, for Trotsky was dead and, as far as Stalin was concerned, the last possible center of resistance was gone. Thus elaborately fashioned assassinations, the surrender to accept punishment, the protection of innocents, the use of an appropriate means at a special moment, poison at the coronation or the pistol at the reception, are marginal to the results—does the victim die? Rather, in a way, a brutal deed may have a greater impact than the niceties of execution by a paragon. The young Arab licking the spilled blood of Prime Minister Tal from his fingers may be intimidating to the enemies of Palestine; and, for those other targets, the uninformed, the impact is magnified: Why? And the answer to hand: No justice for us, no peace for you—look what injustice has made us.

up-country, where conservative sheikhs still raided out of Yemen and Saudi Arabia. The authorities in Aden arranged for a peace conference just on the border and invited the major dissident leaders, many of whom agreed to attend. On arrival they entered a huge tent, the floor covered with rugs, and the rugs with a splendid feast. After elaborate, if insincere, greetings and a beginning on the feast, the "communists" from Aden seemingly were simultaneously stricken with the necessity to relieve themselves. Once out of the tent, they dashed into the dunes to avoid the huge explosion that destroyed the tent, rugs, feast, and sheikhs. Subsequently the wife of the premier sheikh shaved her head, gave each of her warriors a single hair, and swore that when Aden was captured she would weave them into a wig. Alas, Aden remained uncaptured.

IMPACT: MURDER THAT MOLDS THE FUTURE

All changed, changed utterly . . .
—William Butler Yeats
Plus ça change, plus c'est la même chose.
—Les Guêpes

Every visible assassination attempt, successful or not, has *some* impact. At least the selected victim has been warned if not intimidated, at least the guardians of order cannot rest easy, at least the conspirators have offered witness to their aspirations. And often this is the only result—thirty-one attempts, and the most de Gaulle does is lean slightly forward. And equally often that violent witness produces swift and extensive repression, the conspiracy revealed, the plotters imprisoned, the future secure in the hands of the enemy. And failed assassinations, particularly a series of them, may well permit the regime to shore up its defenses, move more swiftly down the road the conspirators wanted to block, as was the case with Mussolini, and, to a degree, de Gaulle. On the other hand, a successful assassination may transform the nation— turning monarchist Iraq into a radical military republic or lighting a powder keg as Princip did at Sarajevo. At times, the deed produces almost exactly what the conspirators intended, as was the case with LEHI and Lord Moyne and Count Bernadotte, or seems to, as with the murder of Hassan al-Banna, which did, for the time being, inhibit the ambitions of the Moslem Brothers. Any assassination that intends to punish is a success on that tactical level if the victim dies; any assassination that intends to remove a piece from the board is a success if the victim dies. At times out of such deaths flow quite simple consequences: the king of Iraq gone, Abdul Karim Kassem in power (and himself first target and then victim of other assassins). At other times, incalculable consequences occur: would American political history have been greatly different if Huey Long had lived, if Abraham Lincoln had lived? Would a live, if elderly, Gandhi have made a difference after 1948? Surely, if Hitler had been killed in 1939, much would have been different. And he could have been. On November 10, 1939, a Swabian carpenter, Johann George Elser, failed in an attempt to set off a sophisticated homemade bomb when Hitler was in Munich. Elser was imprisoned and kept alive in a concentration camp until a grand trial could be held.* In fact, the list of missed targets in this century contains an incredible number of major figures: Hirohito, Nehru, Sukarno, Levi Eshkol, Konrad Adenauer, Chiang Kai-shek and Mao Tse-tung, Kaiser Wilhelm II and Adolf Hitler, Laval and Tojo and Victor Emmanuel, Nasser, Nkrumah, and Castro. Obviously, if each target had been a victim, no matter at what time or place, the seamless garment of history would have a different pattern.

In matters of political murder it is not the lucky living that count —what if? what if?—but the discernible impact of the dead. Again, at the very least, vengeance can be achieved and—perhaps—the objective situation changed. Even if one Somoza is replaced with another, the Nicaraguan situation is adjusted by previous example, if not by much and at the cost of a corpse. The new ruler, seemingly not different, one more Trujillo, may take a different course. The regime may change a little, be harsher or more lenient, less venal or more greedy, sometimes led by the conspirators but often by their opponents. However, real change, revolutionary change, the transformation of the nation as a result of a murder, is obviously rarer and more complex. The Mexican revolution began with a bloodless coup that ushered in the age of assassins. Hitler and Mussolini came to power within a faltering system quite legally. Lenin found power lying in the streets of Petrograd, not at the end of one gun barrel. Some, particularly in the democratic West where the act of political murder is considered aberrant, feel that "If one wishes to institute political change, whether revolutionary or incremental, particularly if one desires to witness that change, let him try some means other than assassination."[6] And yet where are the Iraq of King Faisal II and the empire of Francis Ferdinand, the fiefdom of Trujillo and the Plan of Bernadotte? True, most assassinations that succeed change the players, not the

---

*In the flurry of executions at the end of the war eliminating the imprisoned enemies of the Third Reich, Elser was killed on April 9, 1945.

game—but this is often the desired impact, at least to punish and at most to assume the dead man's power. True, great changes seldom can be traced to a single murder, but, as at Sarajevo, a single murder may have not inconsequential effect—at least giving history a push. A great many men have thought it worth the risk, and the surviving successful still do. For nearly two centuries there have been plenty of volunteers for the role of revolutionary assassin eager to strike at the heart of the state, convinced of the justice of their luminous vision. Whether greedy for power or pure in heart, they have suddenly appeared unannounced on the stage to rewrite the play and even now, even in the secure post-industrial world of the West—democratic, comfortable, sane, a product of consensus and long accommodations—they still appear, determined to change history, to make a revolutionary impact on events.

NOTES

1. Larry Collins and Dominique Lapierre, *Freedom at Midnight,* New York, Simon and Schuster, 1975, p. 459.

2. Pierre Demarte and Christian Plume, *Target de Gaulle,* New York, Dial, 1975, p. 36.

3. Avrahm Yarmolinsky, *Road to Revolution,* New York, Collier, 1971, p. 228.

4. *Ibid.*

5. Max Gallo, *Mussolini's Italy, Twenty Years of the Fascist Era,* New York, Macmillan, 1973, p. 200.

6. Murray Clark Havens, Carl Leiden, Karl M. Schmitt, *The Politics of Assassination,* Englewood Cliffs (New Jersey), Prentice-Hall, 1970, p. 154.

intermezzo II

i

Eldad fits exactly the popular conception of the fanatical assassin, although he never killed anyone. "What should I do with this?" he said, thrusting away a revolver given to him during a prison break. But he knew what others should do. As a leader of the Stern Group in Palestine after 1944, he articulated a mystical belief in a greater Israel, a Hebrew state that was the foreordained child of history, a Biblical gift. He was literally possessed of a revolutionary vision. With a doctorate from the University of Vienna, an expert on Schopenhauer was the *scholare engagé*. In the autumn of 1944, he had sent the two young volunteers into Egypt to kill Lord Moyne. Eldad continued the struggle in Palestine and at the end, after the state of Israel had been proclaimed, he still clung to his vision, his revolutionary dream. On his—and others'—orders on Friday, September 17, 1948, a dark, thin man of about thirty thrust a Schmeisser submachine gun through the window of a United Nations limousine and emptied the magazine into the UN Mediator Count Folke Bernadotte. Today Eldad lives in Jerusalem, a small, seemingly gentle man with a wispy mane of gray hair and a vision no less luminous. Surrounded by a small coterie of disciples, he argues and writes and propounds, defending the killings of the past, denying the rights of the Palestinians to do the same—"So I contradict myself. So I contradict myself."

ii

The Nagant 7.62 revolver used in the assassination of Lord Moyne had been used in the murder of Ibrahim Hassan el Karam in Jerusalem on November 14, 1937, the murder of another Arab whose name was not in the police files, the murder of Constable Caley on March 23, 1943, the murder of Inspector Green and Constable Ewer in Haifa on February 14, 1944, the murder of another constable in Tel Aviv on May 10, 1944, and the murder of Constable J. T. Wilkin on September 26, 1944.

"What, you don't think we would throw it away?"

iii

Israel was about to establish diplomatic relations with the Federal Republic of Germany—much too soon for a group of dissident Zionists living in Western Europe, who, making use of old smugglers' nets, arranged for a display of their disapproval. The Chancellor of Germany, Konrad Adenauer, Der Alte, was sent a splendid, elaborately bound presentation dictionary. The cautious postal clerks unwrapped the book. One ran his hands over the expensive leather binding and, unable to overcome his curiosity about the dedication, opened the cover. The book detonated with a bright flash and a heavy crunch in his hands.

iv

I. EXPLOSIVE

(a) 100 parts potassium chlorate, 20 parts urotropine. *Detonated by ordinary or electric detonator.*

(b) 96 parts potassium chlorate, 12 parts manganous peroxide (pyrolusite). *Detonated by ordinary or electric detonator.*

(c) 88 parts potassium chlorate, 12 parts vaseline. *Detonated by ordinary or electric detonator. A wick can also be used.*

(d) 78 parts potassium chlorate, 12 parts potassium nitrate, 6 parts sulphur, 4 parts carbon, 20 parts urotropine. *A first-class mixture. Detonated by ordinary or electric detonator.*

—Cypriot EOKA "Manual"

v

Ali entered the room, slowly pushing the drinks cart ahead of him. The lieutenant-colonel and his guests were clustered at the window overlooking the Crater district of Aden, the men resting from security duties as the Arab guerillas of NLF and FLOSSY competed with each other in their attacks on the British, the wives avoiding the thought of tomorrow. Ali paused. Underneath the top shelf, the NLF explosives expert had molded plastique and fitted a tiny time switch based on an adjusted stopwatch. All Ali had to do was flick the switch, push his drinks cart near the colonel, mention he had forgotten the ice, and walk out of the room. He would have sixty seconds. His colonel looked up. Ali felt under the shelf and flipped the switch. Instantly there was a heavy roar and an intense light. Ali and the cart were disintegrated as the cone of the explosive ripped upward instead of out. The stunned group of observers at the other end of the room were untouched other than by the sight of the black and twisted drinks cart, the shattered ceiling, and the charred bits and pieces that had been Ali.

vi

Now, when dealing with explosives it is necessary and vital that you adhere to safety precautions and that no matter how long you handle explosives—or how much explosives you handle, that you always treat them with the care and the respect that's due to them. Because you'll only make one mistake. You usually only make one mistake and that's usually a fatal mistake.
—Taped, March 1972, Provisional IRA training session in engineering in Ireland

vii

The lane was narrow and dark. The streetlights had been shot out years before and the security forces never entered the area except in strength, usually in armored personnel carriers. It was raining. The cobbles glistened with water and the two low lines of row houses seldom showed a light. There was a smell of coal smoke and cabbage and few sounds but the rain. The two men, both short with dirty raincoats, wool mufflers, and cloth caps, stood before one of the doors, the third from the corner. The man on the left knocked. There was a muffled sound inside and the clicking of two chains and the thunk of a bolt—they had been expected. The door was pulled inward and the light spilled out on the two. The one on the right held a Colt .45 in his gloved right hand, just above waist level, his left hand holding his right wrist. The man who had opened the door was too stunned to speak. His mouth was open. Behind him down the corridor was his wife, her face draining white, her mouth opening. There was the briefest pause. The man on the left glanced at the door. Number Six.

"God, no, this is Six."

The man on the right squeezed off two shots, the sounds coming almost together. The man in the door was driven back down the corridor, skidding and sliding to end smashed against the kitchen door, his chest already covered with blood. Standing over him, his wife still had not made a sound.

"God, *no,* it was Number *Five* we wanted. *On the other side!"*

viii

Despite nearly two years of bombs and shootings, the commander-in-chief of British forces in the Palestine Mandate did not take what his security advisors felt were completely adequate precautions. On this particular morning, he had left his office and was walking toward his car. Sometimes the car was parked a bit to the left, sometimes a bit to the right of the gate. Today, a bit to the left, a pleasant young woman had paused to tuck the pink blanket up around the baby in her large, English-style pram. She stood back and moved away quietly a few steps, just to the corner. The general turned slightly to the right, away from the carriage, toward the limousine as it drew in to the curb. The young woman stopped at the corner and glanced back. The general was at the door of the car, thirty feet from the pram, too far. Perhaps tomorrow he would be closer. She walked back, leaned over, and with a few seconds to spare, switched back the toggle, tucked the pink blanket firmly around the twenty pounds of explosives and the primer, and pushed the carriage off down the street. The general slid into his car and drove off.

ix

It resembles a .45 automatic, has a large telescopic sight above the barrel, is powered by electricity and is therefore virtually silent, and has a range of about 100 meters. The darts, called flechettes, can carry a poison, saxitoxin, which is instantly fatal. This lethal nerve toxin was derived from shellfish. Cobra venom could be used.

_____

The 180-laser-submachine gun fires a .22-caliber bullet from a drum magazine at the rate of 30 per second with a range of one mile; a silencer restricts the range to 400 yards. The weapon weighs ten pounds, and, in the "undercover" model without stock and/or a nine-inch barrel, is only slightly larger than a regular-issue .45 Colt revolver and can fit in a briefcase. The gun is equipped with a helium-neon gas laser which emits a pencil-thin beam of scarlet light that appears as a red circle on the target— if the red spot hits the target's eyes it is blinding but harmless. Once the spot is on target—a three-inch dot at two hundred yards —the gun can then be fired or not. On automatic the weapon can chop down a telephone pole, blast through sheets of steel, break cinder block, and penetrate the side of an automobile. Using the silenced model, if fired from inside a briefcase as the marksman pivoted in a circle, as many as two hundred people could be hit.

_____

The *Armbrust-300*, manufactured in Germany, is a short-range, disposable, anti-tank weapon. It is silent, with no muzzle flash, no rear blast, no smoke, no infrared signature. It can be fired from a small room or other confined space without detection.

A firearm pipe silencer can be manufactured from a length of galvanized pipe. It is filled with steel wool, which is used as a gas absorbent. If the exit hole at the muzzle end of the device is of the proper size and the quantity of steel wool is sufficient, the silencer can be effective. A barrel extension, wrapped in wire mesh screen and surrounded by a closed tube, acting as an expansion chamber, is sufficient to reduce the sound level up to thirty decibels. The best designs of private manufacture employ perforable plastic, rubber, cork, or leather discs along the bullet path in the device. These discs greatly restrict the gas flow, and, as a result, reduce the audible sound to a great degree.

The new multishot shoulder-fired, squirtless flamethrowers have no fire streams. The weapon fires a cartridge that ignites upon exposure to air or upon impact. It is extremely small and portable—27 inches in length and 35 inches with clip. Total weight: 26–27 pounds, compared with backpack flamethrowers weighing 50–80 pounds.

x

The Nicosia active service unit of EOKA decided to go ahead with a plan to assassinate Field Marshal Sir John Harding, governor-general of Cyprus, despite the concern of their commander, Colonel George Grivas, that they were not properly instructed on the use of time pencils. Grivas could not be reached in time, and the crucial inside man, the Governor's valet, Neofytos Sofocleus, feared that he might be dismissed from his position at any moment. The EOKA Nicosia section leader responsible, Yacovos Patatsos, decided to go ahead and activate the plan that had been hanging fire for months. Patatsos explained the bomb mechanism to Sofocleus—the principle was that if the room temperature remained at a constant 67 degrees, the bomb would explode twenty-four hours after the safety pin was removed. The bomb itself was flat, book-shaped, and less than two inches thick. On Monday morning, with the bomb taped to his stomach, Sofocleus cycled up to the gates of Government House. He passed the guards who knew him well. That night he went to bed and set his own alarm clock for 2:30 A.M. When the alarm went off, he awoke, removed the safety pin from the bomb, and went back to sleep. The device was now set to detonate twenty-four hours later, at 2:30 A.M. Wednesday. The next day while lunch was in progress, Sofocleus strapped on his bomb and went upstairs to clean Harding's room. He took the bomb out, raised Harding's mattress, and slipped the device under it. He then left the room, walked quietly downstairs and out the door, out of the yard, to the road where a car was waiting to take him to the mountains. That evening the Nicosia EOKA waited, listening at 2:30 A.M. Nothing. 2:40. Nothing. Nothing at all. Harding, like most Englishmen, insisted upon fresh air at night. He always threw open the window before retiring. The temperature plummeted. The fusing aborted. Turning back the mattress the next morning, the governor's batman found the device, which was detonated in the grounds of Government House.

xi

A multipurpose, tone-operated, either bi-stable or mono-stable twitcher is an integrated circuit device available commercially. With appropriate battery adjuncts, it can close a circuit up to three years after installation, permitting detonation of almost any variety of explosive device. For more immediate effect, small pocket alarms, made in Switzerland and generally available, marketed for motorists so that when one's parking meter runs out in sixty minutes or two hours the buzz will alert one, have proven effective. So, too, have off-the-shelf model aircraft radio-control equipment modified with a safety circuit so that neither intentional nor random signals will detonate the device. All of these are far superior to chain-store watches with the minute hand removed or gas lighter elements used in a circuit with detonating wire, or even the timers foraged from parking meters.

xii

In order to avoid the problem of mistaken identity, members of the Israeli *Mivtzan Elohim*, Wrath of God, an anti-fedayeen organization, removed the front of the target's telephone earpiece, planted a small shaped-charge with a tone-controlled detonator. When the target returned to his apartment with his girlfriend, a *Mivtzan Elohim* agent, familiar with his voice, put through a call. As soon as he answered and was recognized, the trigger-tone was beeped and the earpiece exploded, almost decapitating him. The girl was showered with blood but unharmed.

xiii

Place 280 grams of TNT and 350 steel ballbearings, pea size, into a metal case (length 13 cm.; width 8.5 cm.; height 6.9 cm.) with two magnetic holders on the top. Place the box and magnets directly to the underside of a parked car beneath the driver's seat. The detonator is connected by a nylon thread to a heavy round flat piece of lead of 700 grams, placed on the exhaust pipe so that the thread is stretched taut. When the motor starts, the exhaust pipe will begin to vibrate. The lead piece will fall off and pull the nylon thread, setting off the explosion. Since the metal case is wider at the top than at the bottom and the lid thinner than the sides and bottom plate, the main thrust of the explosion is directed straight upward at the driver's seat. (Instead of the mechanical thread-and-weight device, a radio-controlled detonator can be used.)

part III

THE THEORY AND PRACTICE OF REVOLUTIONARY ASSASSINATION

Voici le temps des assassins.

—Rimbaud

1

Ogro, Moro, Ewart-Biggs, and Schleyer: Murder in the Streets of Europe

Never Again Without a Gun.
—Motto of the Italian
Nuclei Armoti Proletari

The four young men began the tunnel out of No. 104 Claudio Coello Street in Madrid on December 7, 1973. They were members of a team of the Basque revolutionary organization *Euskadi Ta Askatasuna,* ETA, who had for a year been involved in planning Operation Ogro, the kidnapping of the Ogro, Admiral Luis Carrero Blanco, Francisco Franco's Number Two, who as premier would be responsible for fashioning a post-Franco regime. After nearly a year of investigation, the four had reluctantly decided that Carrero's security was too good, even though they knew his routine between his home and his attendance at mass at the Church of San Francisco de Borja, a Jesuit church on Serrano Street. Their remaining option was to kill him, but without danger to others. The *way* in which Carrero was killed would determine the impact of the deed. And the way the four had chosen was to tunnel out under the street and then dig a chamber that would be filled with explosives. When Carrero's car passed over the mine, guided into place by a double-parked car, the explosives would be detonated electrically from a distance. It was a complex project, perhaps unnecessarily so; and in their year of preparation and surveillance, the four had often shown themselves less than highly skilled professional revolutionaries. There had been adventures and robberies and productive but irrelevant arms raids, accidental shots and botched maneuvers. But on December 7, the adventures were over and the tunnel began.

The pickaxes from the Basque country were too large. One digger suffered from claustrophobia. The first shovelfuls of dirt taken from beyond the wall were permeated with escaped gas and sewage overflow. The tiny room began to stink. The tunnel crept out. The dirt began to pile up in garbage bags. There was a landslide. They found a technical manual in a bookstore but propping and piling seemed to be associated with large tunnels. They kept going, carrying their pistols so that if trapped, they had an alternative to asphyxiation. Work on the bomb chamber guaranteed regular intoxication by the gas fumes. Their skin was ashy green and greasy. They stank. The room stank. But in eight days it was done. On December 15, they rendezvoused with other ETA people bringing explosives from the Basque country. Eighty kilos were placed in the car trunk and brought back to Madrid.

There were fifty sausages of Goma Two, stolen from the Hernani Powder Magazine, and thirty kilos of weaker explosives. Rubber 2E-C (Gelamonite 1-D):

Ammonium nitrate	61.50%	Nitrocellulose	1.20%
Nitroglycerine/		Dinitrotoluene	7.00%
Nitroglycol	28.00%	Sawdust	2.30%

It is dark yellow with brown streaks, with a bitter almond smell and a noticeable discharge.

There were also two-hundred-meter rolls of cord for the detonators, both electric and ordinary. The explosives were placed in the seven-meter chamber, joined by the detonator cord that led back to the apartment, and then, forming an electric cable, the cord was stretched the length of Claudio Coello Street alongside the telephone wires. Then the cable dropped to street level. At the appropriate time, the split cable would be attached to an electric box hidden in a briefcase.

When given the signal that the Carrero Blanco car was over the mine, the man with the briefcase simply switched on the current and set off the explosion. It ought to work, but then none of the four had any experience in explosives. The operation was postponed until December 20 because Henry Kissinger was in Madrid and the area was swarming with police. The four used the time to see a film, *The Day of the Jackal.*

December 20 was a raw, cold winter day. At nine, Carrero Blanco left his house for mass. Within a few minutes he was in the Jesuit church. The ETA commando was in position. At 9:25 a young boy suddenly appeared and asked the man with the briefcase for matches. There was fumbling and confusion and at last matches. A minute of so later another boy made a request for a light. More fumbling. At 9:30 Carrero Blanco left the church and got in his Dodge Dart, license plate PMM 16.4L6, along with Police Inspector Don Juan Antonio Bueno Fernández and his driver, Don José Luis Pérez Mojeda. The Dodge pulled away from the church and moved down Serrana, a one-way street, and then slowed again. It came up opposite the double-parked ETA Austin. There was a muffled explosion and the Dodge seemed to be lifted straight up in a great gout of smoke. It was 9:36, and within minutes the ETA commando had disappeared—and so had the Dodge. The car had been tossed five stories into the air, ripping away the cornice of the Jesuit church and falling down inside the patio to crash on the rooftop of the terrace. There was an enormous hole in the middle of Claudio Coello Street, filled with water from ruptured mains. The escort car was a ruin, its three occupants injured. A taxi was smashed and twenty parked cars tossed about.

Monitored Police Broadcasts, December 20, 1973 (from *Operation Ogro: The Execution of Carrero Blanco,* New York, Quadrangle, 1975)

H-20 wants to find out what happened, what caused the explosion?

It was a gas explosion on Claudio Coello!

Good, H-20 has the message.

R-22. Can you tell us if the premier's car that went by here suffered any damage?

No, Nothing happened to the premier. There are five or six cars that have been damaged. Two badly. It appears that the wounded have been taken to Montesa Hospital . . . water is spilling over.

Has anything happened to the premier of the government? Yes or no? His car must have been in the vicinity. . . . They are trying to locate the president's car to make sure everything is normal.

R-20 over. Please see if you can inform us as to whether anything has happened to the premier's car.

No, got it, no I thought one car . . . but the escort car . . . not his. One of the traffic policemen told me his passed by already.

Can you find out if anything has happened to the premier's car?

We have no information. We will check on the wounded at Montesa . . .

Go over, go over to the premier's house in Hermanos Bécquer and find out if the president's car is in front of the door. Over 16.

We will check it out.

Yes, check it out. To see if anything has happened to the premier.

According to what they tell us, one car got directly hit and is on the roof of the church. The firemen are just coming down. Car had three occupants. Over K-20.

It seems that the car that rose, that the explosion sent to the roof . . . is the premier of the government's car! I can't yet confirm— it appears he is dead.

The car on the roof is the premier president's car! It appears that he is dead.

ETA Communique One

The Basque Socialist Revolutionary Organization for National Liberation, Euskadi Ta Askatasuna (E.T.A.), assumes responsibility for the act which today, Thursday, December 20, 1973, has produced the death of Mr. Luis Carrero Blanco, President of the current Spanish Government.

... Today the workers and people of Euskadi, of Spain, Catalonia and Galicia, the democratic, revolutionary and antifascist people of the world, find ourselves liberated from an important enemy. The struggle continues.

Onward with national liberation and socialism!

GORA EUSKADI ASKATUTA!!

GORA EUSKADI SOZIALISTA!!

Euskadi Ta Askatasuna E.T.A.

The assassination of Admiral Luis Carrero Blanco on December 20, 1973, by ETA was an almost classical example of contemporary practice. The Basque separatists, despite internal schisms and severe repression, had for years been waging an armed struggle, not only to free Euskadi but also to create a socialist state—"We are Basque socialists and nationalists." Those who felt that the time for political organization and agitation had come were regularly shed and new recruits attracted. The milieu for revolutionary violence in the sixties and early seventies was promising. A brutal, authoritarian, fascist state with few friends, Spain had an aging leader and a serious problem of succession; it was a fascist state led by men who could or would make no effort to accommodate Basque separatism and yet were unable to coerce nationalist opinion. ETA was actively supported by only a small proportion of the Basque population, yet was tolerated by nearly all, and its exploits were often regarded with admiration. The two rocks on which ETA was founded, then, were the deep nationalist spirit of the Basques and the equally firm refusal of Madrid—an arrogant and corrupt center—to make any concessions. The ETA struggle, however, had been waged largely in Euskadi with the usual tools and operations of such a struggle: armed raids, theft, arson, kidnapping, ambush, extortion, bombings, and of course murder, usually of members of categories—police or informers or the *Guardia Civile*—rather than prominent individuals. One of ETA's problems was that the struggle was isolated, even from Madrid, and certainly from the Western media. And even the murder of the prominent in Euskadi might only briefly enrage Madrid; and a prime purpose of any armed struggle is to cause trouble, to disrupt the easy life, to embarrass the regime, to provoke and to intimidate. And the extension of the struggle to Madrid—a bleeding out of the geographical milieu—was obviously the next step, and the means, spectacular assassination, was a relatively obvious option.

The leadership of ETA was a mix of plotters and players, as in many small contemporary groups there are often fewer actors than roles; but there was no difficulty in finding volunteers. First, the prisons were filled with ETA people; many had been ill-treated, and some had been killed before reaching prison. The Franco regime had no need to placate domestic opinion and no tradition of gentle democratic repression. There were, then, many within ETA who wanted their own back, wanted to strike a major blow at the system, wanted to kill the real masters instead of the puppet police, kill—always, of course, only as long as there was a proper ideological justification. Even the contingent and unforeseen had to be incorporated into the rationale for murder. Those four young men involved in the planning, then, were most typical; young, innocent at least of Madrid, absolutely dedicated to their revolution and their nation, absolutely assured of their right to kill for the ideal, comfortable with danger, cunning, ruthless, righteous assassins who were also amateurs at their trade. They wanted a pure deed, no innocents injured, an ideologically sound murder, and the logic of the operation appeared obvious.

In 1973 it was clear to everyone, perhaps even to Franco, that Spain was in the twilight of the Franco era. The Generalissimo was old, tired, aging; his grasp was slipping, like it or not. If the existing institutions were to be preserved, if those who benefited from the corporate state were to continue to do so, and if the centrifugal forces of revolution, separatism, secularism, and latent anarchy were not to be unleashed, there would have to be a careful, planned transition. There would be the monarchy, of course; but Franco had ruled by balancing a variety of groups, military, religious, social, political, relying on old loyalists who were dying out. The obvious candidate to begin the structure of the future was the new Ogro, Premier Luis Carrero Blanco. While the prime symbolic target would certainly have been Francisco Franco, the new premier might even return more political advantages. Franco was going to die relatively soon—and the problems of access for Basque provincials were insurmountable.

If ETA were to strike back at the state's brutality, why not logically strike at the heart of the state—Ogro. The victim might be nearly irreplaceable, and other targets would be hit—the ruling elite would be intimidated and disorganized, the Basque people encouraged, the Spanish educated, and the attention of the West attracted. Some of this reasonable logic was strung out after the assassination because, as is so often the case in revolutionary deeds, the realization of the possibility rather than a carefully reasoned plot attracts attention. LEHI did pick out Lord Moyne and Count Bernadotte before the prospect of access could be investigated; but ETA first learned that the premier followed a routine in attending mass. He immediately was vulnerable, perhaps to kidnapping, the first choice, but then surely to murder, the second. Even without this snippet of information, the logic of extending the campaign to Madrid and the need for a major victim were matters of discussion.

Once the discussion went into specifics of killing Ogro, the four men charged with the deed wanted to make the murder spectacular. They certainly made it most complex, and put themselves at risk over and over. To begin with, they knew nothing of their trade, and were dedicated, determined, and untrained. They wandered about losing their guns—guns which they need not have carried—becoming involved in armed operations irrelevant to their task, and finally selecting a means to murder that required skills they did not have and would put the whole affair open to discovery—if the double-parked car needed to force the limousine over the tunnel-bomb had been a car-bomb detonated by radio, there need not have been a tunnel nor innocents put in jeopardy. In any case, all the compensating errors worked out, the premier was killed, and the size of the crater and the car tossed in the air were spectacular. And the assassins had escaped.

Spanish security forces made a concentrated effort to avenge the premier's death, even—rather quickly—seeking out ETA leaders abroad. For example, on December 21, 1978, José Miquel Peñoran—"Argola"—a twenty-eight-year-old "suspect," was killed in the southern French town of Anglet when he pushed down the accelerator of his automobile and detonated a bomb.

The impact for ETA and for Spain was real but, as always, difficult to judge. The advocates of the operation were delighted: the premier proved irreplaceable, and Franco faded and died in November 1975, and with him the system. A new Spain began to emerge. Those less enthusiastic about the results of murder feel that such change was inevitable, that both King Juan Carlos and progressive forces under Premier Adolfo Suárez had simply waited until Franco was gone in order to move Spain toward Western democracy. If the Ogro had lived, he would have been irrelevant. The old system might have been punished for excesses against the Basques, but it had not been killed with one bomb. More to the point for ETA, the new Spain, free, democratic, compassionate, the repressive security forces dismantled, the old oppression gone, held few charms. Spain was Spain and Euskadi was still oppressed. In a real sense a new democratic Spanish government that offered concessions to the Basques was a greater danger than the old discredited Fascist regime: damn your concessions, we want our country.

The result has been that the military militants of ETA have refused to accept accommodations offered by Madrid and have continued their armed struggle of direct action, action that includes murder. Between June 15, 1977, when the first free elections in forty-one years for the Cortes took place, and the following July—the year of democracy—ETA killed twenty-five people, mostly police, but also two army officers in Madrid. It is no longer clear that it is logical for ETA to strike at the heart of the state in Madrid, but there is no indication that the campaign of national liberation will be abandoned—rather the reverse—nor that its local support is eroding, nor that the central government will concede absolute independence. Madrid may, of course, concede enough on the national issue to isolate ETA, whose revolutionary political program has little support in the conservative Basque provinces. At the moment ETA soldiers on, in an atmosphere of turmoil and uncertainty, determined on the salvation of the nation through direct action.

Although ETA's separatist campaign has been the most violent and, after Operation Ogro, one of the most visible, the problem of submerged nationalities and dissident ethnic groups is a very real one in Europe, in the United States with the Puerto Ricans, and in Canada with Quebec. Nearly all of the separatists share certain basic assumptions: (1) the direction of events is toward an homogenized culture: Frenchmen working in Holland wearing Italian shoes, driving German cars, speaking to their colleagues in English, and returning home to watch American programs on Japanese television sets; (2) the certain losers in this centralized society, with bounds determined by the iron laws of economics, will be those in the periphery, the outlands, the islands, and marginal rural areas, where the population will be sucked away into the Saar or the Midlands, and the unprofitable farms purchased as summer retreats; (3) the pace of this trend is sufficiently swift and so far advanced that the culture and language of the small minorities are being destroyed, the young are deserters, the old ways are no longer of pragmatic use, the hidden nation is eager to be absorbed in the new system. Thus something must be done, and done swiftly. A great many of those in such a nation-culture will support, and all tolerate, those differences that appear to have practical advantage, such as local color for tourists, or engender special pride, such as kilts or hurley or a private language. This base of the pyramid supports those who want greater regional power, special aid for the language, federalism, and who establish nationalist parties or refuse to plead in court in the language of the oppressor. Then come the separatists, who see no solution but independence, perhaps in a European federation, perhaps as a completely free nation. The pyramid has narrowed greatly, and most separatists seek change by political means—parliamentary politics, agitation, civil disobedience. A few go further and opt for symbolic bombing directed by a liberation front, and, finally frustrated, a few choose direct action, the national liberation struggle. Most of the last lot, the tiny minority of militants, rise from the revolutionary Left, although not always. In the South Tyrol during the bombing campaign—an irredentist struggle to unite the German-speakers in Italy with their colleagues in Austria—the language was of the Right, as has been the case with the similar Alsatian Autonomist Movement, whose speakers employ the language of anti-Semitism as well as German nationalism. The basis of most separatist movements, regardless of the language of the Left, is the plinth of nationalism.

The number of linguistic or ethnic minorities scattered about Europe is impressive. Some nations are stitched together from two or more diverse groups, such as Belgium, with its Flemings and Waloons; others are like Spain, which contains a variety of "nations," ranging from the Basques—with an ancient and unique language unrelated to any other, and a history of cultural separatism—through the Catalans, with a romance language of their own, on to the small, distant, obscure different regions. Modern Spanish history has been a mix of long periods of centralized authoritarian control, interrupted by periods of centrifugal chaos that permit peripheral freedom. In France there have been increasing tides running against the center—languages to be saved or economic deprivation to be corrected or an almost forgotten culture to be revived. In at least two cases, Brittany and Corsica, the agitation has reached the stage of symbolic bombing. In the first case, a variety of militants have been involved since the mid-sixties with a sporadic series of bombings, mainly in Brittany, but very few indeed seem ready to kill for a Breton Republic. In the case of Corsica, the campaign began as much as a protest against neglect—a few bombs to attract the attention of Paris—as a separatist movement; but by the summer of 1978 the campaign had accelerated—thirty-three bombs on a single day—and appetites were whetted. In all these campaigns the movement, however halting, is toward a milieu that would encourage revolutionary violence and concurrently assassination. The border can be crossed without planning—a guard killed in a prison escape, a policeman shot at a roadblock. And once a murder is factored into the situation, another comes more easily; and the attraction of killing at the center, striking at the heart of the state, often seems obvious and logical. Thus, besides being arenas for international operations and transnational terrorists, many Western states could be threatened by their own gunmen of redemption seeking to build new nations by dismantling the old forms.

Of all the submerged nations, Poland included, Ireland has seen the longest struggle to achieve absolute freedom. Many Irish nationalists insist that the fight began when the Normans were invited into the country and London sought to impose control on the Celtic island. After that, there were centuries of invasion and absorption, rebellion and repression, imposed settlers and armed rising—and, of course, long periods of prosperity and accommodation. Modern Irish revolutionary history, however, begins with a confluence: (1) the ideas of the French Revolution; (2) the historical forces of Irish nationalism; and (3) the effort of Britain to rule directly without the existence of a Dublin parliament. There followed a litany of revolt: 1798, 1802, 1848, the Fenians, the Invincibles, boycotts and bombs, the Irish Republican Brotherhood, and even an invasion of Canada—and at last the blood sacrifice of the Easter Rising in 1916 and the Tan War of 1918–1921, culminating in the Irish Free State in twenty-six of the thirty-two counties. Although some thought the battle half won, for militant Irish Republicans the battle had just begun. They saw the Free State as a British pawn and the six-county Province of Northern Ireland, fashioned around the two-to-one Protestant majority of loyal Unionists, as an artificial enclave. In 1938–1939 the Irish Republican Army carried out a futile bombing campaign in England, withdrew to organize, and between 1955 and 1962 launched a very low-intensity guerrilla campaign in Northern Ireland. In neither the bombing campaign nor the Northern campaign did the IRA really employ specific murder, assassination, as a weapon—although such an operation was hardly alien to Irish tradition.

In point of fact, almost no variant of violence had lacked advocates in Irish history, and the generations of revolt were sprinkled with assassins. Some were singular and spectacular, such as the Phoenix Park murders in Dublin, when the secret Invincible Society stabbed and killed Lord Cavendish and his Permanent Secretary Thomas Henry Burke on May 6, 1882. Others were of a lesser category—as when British intelligence agents were killed during the Tan War—or of more import, as when the British military commander Lord French escaped a road ambush and the chief of the Imperial General Staff was shot and killed in front of his door in London. Within the Irish Free State, the Minister of Justice Kevin O'Higgins, blamed by many for the judicial executions that occurred during the IRA–Free State War, was shot down and killed in a Dublin suburb in 1927. Yet the IRA Army Council in the bombing campaign and their successors in the Northern campaign never seriously considered assassination—although one chief of staff, Tom Barry, proposed machine-gunning members in the House of Commons instead of setting off infernal devices in mailboxes. Then, in 1968–1969, the civil disturbances in the North and the vulnerability of Northern Catholics revived the IRA, to the extent that a split occurred between the more political Officials and the more traditional Provisionals (Provos); there were two secret armies pursuing the Republican dream of a single united Ireland achieved by physical force.

As far as Northern Ireland was concerned, since 1921 there had been a potential for political violence instigated by the Republicans or by militant Protestants provoked by imagined grievances or simple spite. For a century there had been examples of the latter, Protestant pogroms; but Republicans were more cautious— they were based in practice, if not in theory, on the Catholics, who were in the minority. During the 1955–1962 guerrilla campaign the flashpoint of Belfast had been avoided. In 1968– 1969, however, matters had changed. The Nationalist population, led by a new young generation of university students, was willing to risk a challenge to the institutionalized injustices of the provincial Stormont regime. The Protestant militants, not unexpectedly, had assumed that civil rights was a code word for united Ireland and rioted. Civil order collapsed—a police state with too few police. The army was sent in and stayed in the province, unable to impose order, and gradually becoming alienated from the Nationalist population. The Provos, increasingly seen as Catholic Defenders, exploited the situation with a cunning blend of provocation and guile and began their campaign. In uneasy alliance with other Republican secret armies, the Provos employed a classic mix of urban and rural actions, which the leadership in the Army Council saw as essentially a military campaign combining attacks on the security forces with the bombing of commercial targets. Although the Official IRA undertook one—flawed—assassination attempt, the Provos saw no need to do so until their campaign peaked late in 1972. When they ran into difficulties in the North, they began bombing in England as a form of escalation. There control was more difficult, and an active service unit of four, in an ill-advised move, killed Professor Gordon Hamilton-Farly by mistake and then shot and killed Ross McWhirter, who had offered a reward for information about IRA bombers—felon setting, in Irish terms. In the North there were scattered attempts on specific, symbolic foes —foreign managers of plants or those connected with the judiciary —but assuredly not a campaign of assassination or the selection of a target-victim of note. The Protestant-Loyalist paramilitaries could not reach their avowed Republican foes and were content with the random murder of Catholics—and each other—in internecine feuds. On the Republican side, similar feuds developed between the Provos and the Official IRA, and then between Seamus Costello's break-away Irish Republican Socialist Party and the Official IRA that killed more Republican volunteers than had the loyalist paramilitaries. The Provos soldiered on, however, their campaign of ambush-and-bombing interrupted by truces, waxing and waning according to repression and political shifts. Yet between 1969 and 1976, with over 1,500 killed, bombs in England and the Irish Republic, thousands arrested, the centers of Derry and Belfast blown down, large areas of the countryside turned into bandit zones, and no end in sight, there still had been nothing to equal the Ogro Operation.

On the morning of July 21, 1976, Ambassador Christopher Ewart-Biggs prepared to drive from his residence in the Dublin suburb of Sandyford to the Embassy in Merrion Square with Brian Cubbon, the Permanent Under-Secretary of the Northern Ireland

Office, who was down from Belfast conferring. Ewart-Biggs was new to Dublin, and a striking choice. He had lost his right eye in the Battle of Alamein and wore a black-tinted monocle. He looked and sounded like an eccentric squire. He had written thrillers banned by the Irish censors, been threatened by the OAS during the Algerian troubles, and served in posts from the Middle East to Paris. Ireland was his first ambassadorial posting, and many thought this indicated that the British Foreign Office wanted to upgrade Dublin by appointing a substantive instead of social ambassador. Although the Irish newspapers tended to characterize him as a cross between Bertie Wooster and Colonel Blimp, his colleagues thought he was an exemplary taskmaster, a keen negotiator, and an enlightened friend. It soon became clear in Dublin —a very small city—that he was exceptionally well briefed about Irish matters; so much so that the more suspicious, including the perpetually suspicious Republicans, felt his brief was more than diplomatic. The presence of Cubbon from Belfast certainly indicated that the new ambassador was going to be more than a social cipher.

After breakfast Ewart-Biggs and Cubbon came outside—it was a sunny summer day—and got into the 4.2-litre Jaguar. The ambassador was on the left side of the back seat, Cubbon on the right. In the front Judith Cooke, Cubbon's private secretary, sat on the left of the driver, Brian O'Driscoll. The Jaguar turned left out of the grounds of Glencairn onto the Murphystown Road, followed by an escort car of the Irish Special Branch. A few hundred yards from the residence, the Jaguar passed over a culvert stuffed with over two hundred pounds of commercial gelignite. The road-mine was triggered by an electric detonator operated from bushes one hundred and fifty yards away. There was a tremendous roar and a bright flash. The Jaguar was tossed into the air, flipped over, and crashed back into the smoking crater. The left side hit first, crushing Judith Cooke and Ewart-Biggs. She died instantly with a fractured skull and broken ribs. He, with his neck broken and sternum smashed, was dying by the time the detectives from the escort car could reach the crater. Unlike the Operation Orgo blast, most of the force of the explosion had gone out the sides of the culvert, but there had been enough lifting power to toss the Jaguar over on the left side—O'Driscoll and Cubbon were injured, but would re-cover.

Two men carrying FN rifles were seen leaving the area. A huge police and army sweep through the area found a few clues that led nowhere. For weeks an intensive hunt for the killers continued, without results. No one claimed responsibility for the murder, and as time passed police were assigned to other duties. Much of the horror and outrage of the Dublin government, of the British, of all those appalled by the long, violent agony of the North, slowly dissipated. Everyone, of course, knew who was responsible—the IRA: if not the Provisional Army Council or the Official Army Council or some "army council," then IRA people acting independently. Everyone also knew why Ewart-Biggs had been killed: he was the official British presence—symbolic of the continued occupation of the six counties—and he might even be in a position of power and influence. He was the Lion made manifest, Colonel Blimp with a black monocle, a provocation to Republican opinion. And he was dead—and for the assassins this was largely sufficient, an immediate impact, a warning to London that the war was still on. The murderers did not care about the editorials in Irish newspapers and the indignation of Irish politicians, nor had they given much thought that the ambassador's death would unite their enemies in Dublin and London, and might begin a groundswell for peace in the North. They knew their enemies already, and there would never be peace in the country until Ireland was a nation once again. In fact, in retrospect, the only thing that was remarkable about Ewart-Biggs' death in 1976 was that so few important British officials had so far been a target, and none a victim. Mostly —not entirely—the Provisional Army Council was running a military campaign that might include commercial targets—pubs and clothing factories and buses—but not individual officials as targets. This did not mean that priorities and targets might not shift, and could do so at any time; but the physical force campaign was built around not assassination but attacks on security forces and the "artificial economy" of the six counties—plus bombing excursions into England.

The Irish experience, founded on the rock of unrequited nationalism thwarted by illicit regimes in Dublin, Belfast, and London, presents a classic milieu for violence where assassination occurs but, given all, is hardly endemic. Many of Europe's other national-based grievances, such as those of the Bretons or Corsicans, have gone no further than bombing. ETA is an exception. There are, however, strange new pools of ethnic dissent, real or potential, that have engendered murder and could do so again. Scattered in clumps are alien workers, recent immigrants, and refugee communities: the Aryans in Sweden, Mexicans in the United States, West Indians and Asians in England, South Moluccans in the Netherlands, and Turks in Germany. In France there are more Moslems than Protestants. Some of these aliens are transient, going home regularly. Some can never go home again, such as the South Moluccans, who have resorted to kidnapping and murder to persuade the Dutch to assure their dream republic in the Spice Islands. Some are not yet integrated, such as the Turks in Germany. And when some try to dissolve in the new melting pot, they provoke violence against their alien presence, as has been the case with Indians in Britain. So far, the South Moluccans excepted, the immigrants have tended to be the victims of violence; but their presence, like the bacillus of submerged nationalism, may present efficient democratic countries with an unexpected challenge.

Even more startling than the revolts of traditional nationalists in Euskadi and Ulster, or the seething of ethnic dissent, has been the rise of revolutionary violence—urban terror—in one of Europe's most efficient democracies which, the problem of a united Germany aside, has no nationality problem. It is understandable that Germany might be used as a terrorist arena, as was the case at Munich, or even that idealist Germans might volunteer in alien causes and be shot down in distant places like Entebbe; but most observers, especially German observers, cannot understand what the militants of the Red Army Faction or the June 2 Movement *want*, where they came from, or what is to be done in a society that is stable, successful, open, and efficient to a fault.

Where the ideological revolutionaries of Germany came from is patent: the wilder shore of the generation of 1968, epitomized by the Paris Spring, protesting against bureaucratic rigidity, the errors of the elders, the slaughter in Vietnam, the complacency of those who cherished things rather than ideas. The student protests of the West produced a New Left (a collection of ideas rather than a movement) that apparently radicalized a generation. On the far, far New Left were those who wanted to turn the rhetoric into revolution. In Germany, a small group collected around Andreas Baader and Ulrike Meinhof turned to direct action to protest the imperialist war in Vietnam.* They set fire to a supermarket on April 2, 1968, a "political" act that most of their more orthodox colleagues regarded as infantile romanticism. Two years later, on April 4, 1970, Baader was arrested. He was freed on May 14 in a prison break and was soon involved in a series of bank robberies. On December 22, 1971, a police officer was shot during a raid: ". . . shooting is taken for granted." And so was bombing. On May 11, 1972, fifteen bombs exploded on six targets. At the United States military headquarters in Frankfurt, an American army officer was killed. The Red Army Faction, RAF, of Baader and Meinhof had passed the crucial hurdle. They had killed, if at a distance. On May 15, Federal Judge Wolfgang Buddenberg was killed and his wife injured in a bomb attack in Karlsruhe. The bombing deaths soon totaled five, including four United States servicemen.

The RAF, along with the largely Berlin-based June 2 Movement, were totally isolated politically. While symbolic bombing might have been tolerated by the New Left, murder was not—especially murder by those who thought in slogans. Briefly it appeared that the new German terrorism was a matter of the moment. Baader, Meinhof, and several other leaders, including Hölger Meins, were arrested. The next year, 1973, was relatively quiet, with most attention focused on the forthcoming trials. But there were those who intended to continue "even without prospect of victory," and who could do so more effectively than the nominal RAF leaders. In 1974 Meins died after a hunger strike, the focus of resistance

---

*One of the groups closely connected to the Baader-Meinhof group in the early seventies was the Socialist Patients' Collective, located in a Heidelburg psychiatric-neurological clinic. They insisted that capitalism was the cause of mental illness, and that only the maladjusted could exist in the existing German society: the insane are too sane to live under the existing social conditions. The cure was the violent overthrow of the existing social order.

apparently still the prisons. Then, in November, Dr. Gunter von Drenkmann, Chief Judge of West Berlin, was assassinated. In February 1975, Peter Lorenz, the Christian Democratic leader in West Berlin, was kidnapped and, through the manipulation of the media, his release was negotiated in return for five prisoners, who were flown out of the country. In April there was an attack on the German embassy in Stockholm that resulted in three deaths and thirty injuries; the targets were no longer linked to the security-judicial establishment. The aim now announced was to "hit the imperialist apparatus, its military, political, economic and cultural institutions, its functionaires." And the RAF–June 2 people, although with limited capacity, had apparently found like-minded friends outside Germany, especially in the Middle East. Wilfried Rose was in the group that hijacked the Air France jet, and he was killed at Entebbe in July 1976. In fact, 1976 was not a good year for the RAF, for Ulrike Meinhof had hanged herself in prison in May, and there were constant arrests—and constant escapes. There were 110 accused or convicted terrorists in German jails, and only fifty to sixty still wanted by the authorities. There might be a few thousand sympathizers, but no more, and the activists did not seem to be able to recruit a new generation. With few exceptions, most were in their thirties: Baader was thirty-four, Gudrun Ensslin thirty-seven, Jan-Carl Raspe thirty-three. The worst might have been thought to be over—but 1977 became the year of terror for Germany, the time of assassins.

On April 3, 1977, two German radicals were turned over to the Bonn authorities after the Swedish police had discovered a plot to abduct former Immigration Minister Anna-Grete Leijon in order to trade her freedom for that of the RAF people in West Germany. On April 4, in Germany, Chief Public Prosecutor Siegfried Buback held a news conference to announce that warrants had been issued against the two extradited men. Coming just as the twenty-three-month trial of Baader, Ensslin and Raspe was drawing to a close and an inevitable judgment of guilty, it appeared to be further evidence that the day of the German "urban guerrilla" had passed. At 8:45 A.M., on Thursday, April 7, three days after Buback's news conference, a young couple pulled their Suzuki motorcycle into a service station in the middle of the city of Karlsruhe, not far from the German Constitutional Court. At 9:15 Prosecutor Buback's official limousine drove up, slowed, and stopped at a traffic light near the service station. The couple swung the Suzuki around behind the limousine, idling just back of the car's left rear fender. When the light turned green, the motorcycle's rear-seat rider produced a submachine gun and fired a long burst into the back of the limousine, sweeping the cone of fire through the chauffeur as the Suzuki sped away. The limousine was stalled, punctuated with bullet holes, the windows shattered.

The three men inside were slumped over, motionless. Thirteen spent cartridges rolled on the street. Buback and his driver were dead. Buback's bodyguard was mortally wounded. The rented Suzuki was found abandoned near the Karlsruhe-Frankfurt autobahn. The West German news agency, DPA, received a call from the Ulrike-Meinhof Special Action Group taking responsibility: "You'll hear from us again." No matter; Baader, Raspe, and Ensslin received life sentences and would remain in the huge, new, expensive, top-security Stammheim prison in Stuttgart, a facility built especially with terrorists in mind.

On July 30, 1977, Susanne Albrecht and two other young ladies appeared at the door of Jürgen Ponto's house near Frankfurt. He was chairman of the Dresdner Bank and his daughter was a friend of Albrecht's, who had brought him red roses. When he appeared, the three attempted to kidnap him; when he resisted, they shot and killed him. The roses were left scattered on the floor. The three women disappeared. Widespread searches and sweeps produced nothing. Then, in August, eleven convicted terrorists in widely scattered prisons went on a hunger strike. Unexpectedly, on September 1, the strike ended, again simultaneously, although these prisoners supposedly could not communicate beyond their own cells. On September 5, Dr. Hans Martin Schleyer, sixty-two, president of the West German Confederation of Employers Association, a member of the board of Daimler-Benz, stepped into his Mercedes. In a meeting with his colleagues after the murder of Ponto in July, he had predicted that the next victim would be someone in the room, capitalists all. His car, however, was not bulletproof, nor was there safety glass, although he now had a police escort traveling behind him. Schleyer was in most ways an ideal symbol of German capitalism, with a huge solid block of a face cut with dueling scars. A "fat magnate," he had joined the Nazi Party and the SS in 1943, and prospered after the war; he showed neither guilt nor remorse over the old days, over his own —and Germany's—success, and he was always ready with the hard word to silence the critics of the Left. His Mercedes moved smoothly through the traffic of a Cologne suburb, with the escort car and two policemen directly behind. For Schleyer there would be no roses.

Suddenly a baby carriage was pushed across the street in front of Schleyer's car. The chauffeur braked to a halt alongside a yellow minibus. Five people appeared, snatched submachine guns out of the baby carriage, and opened fire on the two stopped cars. The security submachine guns had been carefully locked in the luggage compartment. The five gunmen continued to spray the two cars, back and forth, missing only Schleyer. Over two hundred rounds were fired. The driver was killed, as were a security agent in the Mercedes and both police officers in the escort car. The two vehicles were riddled, the window glass scattered across the road. One body tipped out and fell into a gutter. The firing finally stopped and Schleyer was hustled away by the ambushers. The RAF wanted eleven prisoners freed—those who had gone off the hunger strike to build up their strength. The list included Baader, Ensslin, and Raspe, in the Stuttgart prison for life, and those who had participated in the attack in the Stockholm Embassy in 1975, who were in prison in Cologne. The eleven were to be moved to the Frankfurt airport; each was to be given $43,000, and then they would be flown out of the country.

The immediate German response was outrage and indignation —"ice-cold killer-technocrats" and "perverted offspring of the new left." Chancellor Helmut Schmidt demanded that they end their "insane undertaking. We will not permit ourselves to be infected by your insanity. You believe yourselves to be a selected elite, chosen to liberate the masses. You are mistaken; the masses stand against you." So did the authorities. A Crisis Staff was established in the Interior Ministry. The German borders were closed. Thousands upon thousands of "suspects" were questioned. Roadblocks were set up. Millions of wanted posters were printed and distributed. The streets were filled with police shouting through bullhorns and with armored personnel carriers rumbling back and forth. A budgetary addition of $500,000,000 for security was announced. Government buildings were protected with long sausage rolls of barbed wire, killer watchdogs, army checkpoints, sandbagged gun emplacements, and armored vehicles. The chief of the Federal Criminal Bureau, Horst Herold, estimated that there were 1,200 hardcore terrorists plus 6,000 sympathizers at the root of the problem—and most thought this estimate rather generous; but although the government had announced they did not want a "military solution," this vast array of security forces, the clicking computers churning out data on suspects, the air of high crisis, to a great many observers seemed an overreaction to the kidnapping of one man. In any case, no one could track down the kidnappers or Schleyer, and tentative negotiations with extending deadlines continued through a Swiss contact.

On Thursday, October 13, thirty-eight days after the kidnapping, Lufthansa Flight 181, a Boeing 737 with eighty-two passengers and four crew members, took off from Palma, Majorca, for Frankfurt. Among the passengers were forty-six women and children, including eleven beauty queens. Over the French Riviera, four Arab hijackers, members of the rogue Popular Front for the Liberation of Palestine, Special Operations, using the name Organization of Struggle Against World Imperialism, took over the flight without opposition, which was Lufthansa policy. The plane was directed to land and refuel in Rome, where, despite pleas by the German authorities, the Italian officials refused to attempt to abort a takeoff. Then began the long odyssey of Flight 181—on to Larnaca in Cyprus, back and forth over several Mideast countries that refused landing rights, on to Bahrain, and then to Dubai on October 14, for two days. By then a rescue operation had been mounted by the Border Protective Group 9, set up after the Munich massacre in 1972, under the command of Lieutenant-Colonel Ulrich Wegener. The Germans soon knew that the hijackers wanted the eleven prisoners on the Schleyer list plus two Palestinians in jail in Turkey (and $15,000,000 for expenses)—a truly international operation. The Germans did not intend to concede anything. So they dithered in public while Wegener and his sixty commandos flew after Flight 181. The hijacked flight took off for Aden on October 16, where the pilot was shot and killed for no apparent reason by one of the Arabs in a moment of hysteria. The Boeing was then moved on to Mogadishu in Somalia, where many of the passengers were losing hope of escape. With Somali permission, Wegener's plane arrived soon after dark on October 18. The crew and passengers by then had been on a 106-hour, 6,000-mile junket; and according to the hijackers, there were only ninety minutes until the latest deadline expired and they would all die. Then came the word that Germany had conceded. The prisoners had been released and were on the way. The Organization of Struggle Against World Imperialism had won. At this moment of triumph, Border Protection Group 9 sucked off the doors with a new device, tossed in shock-flash grenades, and opened fire. The three Arab men were killed and the woman wounded within seconds. German euphoria knew no bounds. Justice had been done, murder thwarted, the wicked punished, and German efficiency had matched that of the Israelis at Entebbe. The campaign against terrorism had won a massive victory. The friends and family of Schleyer were less enthusiastic; victory in Mogadishu implied a death sentence for the hostage. And death there was, almost immediately.

In his cell in the high-security prison in Stuttgart, Andreas Baader took out a hidden 7.65-millimeter Heckler and Koch pistol and shot himself in the head minutes after the failure of the hijacking had been announced—and picked up on his secret radio. Raspe shot himself with his pistol, a 9-millimeter Heckler and Koch; Gudrun Ensslin hanged herself, and Imgard Möller stabbed herself with a bread knife but did not die. German euphoria immediately disappeared into recrimination. The prisoners had pistols, private communication systems, links with other prisons and their friends outside. And worse, the European Left instantly assumed that the three had been murdered, in advance retaliation for Schleyer. On October 19, the French police in Mulhouse opened the trunk of a green Audi, and found Schleyer, who had been shot three times in the head, apparently as soon as news of the Mogadishu operation reached the kidnappers, who announced they had slain him "in pain and anger." The intensified manhunt produced little more than a growing uneasiness as an efficient, democratic country filled the streets with police, monitored all cross-border traffic, covered the walls with nearly four million posters, and transformed the seat of government into an armed camp.

During the decade 1967–1977 terrorism in Germany had cost 27 lives; there had been 102 target-victims, 92 injured in bombings and shootings, and 100 people held hostage. There were 94 terrorists in prison, 30 sentenced and 64 waiting trial, and there were 41 warrants out. All told, 550 suspects had been investigated, and 14 terrorists killed—all over a ten-year period. In 1977 Federal Police Director Erich Strass reported that narcotics had killed 380 people in Germany; there were no headlines or outraged indignation, only some satisfaction in official quarters that the fight against drugs was succeeding. Germany, an efficient democratic state without a nationality problem, did *not* have a serious revolutionary terrorist problem; but the politicians and the public assumed that they did, acted as if they did, and thus assured that they would. The Schleyer affair dominated the German mind for months—why us, why these fanatical young people, what is to be done? For the RAF—given that Schleyer was not a major figure —one murder of a "miserable and corrupt" Nazi-capitalist, the sacrifice of three of their own, and the spectacular end run of the four Arabs had struck deep into the heart of the state, an impact even the most optimistic terrorist could not have foreseen.

The German body politic simply seemed unable to withstand random, disorderly, inexplicable violence, and thrashed about *in extremis* clasping the old authoritarian ways—more police, bigger computers, better commandos, and the erosion of civil liberties of all. In time, fortunately, the crisis mood faded, but not the RAF. There were more escapes, another major kidnapping in Austria, more shots at officials, and more efforts to abort the German justice system. On April 11, six men charged with the murder of Judge Drenkmann in November 1974 and the kidnapping of Lorenz in February 1975 went on trial. One judge dropped out because it was revealed he was a 1974 target of assassins; one court-appointed defense lawyer, Eckhard Krummheuer, found a time bomb in his car on May 31; another lawyer, Dietmar Hohla, was shot in the foot on the way to court. The trial continued, and the security forces began to achieve major coups—suspects found in Yugoslavia, in Bulgaria, in Paris; guilty verdicts in Switzerland; captures in Holland and the United States. The hard core was badly eroded—and there were few second-generation militants. Perhaps there would be no more after them, the last who would murder "even without prospect of victory."

What seemed inexplicable, especially to the Germans, was the lack of an appropriate milieu for political murder, murder without point or prospect. There were those who felt the RAF were pathological rather than political killers. And certainly it was quite possible to explain their acts solely by examination of their personal histories. Self-destructive, guilty for others' sins, intense without discipline, clinging to revolutionary rhetoric in order to rationalize acts without revolutionary content, driven and desperate, the core of the RAF ultimately found peace in their own deaths—Baader, Meinhof, Ensslin, Raspe, Meins—all suicides.

Their perception of German reality—a capitalist-imperialist culture that bemused the workers with consumer goods, television as the opiate of the masses—created a murderous milieu only for them. Someone must strike the first blow. And they were willing, eager, to make the blood sacrifice. From that premise the logic of the Schleyer kidnapping is obvious, the impact almost exactly what the most optimistic would have wanted: the bland patina of Western democracy stripped away to reveal the Ugly Germany, Nazi-Imperialist-Capitalist. Very few Germans were willing to accept their original premise or felt that, given the provocation, the government had been "revealed" to be anything but determined to stamp out terrorism. Murder was unneeded in an efficient democratic country.

While the Germans might feel that they had coped reasonably well with the lunatic fringe of the generation of 1968, to the south in Italy, no one was at all sanguine. Whatever the impact of the postwar economic miracle, Italy was assuredly *not* an efficient democracy. Still, Italians did not expect efficiency, order, and discipline, as the Germans did. They had, in fact, been amazed at the wondrous transformation of a shattered, war-torn Italy into a major industrial power ruled smoothly year after year by the

Christian Democrats. From a near-zero point after the war, Italian economic growth had averaged 5.6 percent a year. In 1968 the gross national product was $74.8 billion—an increase of 370 percent since 1953. During the same period, the dominant Christian Democratic party ruled alone or in alliance with the small parties of the center, gradually involving the noncommunist Left, first the Italian Socialist Democratic Party of Saragat and then the Italian Socialist Party of Petro Nenni. Italy was transformed. A pedestrian had first a Vespa motorscooter, then a Fiat sedan, and finally drove a second car to a summer home. Two million workers moved from the impoverished South to work in the new industries of Turin and Milan and Genoa. In return, billions of dollars were invested in the South and in the islands. Vast new high-rise districts spread out from the major cities as Italy became an urban country. Italy was a vital link in NATO, a member of the EEC, a success.

In 1967–1968, behind the success, the highways, and tall buildings was another, more familiar, Italy. Great numbers of people, especially in the South, lived outside the new economy. All the Southern workers had not been integrated in the North, nor had the billions invested in the South been effective. The central bureaucracy was huge and inefficient. The educational system was rigid, unresponsive, and increasingly crowded, and its standards were decaying. The new wealth was not only unfairly distributed but also, in many cases, untaxed. The housing shortage seemed permanent, the lira soft, the state industries unprofitable. There were repeated scandals and continuing incompetence, with no one ultimately responsible. Yet the country puttered along, the same old faces appearing in the revolving cabinets. The tiny neo-Fascist Movimento Sociale Italiano, MSI, was isolated on the far Right, and the huge Italian Communist Party, PCI, dominant in many local elections, was also isolated, unable to win a national poll. The few nationality problems were minor; the German-speakers in the South Tyrol had gradually accepted accommodations from the center, and most other potential separatists had been defused by regional agreements. Italy was a more-or-less efficient democracy without a serious nationality problem; but it was also a country on the edge of real trouble.

The first signs came in 1967, a year before the May Days in

Paris, when the secondary-school students rioted in protest of the archaic educational system. Unlike the riots of gesture in Paris, with their elegant graffiti and endless seminars, the Italian riots were smashed swiftly and without dialogue. The more radical students began to suspect that the system could not accommodate real change: the system was the culprit. Independently, they abandoned conventional Marxist-Leninist positions—in particular, the Communist Party—and moved beyond parliamentary politics. One center of disenchantment in 1969–1970 was the School of Sociology in Trento, but there were other groups. In 1969 the Metropolitan Left split with the Communists. In January 1970, a group from Trento led by Renato Curcio, his wife Margherita Cagol, Paolo Maurizio Ferrari, Roberto Ognibene, Alberto Franceschini, and a few others formed *Brigate Rosse*, and for their first direct action burned three Pirelli trucks. Hardly anyone noticed. By April 1969, a series of bombings that had begun the previous year totaled seventeen. Again, few noticed and few seemed concerned with who was responsible. In August bombs detonated simultaneously on seven trains, injuring twelve people. Then, on Friday, December 12, a bomb exploded in front of the Banca Nazionale dell'Agricoltura in Milan, killing sixteen and wounding ninety. Bombs had gone off simultaneously in Rome. The 16 dead and 140 wounded could not be ignored and could not be easily explained: anarchists, Fascists, provocateurs? A decade of political violence had begun in Italy, and, it would eventually become clear, without the aid of the self-proclaimed revolutionaries of the new Left. On the right of the MSI, new Fascists equally beyond parliamentary politics arose—the New Order, the Black Order, the Mussolini Action Squad, the Steel Helmet—and began their armed struggle.

For years none of the conventional Italian politicians, Christian Democrats or Communists, wanted to accept the reality of the new political violence—terrorism—except as a stick to beat their political foes. The Communists insisted that the communiqués from the *Brigate Rosse* or October XXII were the work of provocateurs, CIA agents, or Fascists, and the *real* Marxist-Leninists were to be found only within the Party. The Christian Democrats blamed the Left, the anarchists, the Marxists. Everyone from time to time blamed the Fascists. Everyone devoutly wished the entire problem would go away. Bombs and murder were an aberration, irrelevant to the Italian system, the work of madmen or alien fanatics, without precedent, logic, or relevance. This was obviously not the case, but rather wishful thinking by the threatened. Political violence was to become endemic to the Italian system.

On the Right the new Fascists had sensed a slackening of purpose in the Republic—old tired men with interchangeable faces, no ideals, no call for sacrifice, ready to permit the atheists, the aliens, the Communists to edge into power. The new Blackshirts called to old memories and offered the young a chance to sacrifice for the real nation. Some were unsavory indeed, leather-coated gorillas lured by a slogan; some were silly anachronisms, such as Prince Julio Valerio Borghese, the Black Prince, dreaming of a coup; some were powerful, embedded in the heart of the state security forces; and there were doctors and lawyers and always the impatient young. They believed that the Italian system was fragile, that if a strategy of tension were employed the government would be unable to rule. There could then be a coup or the appearance of a man-on-horseback. After all, there had been the March on Rome, and in 1967 the Colonels had taken over Greece. Italy did not work well. They would give the country a push. Their Left counterparts agreed with the analysis, in large part. Italy was the weakest of the imperial powers, vulnerable to violence. The center was rotten; the Communists had sold out, and by the end of the decade were allied with the Christian Democrats. There was no question of violence without hope of victory, for *real* victory was possible by striking at the heart of the state.

So both ill-assorted groups struck at the state. There were bombs without warnings, Prince Borghese attempted a coup, and the *Brigate Rosse* kidnapped Mario Sossi, the deputy public prosecutor in Genoa—"a fanatic persecutor of the working class." And the years passed in an atmosphere of general disorder, the burning of schools, bombs in factories, student disorder, sniping, murder, kidnapping, and criminals copying the gunmen's tactics. The police—200,000 of various varieties, one for every 275 Italians—could do little; in fact, some of the commanders seemed to be more involved in fomenting violence than in quelling it.

In 1975 there were 702 terrorist incidents, kidnapping had become a criminal cottage industry, and the old political rigidity began to crack under demands for reform—new divorce laws, even abortion laws, had become radical causes. The police had had some success the previous year. The informer Silvano Girotto, who either was or was not a Franciscan but was known as Brother Machine-gun, led the police to Renato Curcio and several key members of *Brigate Rosse*. Then, in June 1975, the police killed Margherita Cagol Curcio in a shoot-out at a farmhouse being used as a secret prison for the wealthy vermouth manufacturer, Vittorio Vallarino Gancia, kidnapped the day before. Next, there was an indictment against forty-seven members of the Left—a conspiracy to overthrow the government. In November seventy-eight people were ordered to stand trial on charges connected with the coup of the Black Prince. Thus the police seemed to be making some progress against the militants of both the Left and Right—not that the violence ebbed; rather the reverse. There would be 1,198 terrorist incidents in 1976.

The number of revolutionary groups continued to multiply— over one hundred, with many often claiming credit for a single incident. Some, such as *Prima Linea* and *Azione Rivoluzionaria*, were real enough, but others, such as October XXII, were all but wiped out by arrests. In 1975 in Naples, a new variant had appeared in the *Nuclei Armati Proletari*, NAP, formed by a mix of prisoners and people of the new Left. In May they kidnapped Judge Guiseppe di Gennaro and released him after their rather limited demand for legal aid for prisoners was accepted over the state radio and television. The state had seemingly compromised before when it agreed to release certain prisoners for the return of Sossi, but Genoa Public Prosecutor Francesco Coco had called off the deal. In 1976 terrorist incidents still were largely regarded as spectaculars, nine-day wonders. Real interest, however, was focused on the transformation in the Italian political scene.

The abortion referendum had been passed overwhelmingly, despite the opposition of the Church and of the orthodox within the Christian Democrats. In a non-parliamentary election, the old percentages had no relevance. In the regional elections the Communist Party made startling gains—some dared to think of a national triumph that would bring the party to power, perhaps in the much-bruited Historical Compromise, a coalition with the Christian Democrats, perhaps even a Popular Front with the Socialists. The direction of these currents enraged both the far Left and far Right, *Brigate Rosse* and New Order; for the former the Communists were selling out the masses for power, and for the latter the Christian Democrats were selling out the nation in order to cling to power. Premier Aldo Moro's minority Christian Democratic government held on for a while, during 1976, but with eroding support and rising violence. Then it was announced there would be June elections and the crucial confrontation with the Communists. On May 28, south of Rome at Sezze Romano, MSI held a rally that collapsed into violence. Sandro Saccucci, a member of the chamber with a long record of violence, was sought for the murder after a young Communist was killed in the melee. Saccucci fled the country. On June 8, in Genoa, the *Brigate Rosse* caught up with Francesco Coco, who had reneged after the Sossi kidnapping. When Coco left his car and driver and began walking toward his home, as he always did at lunchtime, several young men appeared. The driver was shot and killed. The single bodyguard was shot and killed. Coco was shot and killed. In Turin at the trial of the *Brigate Rosse* leadership, betrayed and arrested in 1974, Prospero Gallinari accepted responsibility in the name of *Brigate Rosse*. No one could judge the impact of the deaths on the electorate; but on the morning after the final polling, it was clear that the country had been polarized. The Christian Democrats kept their place as the largest party, with approximately the same number of seats, but the Communists made huge gains, in large part by decimating the smaller parties. A monochrome, single-party minority Christian Democratic government under Giulio Andreotti emerged, made possible by Communist abstention, a most radical innovation. No one knew what would happen next. The government needed the Communists in order to rule effectively, but would collapse if they demanded ministries. Moro, five times prime minister, once foreign minister, the dominant Christian Democratic figure—*Il Cervello,* The Brain—out of sight behind the scenes, began to weave those wondrously vague formulas with rigorously explicit language that had been the glue of Italian centralist politics for so long. Somehow the Communists would share power but not have it, be in control of arenas of power but not seem to be. Everything would go on as before. And of course, Italy being Italy, everything did. On July 10, the Roman public prosecutor Vittorio Occorsio was machine-gunned while sitting in his car. Fascist New Order pamphlets were scattered over his shattered body. He had been "guilty" of serving the democratic dictatorship and persecuting New Order militants. The Right claimed it was a *Brigate Rosse* trick. The Left pointed out the dangers of neo-Fascism. The police could not discover the culprits.

Somehow the Italian spectrum still tried to assume that terror was an aberration, not an outward sign of ignored systemic faults. The old rules should still apply. Moro would find a formula to allow the same people in the Christian Democrats to rule in an invisible alliance with the Communists. Finally, after ten years, in March 1977, the penny dropped. The university students, embittered by certain unemployment on graduation and the loss of their student stipends, angry with the huge enrollments, unresponsive regulations, small and often part-time faculties, and archaic facilities (the Universita di Roma had 100,000 too many students) took to the streets. On March 11 in Bologna, a student leader of the radical left *Lotta Continua* was shot and killed by the police. A weekend of rampage and violence followed. Students in Turin, Milan, Florence, Naples, and Rome ran amok, tossing firebombs, ransacking stores, and attacking the police. In Bologna police moved in armored vehicles. The city center, with swirling clouds of gas, squads of police carrying rifles, and masked demonstrators, often armed, became a war zone. Fifty thousand demonstrators appeared in Rome. Many brought firebombs. The next morning the center of the city looked like a battleground—gutted cars, ruined stores, the streets littered, and everywhere the lingering odor of burnt rubber and gas.

Everyone was shocked. In Rome, Interior Minister Francesco Cossiga announced that the government would not tolerate further violence: in 1977 there would be 2,128 terrorist incidents. The secretary of the Communist youth organization, Massimo d'Alema, condemned the violence and announced that Italy faced a new phase of tension and provocation that might throw the country into a dramatic crisis; when Communist speakers went to the universities to explain this to "their" students, they were hooted at and stoned. The walls of Bologna, long a Communist-run showplace, were covered with the graffiti of the March rebels: "We want everything. We want to destroy everything." What was to be done with this new and violent breed who wanted everything, who had smashed the center of Rome and Bologna, who were not amenable to the old slogans and admonitions? No one knew. There was so much to be done: build new housing, stabilize the lira, cut down unemployment, reform education, bring the invisible part of the population into the system, find a compromise on an abortion law, keep the country puttering along. And, in the case of the universities, if the money could be found and could be wisely spent to reform the system, enrollments would have to be cut. And the embittered rejects would still turn to the streets or, worse, go underground, where the *Brigate Rosse* and the others waited. And if nothing were done and order decayed, there on the Right waited the New Order, the Black Order, the Fascists with their solution.

And the violence continued and order decayed. *Brigate Rosse* introduced a new technique of violence, called kneecapping in Northern Ireland and *azzoppamento* or laming in Italy, the wounding of the enemies of revolution. Local Christian Democratic politicians, managers of major industries—Fiat especially—journalists and editors, police and prosecutors were shot in the legs or arms, maimed but not murdered. The police seemed helpless. There were 115 identifiable extremist groups, 94 of the Left and 21 of the Right, and for two years almost no important arrests had been made. The *Brigate Rosse* trial of Curcio and the rest dragged on, a spectacular circus regularly postponed because of violent attacks on those involved. Then, as they had so often promised, the *Brigate Rosse* truly struck at the heart of the state.

On Wednesday evening, March 15, 1978, someone slashed the tires of the van of the Roman florist Antonio Spiriticchio. He would be unable to sell his flowers in his stand on Via Fani in Monte Mario the following morning. One witness removed. At 8:55 the following morning, Thursday, March 16, Aldo Moro left his home on the Via del Forte Trionfale in the Monte Mario district of Rome. Like all important Italian political figures, he was guarded, but unlike some, he did not have a bulletproof limousine. President Leoni's car was practically an armored personnel carrier, but then plots against his life had been discovered. With Moro was Oreste Leonardi, who had been his bodyguard for fifteen years. Outside was Moro's Fiat 130 with driver Domenico Ricci and the escort car, an Alfetta with three agents. The two cars moved off down Via del Forte Trionfale and then into the narrow Via Licino Calvo. A Fiat 128 with diplomatic plates was directly in front of the two. Suddenly it slammed to a stop. The escort car smashed into the back of Moro's Fiat, slamming it ahead into the Fiat 128. Instantly, a man and a blond woman rushed back alongside Moro's car. Standing directly beside the hood, the two emptied submachine guns into the front seat, killing Domenico Ricci and Oreste Leonardi before they realized what had happened. Four other men dressed in Alitalia pilot uniforms, who had been waiting next to a closed bar, rushed out and began spraying the escort car with fire. One agent, Raffaele Iozzino, was killed immediately, and another, Zizzi, was mortally wounded. Somehow the third agent, Giulio Rivera, managed to get out of the shattered car and draw his revolver. He managed to get off three shots before he was hit in the middle of his forehead and killed. At 9:06, Moro was shoved into a waiting blue Fiat 132 that had been used to block all traffic in Via Stresa, the cross-street. In a convoy with two other cars, the Fiat 132 drove off. At 9:30 the *brigatisti* abandoned first the Fiat 132 and then their Fiat 128—the third car, a blue 128, would be found the day after near the site of the kidnapping.

Within an hour, the police had three thousand men assigned to the case. On the spot they found sixty spent bullets from a mix of weapons—Italian, a Czech Nagat, an odd Soviet gun. That day and the next they found the cars. That was all. There were three thousand special searches in twenty-four hours. Fifteen thousand police spread out; roadblocks, appeals, armored personnel carriers on the roads, anguish in high places—and nothing. At least eleven people had been involved in the actual kidnap operation, and certainly as many elsewhere. Cars had been stolen, used, exchanged. Safe houses were necessary. And the police could find nothing. On March 18, *Brigate Rosse* issued a communiqué affirming responsibility and stating that Moro would undergo a "people's trial." A photograph of Moro was enclosed showing him in front of the red star flag of the *Brigate Rosse*. The following day the Italian government decided to continue the Turin trial. They would not be intimidated; furthermore, in the past, political hostages had been kidnapped and then released. On March 29, another letter arrived, this time from Moro to Interior Minister Cossiga asking the government to negotiate his release and naming the Vatican as a possible mediator. On April 4, there was still another *Brigate Rosse* communiqué and another letter from Moro: "I am a political prisoner and your brisk refusal to enter into any kind of discussion about the fate of other, similarly detained persons gives rise to an untenable situation. Time passes fast. Any moment may be too late." Time passed. There was a heightening feeling of crisis. Moro's family was outraged by the government, composed of old friends. Observers felt that as the days slipped by, Moro's chances of survival diminished. On April 18, a message arrived saying that Moro had been executed after the people's court passed a death sentence. His body could be found in Lake Duchessa, five thousand feet high in the Abruzzi Mountains, seventy-five miles northeast of Rome. There was no body. On April 24, one day after a special plea by Pope Paul VI, a *Brigate Rosse* communiqué announced that unless thirteen imprisoned colleagues were released—those on trial in Turin—Moro's sentence would be carried out. Moro's enclosed letter stated, "We are almost at zero hour, seconds rather than minutes from the end." Then there followed eleven days of silence. On May 5, a *Brigate Rosse* communiqué announced, "We concluded the battle begun on March 16 by carrying out the sentence to which Aldo Moro has been condemned." Two days later Moro's farewell letter to his wife arrived. "They have told me they are going to kill me in a little while, I kiss you for the last time." On May 9, after fifty-four days, Moro's body was found in the luggage compartment of a French burgundy-red Renault R-4 parked in the center of Rome on Via Caetani, three hundred yards from Communist headquarters, two hundred from those of the Christian Democrats. He had been shot ten times in the chest early on May 8.

The kidnappers were still at large, despite a series of arrests. Not only had they evaded capture, kept Moro for fifty-four days, and maintained simultaneous communications in three cities with the authorities, but they had also continued their operations: wounded a former mayor of Turin, killed a police officer assigned as a guard to the Turin trial, and shot a Christian Democratic politician, two Fiat officials in Turin, and industrialists in Genoa and Milan. Two days after Moro's body was discovered, the twentieth shooting of the year took place when the Italian manager of the Chemical Bank of New York, Marzio Astarita, was wounded. Still, there were arrests and discoveries of *Brigate Rosse* houses. The trial at Turin continued and sentences were handed down. Many, if not the Moros, had praise for the government's stand. The fragile arrangement with the Communists continued. And if anything the Communists were as firm on no-surrender-no-compromise as the Christian Democrats—and so one of their officials was shot and wounded. Italy trundled along into the next crisis when President Leone was forced to resign under public criticism of his finances, resulting in one more of Italy's marathon presidential elections with all the old maneuvers, deals, and backstage dickering. Italy still was not very efficient, but then the country has always seemed on the lip of the precipice and nothing ever did work very well.

Unlike their German colleagues, the *brigatisti* discovered and exploited a milieu for murder. Unlike the RAF, they did not begin direct violent action, as the Fascists did in 1969 with the Milan no-warning bomb; but they too started with symbolic arson, brief kidnappings, and violence short of murder. They were encouraged, justly so, by the fact that the visibly rising level of violence coupled with the inequalities and inherent injustices of the Italian system would destabilize the country, the weakest link in the larger imperialist-capitalist world. They acted with firm hope of victory, although recognizing that few accepted their analysis and fewer still their means. They were hardly as isolated as the German RAF, but of all those thousands of rioting students only a very few would go underground instead of back to classes. What they did have going for them in their analysis of the milieu was that Italy was really inefficient—for example, the police were a positive *Brigate Rosse* asset, a form of outdoor relief for needy Southerners.

There were real grievances. And if the future offered by the *briga-tisti* was as vague as it was luminous, Italian conditions were ame-nable to violence.

Logically, then, with the same absolute tunnel vision and single-ness of purpose, the righteous assassins, brutal, ruthless idealists, whose acts could *not* be as simply explained as those of the RAF killers with their flawed personalities, struck at the heart of the state. The perfect victim was Moro, the Brain that stitched that state together. Five days before he was kidnapped, Moro had arranged an understanding: there would be a new Christian Dem-ocratic government with the Communists as part of the governing majority, but not represented in the Cabinet. Even more than the pompous and possibly corrupt President Leone or the bland pre-mier Giulio Andreotti, Moro represented what the *brigatisti* liked least. As a symbol he was ideal, as a man he might be nearly irreplaceable. Dead or alive, once kidnapped Moro would be removed from the system, released as the result of a deal, and after the series of anguished letters he would be politically emasculated. Dead, even as a martyr, he would be of little use to the "guilty" colleagues who abandoned him. The *brigatisti* on that level could not lose. As far as the real target—the state—was concerned, Moro was at the heart of the system, and the long kidnap siege would put a severe strain on that state. Just as the kidnapping of Schleyer seemed to bring out the worst in the German psyche, so did Moro's kidnapping show up the Italians' bumbling: hesitant leadership, the inefficiency of the security forces, a lack of responsibility in high places, and the moment Moro was buried back to politics as usual. As propaganda of the deed, the impact of the Moro murder was impressive, yet simply *because* Italy was inefficient, there was no overreaction and no dawning realization that the *Brigate Rosse* fed on real grievances, that substantive change would be needed, not simply police who knew their job.

In each of these four special cases—Spain, Ireland, Germany, and Italy—there is an almost classical example of political murder. Spain at the time of the assassination of Admiral Luis Carrero Blanco was a rigid, unsavory dictatorship adamant against regional autonomy, and ETA was a typical liberation movement cloaked in revolutionary rhetoric but based on purely national aspirations. Ireland has for two centuries engendered violent efforts by the men of physical force to forge the mystical united Irish Republic of their dreams, assured always that there will be some support for the struggle until *Beir Bua,* Final Victory. In Germany, the RAF was the last froth of 1968, was on the very cusp of those who revolt without hope of victory, rebels who found personal therapy in terrorism. And in Italy the rebels are real, the political grievances real, the prospect of a new and more ruthless generation of gunmen real, for the *brigatisti* operate in the congenial milieu of a faltering democracy. And democratic institutions are, if open, vulnerable to violence—although, if the democracy is effective, indigenous violence, being illicit, is rare. The Spanish case, the shift from authoritarian corporate dictatorship to parliamentary democracy and constitutional monarchy, reveals that the label "democratic" is insufficient to immunize the country from national-based violence—ETA killed two Spanish army officers in Madrid on July 21, 1978, "democracy" or no, and the Basque militants continue to murder, and not only in the Basque country, despite the promise of regional concessions by the "democratic" center. In Ireland, refusing to recognize the puppet democratic regimes in Dublin and formerly Belfast, and certainly not recognizing the Irish suzerainty of London, the IRA has for decades fought on a nationalist base, on a nationalist issue. Anyway, as Eamon de Valera once said, "The people have no right to do wrong." While on one hand submerged nationalism creates the appropriate milieu for political violence in Ireland and Spain, the existing or perceived system—and its function—encourages revolt in Germany and Italy. In the former case, the motives of the rebels can hardly bear scrutiny, while in the latter the existing system can hardly operate effectively. Each case, of course, is special, but there are certain general conditions in advanced Western societies that can be noted.

There is presently a concept that a transnational imperialist-capitalist order exists in the world, exploiting the Third and Fourth Worlds and increasingly aligning with the Socialist Second World—even China. This system can be attacked anyplace—there are no innocent people or institutions, democracy is an illusion.

Violence must be used, even without victory, in order to release the slumbering power of the masses—if not this year, then next. Those very few who have raised their sights from national liberation to transnational deeds have perforce opted for spectacular terrorism: hijacking, kidnappings, and assassination. They have given the others a model, often seized by the mad and the criminal. There is very little that the threatened in democratic countries can do to smash the model, dispute the analysis, or even in most cases plug up the vulnerabilities of open societies without endangering the civil liberties of all. The problem is that there is no solution, although there are assuredly incremental advances, better safeguards, that will restrict the incompetent rebel. Much the same was true with the revolutionary assassins before World War I. When a worldwide revolutionary milieu encouraged individuals and groups to kill the powerful and treacherous, violence became part of the king's trade until revolutionary fashions changed. Presently, at least, the band of transnational revolutionaries recruited out of the Japanese Red Army, the Palestinian fedayeen, or the mercenaries who can be hired with a slogan, is small. They will kill, but to no great purpose—as long as democracy is not closed down to protect itself.

A second problem without a solution for the West is the arena-assassin, the international operator who finds access to a victim easier in London or Paris or Vienna than at home. Regimes reach out to remove an old foe, rebels kill symbolic victims, conspiracies are organized in exile, and democratic societies have to deal with political crime that has nothing to do with their politics: Israelis tried in a Norwegian court for killing the wrong Arab, or Croatians hijacking an American plane for a Balkan purpose. The solution to this problem, however, is much simpler, since it is clear that the arena is not politically threatened, an open society not the target but only the venue. Murder in Norway or hijacking over New York remains quite simply a crime and can be so treated. It may not have even in the short run any more effect on security than punishing the transnational terrorists, but arena-murder is seen even by an easily outraged population as an alien—unthreatening—event.

A great many political murders, however, are not alien. The

rebels, with or without a cause, are home-grown. The most likely field of growth is always in a submerged nationality of a Western society, a danger that may be accommodated, as the Italians did with the South Tyrol, postponed in hopes of a democratic solution or an ebbing of sentiment, as is the case in Quebec, or fought for lack of any viable alternative given old commitments, as Britain has done in Ireland. The real danger is in not recognizing such a nationality problem—however small, as is the case with Puerto Rico; however quixotic, as seems to be the case in Brittany. Secondly, the emergence of terrorists of whatever ideological persuasion who seek to overthrow a democratic system is an indication that the system may not be efficient, that there may be real grievances—in Germany, however, it is that the system is so efficient, so materialistically successful, so generally accepted at the polls, that alienates the very radical and very curious RAF and June 2 Movement. There may, of course, be turmoil, riots, direct action, and symbolic bombing—the background music of the West, but not revolutionary violence. In the United States during the years of the unpopular Vietnam War, in the midst of a racial-social transformation of the widest proportions that unleashed new appetites, with a population curve that brought to maturity at their most volatile years a huge mass of young people, almost no one was killed, and most of those were victims of their own bombs and mistakes, or psychopaths adopting the terrorist model.

Consequently, at present, the West appears certain to be invested with the small but virulent transnationalist terrorists feeding off fantasies and grievances twice-removed, and appears certain to remain an arena for gunmen killing for alien causes. Perhaps the ideological assassins of the 1968 generation will find no successors, perhaps Spain will move solidly into the ranks of legitimate democracies, perhaps Italy will find solutions to inefficient institutions. Perhaps the aspirations of the Corsicans or Puerto Rican extremists or Welsh nationalists can be accommodated. Perhaps the South Moluccans and the Turks will be peacefully integrated. Perhaps not.

2

The Past as Prologue

Assassination has never changed the history of
the world.
—Disraeli in the House of Commons, May 1,
1865, on the murder of Abraham Lincoln

Every assassination, no matter how demented the killer or how
slight the impact, changes history: one special and peculiar piece,
one unique human being, is gone from the board, and his passage
was violent. And a failed attempt—as long as the authorities realize the threat—also has an impact, albeit less significant than if the
victim died. Obviously and often, the impact may not be exactly
as intended or sufficiently impressive to warrant grave concern on
anyone's part. Still, political murder, especially by those who attack the system, always has *some* repercussions. When one tyrant
replaces another, when one member of a revolving elite replaces
the next, at the minimum the new man, a beneficiary if not the
director of murder, is apt to be more wary. At times repeated
attempts on a ruler's life may not only make him more wary but
also embellish his reputation for invulnerability, each flawed deed
underlining the power and perhaps the legitimacy of the regime.
Sometimes, too, when the deed has exactly the impact intended
by the conspirators, the shift is so slight as to seem not worth the
effort or, particularly, the lost life: the attempt on German Chancellor Konrad Adenauer by militant Zionists as a warning against

pursuing a policy of rapprochement with Israel was structured
from the first with the realization that the bomb would never get
to him but kill someone along the route, German lives not being
of prime concern to those involved. Matters went as planned and,
as might have been anticipated, the "warning" had no effect but
to improve German security measures. Certainly, given the remarkable number of assassination attempts, the general impact is
not great; yet at times—from Henry IV until the present—a single
murderous deed has what appears to the disinterested very considerable impact. And for the speculative mind, if some of the
failures had succeeded—such as the attempt on Hitler in 1939—
history might have been given a considerable push. At the end it
is not whether the observer feels that history has been changed,
but rather that in generation after generation under certain circumstances, in a special milieu or in isolated horror, men and
women have chosen to kill for their cause. And there is not the
slightest reason to suppose that they will not continue to do so,
encouraged and emboldened by their analysis and their logic,
frustrated with all other options, righteous, indignant, deadly.

The single revolutionary assassin acting alone, often from motives suspect to the threatened, can rarely anticipate that one
murderous deed alone will change the board. Most such killers
recognize that they can punish, perhaps when the victim and the
symbol are one, and in so doing warn. At times, of course, they can
assure the end of a special tyrant, even if they will not be able to
choose his successor—can anyone be worse than the incumbent?
At times, as in the case of Huey Long, who was perceived as a
threat to a national system rather than as a local despot, the irreplaceable man could be eliminated. Someone could replace Tsar
Alexander, or certainly inherit the title and powers, but no one
could replace Huey Long, no one could have replaced Charles de
Gaulle or Hitler or Mussolini. They *were* the system. Yet the lone
assassin by and large has been most concerned at the two far ends
of the scale—to punish a single wicked man or to kill a king or
president, any king or president, and undermine the entire global
system in the name of a transcendental cause—an anarchist millennium. The difficulty with the lone assassin is just that—he is
alone, may step from the shadows tomorrow to punish on his own,

to kill for a luminous if uncertain cause. In an open society any of the prominent are vulnerable, particularly when there is an encouraging international milieu, no matter how unpromising local conditions may be.

Conspiracies to murder for political cause are more easily predicted in time and place, the logic of the deed more amenable to analysis. The same motives exist for the several as for the singular—punish, warn, replace, erosion of the system or regime. More likely, however, conspirators seek not only to change history, as was the case with the murder of Lord Moyne and Count Bernadotte, but also to secure power. There is the swift coupassassination, a normal way of political succession in many parts of the world, or campaigns to grasp power over time, often to rule no differently, but at times under different banners, and in some cases to change everything. When there is a consensus in society, when the means of succession are legitimate, when there are few pressing issues or turmoil in the streets—and especially when there is no hope of success—conspiracies to murder are rare.

Unfortunately for those seeking the easy life, over much of the globe such idyllic conditions do not exist. The present transnational terrorist milieu has created a striking and compelling model for political violence. The existing transnational system of rapid travel, instant communications, shifting populations, and, in the West, open societies, has created an effective medium of access not simply for the new jackals but also for the traditional rebel who can now kill abroad for distant purposes. Most assassinations, however, including those in the international arena, are still nationalbased, reflecting specific national conditions. Thus there are certain states and certain regimes that invite rebel conspiracy. Some regimes have no real means of legitimate succession or even logical elite replacement. Who replaces the military dictator in Yemen or Ethiopia? At times an *ad hoc* formula may be worked out by which the military elite choses each successor—as in Brazil —or seeks a return to the electoral process—as in Peru and Bolivia —but the difficulty remains, and the impatient or denied may strike—Bolivia again. Even more to the point, a regime may not be a closed elite but a single man ruling through fear and repression, his regime founded on dread and charisma: Idi Amin in Uganda is a classic tyrant. In many countries, however, there are not cannibal kings or mad ministers—rather, presidents of one-party states, who, unlike the generals, have fashioned the form for succession without assurance that the process will work. In British East and Central Africa, excluding the special example of Rhodesia, four states have, since becoming independent, been directed until recently by a single man and ultimately a single party: Kenneth Kaunda in Zambia, Hasting Banda in Malawi, Julius Nyarere in Tanzania, and Jomo Kenyatta in Kenya. Each is quite different. Zambia is a radical front-line state maintained by expatriats. Malawi is a patriarchial fief with all power and 4.7 percent of the tobacco holdings in presidential hands. Tanzania is the great and unsuccessful experiment in African socialism. Kenya is capitalism incarnate with lardings of corruption. There is no certain individual successor to each president, no great faith that the "system" will produce a swift and legitimate transfer of power, and most of all to the west there was until recently the grisly example of Uganda and the grotesque Amin. Of course, some countries have moved smoothly—or nearly so—and the new institutions have managed to cope, as with Sadat following Nasser in Egypt. But nowhere is there real certainty when the system rests on one man, and consequently the threat of murderous change exists, even after a decade of peace—especially if the ruler is a demonstrable tyrant, always if he is both brutal and inefficient.

One-party states that are potentially vulnerable to a conspiracy of assassins are better off than those areas that have slipped into endemic violence, no matter what the form of the existing institutions. In revolutionary Mexico it took three decades before the new institutions could bear the weight of succession. In Argentina, the state has shifted for three decades between civilian incompetence and military brutality, with a high, if at the moment ebbing, level of violence. In the turmoil of rampant inflation, uncertainty at the center, guerrilla armies in shoot-outs with the police, it is hardly surprising to find a high incidence of assassination. The same is true in Ethiopia, and probably could become the case in Turkey, where between January and July 1978, 235 people, mostly students, have been killed—sooner rather than later, someone more important than a student may be a victim unless the disturbances can be curtailed. In some areas of the world there have been decades of endemic violence that may sweep into the capital of Chad or Burma or the Philippines. In other places, despite the most legitimate of institutions, the most democratic of systems, the prospect of murderous violence may remain present because a nation remains submerged, denied. For the rebels, killing for such a cause in Ulster or Spain or Ethiopia is a clearly defined responsibility.

Thus, in the broadest terms, the areas most likely to encourage assassins are those of the Fourth World, the collection of basket cases with unviable economies, only one crop or commodity (or none), new and irrelevant institutions, a tiny elite divided by custom, tribe, and ambition. Politics may be a dangerous career but it does pay dividends, and several of the most dreadful despots have long outlived their opponents, even, in the cases of Haiti and Nicaragua, passing along the family fief to the appointed heir. For much of the Fourth World the gun is the only means to power. In the larger, more stable and more hopeful Third World of developing nations as diverse as India and Iraq and Brazil, the major factors that create a murderous milieu have been (1) separatism, usually tribal in Africa but linguistic and religious elsewhere: Ceylon and Cyprus and Nigeria and Lebanon have collapsed into a violence that has encouraged gunmen; and (2) succession: how is the Ba'athist president of Iraq to be replaced, or the Chilean junta? And (3) recently in Iran the very impact of "developing"—coupled with the arrogance and corruption of the Shah—led to turmoil and chaos. Some nations have managed to scramble through violence engendered by revolutionary aspirations—as the Naxilities in India did—or the simple decay of order—as with *la violencia* in Columbia. Some seem fairly stable at present, but the vulnerability remains—too many problems, too many conflicting ambitions, uncertain institutions.

Yet it is in the First World of the West, where most problems seem solved, where on most issues there is a consensus, where the institutions are stable and legitimate, that the assassin is everywhere to be found. In open societies gunmen of varying hues may move freely, strike easily, carry the war abroad—or, in the case of the new terrorist, to the evil system. And not all Western states are efficient or have, indeed, reached a consensus on their internal nationality problems. It is rather the Second, Socialist, World that has so far been invulnerable to the righteous gunmen: few care to die certain that the cause will never triumph—dying without sight of victory is one thing, but dying with the sure and certain knowledge that there will never be a victory is another. And the technical problems of killing within a closed society are formidable. So Soviet Russia has potential nationality problems that make Madrid's problem with the Basques or London's with the Irish appear child's play, but Moscow will respond with ruthless and brutal force—destroying the "nation" or rooting out and exiling the separatists, if need be. There has been and may again be murder within the elite to assure succession, but this is a deadly quarrel at the top, and one that after fifty years of practice has become somewhat less deadly, if no less important. The institutions of the Second World have increasingly become more legitimate, even when the most brutal repression is institutionalized, tolerated if not admired. The key, however, for the Second World is that such institutions must be efficient—submerged nations can be intimidated and potential rebels disheartened only so long as the system works. When there has been an opening—the German invasion of Russia in 1941, for example—the nationalist and the ideological gunmen enter politics; but presently even the most sullen are silent—one Budapest or one Prague every ten years seems sufficient. Still, the Second World excluded for the moment, there seems ample international scope for the assassins. There exists a global milieu for murder, any number of volunteers to kill for the nation or the cause, to grasp for simple power or to punish evil.

Violence, of course, may not pay at all, but it may pay very well —and this has long been the argument of the threatened, of those involved in less lethal politics, of those convinced that democratic institutions can accommodate legitimate demand for radical change. As Austin Currie, an Ulster politician, insisted, the latest Irish Troubles have indicated at least one thing: that violence does not produce political change—or so it seems to many observers. Yet the Stormont regime is gone—but the reason is not because of the gunmen. And according to Conor Cruise O'Brien, even the twenty-six-county Republic would have come without the Easter Rising in 1916 or the Tan War. Violence within a democracy is always illicit and unnecessary. There are cogent arguments opposed to those presented by Currie and O'Brien; but the real point is that they do not convince the men of violence. Again, for the next and future assassin, it is his *own* logic that becomes so compelling—given the existing situations and potential options that will obviously be required for the murderous deed.

And there are abroad now, and appear likely to be in the future, men who will resort to violence—"treacherous" violence, if you are the target. They have grasped the theory of the dagger; they deny the legitimacy of the powerful, point to old heroes, such as William Tell or Mazzini or the Swabian carpenter Johann Georg Elser, look into their own hearts to discover the will of the people and the needs of the masses, and go forth to change history. For them to kill is not a crime but a duty. And at the very least, they strike at one man—they do not dump cluster-bombs on villages, or drop incendiaries on major cities, or slaughter everyone wearing a tie or owning land. They kill one at a time, usually by hand, and while they may unleash the dogs of war, as did Princip, their single deed is a narrow one, usually futile, often unsavory, all but inexplicable—as in the cases of Moro, Schleyer, Ewart-Biggs—but those of the state are often brutal beyond measure: remember Gulag and Hiroshima, Dachau and Cambodia. This may be cold comfort, indeed, with the righteous gunmen among us. Yet in much of the West assassination for political purposes has become aberrant, the tool of the distant or the fanatical few. There are national problems, but accommodation may be possible in time. There is need for radical change, but even in Italy there is reason to assume, again in time, that sufficient improvement can be effected to make the gunmen obsolete or irrelevant, a maladjusted few using terror as therapy. Apparently the psychotic lured toward murder as a cure to intolerable personal anguish will be with us always, each inexplicable deed causing ripples of irrelevant concern that need not produce systemic adjustment. But the revolutionary gunman may have outlived his day in the open societies of the West.

Beyond the Socialist Second World, for the moment, the assassin's vocation beckons, for power does come from a gun barrel—often one man's gun. Violence does pay, even if the wages are uncertain. Assassination is and will remain one facet of revolutionary politics, a conventional tool of the rebels' trade. Those distant murders of unspeakable people by those with unpronounceable names may be simply an unattractive spectator sport for the West, one cannibal king replacing another. Sometimes the slaughtered have real assets—geography to command, oil to sell, tribes to unleash—sometimes not. No matter if the heartland of the West or that of the Socialist camp are relatively secure—not immune in the West, but inured—there will be ample scope for murder elsewhere. And some of those gunmen from the far parts will come into the Western arena to murder in the name of strange ensigns. And again, no matter—open societies have long lived with the psychotic murderer, and can do so with the righteous gunman and his irrelevant cause. For us—and for the Marxists—history cannot be changed by righteous murder—at least, not often and not by much.

 sources

There is no practical possibility of attempting even a vaguely comprehensive bibliography of assassination in general or even certain spectacular assassinations in particular. The murder of President John F. Kennedy alone has engendered a vast cottage industry of experts, official records, special institutions, enormous numbers of articles from the lurid to the scientific, books, dissertations; whole careers, some unsavory, have been founded on that day in Dallas. For American assassinations there is even an Assassination Information Bureau and by now bibliographies of bibliographies. What can be done briefly is to sketch the kind of material available, especially the more recent material, for the subject has for centuries held a considerable fascination for writers of all sorts and conditions.

Fairly regularly over the years books have appeared dissecting the whole subject of assassination. Normally they begin at the beginning, include the more dramatic murders—Caesar or Lincoln or Kennedy—and in a coda draw some conclusions, often moral:

Bornstein, Joseph, *The Politics of Murder*, New York, William Sloan, 1950

Horowitz, Irvin M., *Assassination*, New York, Harper and Row, 1972

Hurwood, Bernhardt J., *Society and the Assassin, A Background Book on Political Murder*, New York, Parents' Magazine Press, 1970

Hyams, Edward, *Killing No Murder, A Study of Assassination as a Political Means,* London, Nelson, 1969

McConnell, *The History of Assassination*, Nashville (Tenn.), Aurora Publishers, 1970

Paine, Lauran, *The Assassin's World,* New York, Taplinger, 1975

Porterfield, Austin L. *Cultures of Violence,* Fort Worth (Texas), Manney Company, 1965

These vary greatly in quality, and the best general work remains the slender *Assassination and Terrorism* (Toronto, Canadian Broadcasting Company, 1971) by David C. Rapoport. There have been some more rigorous academic approaches as well, such as Stephen Schafer's *The Political Criminal, The Problem of Morality and Crime* (Glencoe, Illinois, The Free Press/MacMillan, 1974) and Doris Y. Wilkinson's edited volume *Social Structure and Assassination,* (New Brunswick, New Jersey, Transaction Books, 1976); but certainly the most bizarre exercise is Sandy Lesberg's *Assassination in Our Time* (New York, London, Peebles Press, n.d.)—a pictorial study of the major assassinations of the twentieth century.

There are as well works on a certain series of assassinations—the best on the Americans being James F. Kirkham, Sheldon G. Levy, and William J. Grotty, *Assassination and Political Violence: A Report to the National Commission on the Causes and Prevention of Violence* (New York, Praeger, 1970), but there have been others, such as Hugh Byas' *Government by Assassination,* that are somewhat more biased (published in London in 1943, this was an anti-Japanese tract). By far the largest genre is single volumes on single victims, from Roland Mousnier's splendid *The Assassination of Henry IV, The Tyrannicide Problem and the Consolidation of the French Absolute Monarch in the Early Seventeenth Century* (London, Faber and Faber, 1973) to the revelations of the journalists Pierre Demaret and Christian Plume in *Target DeGaulle* (New York, Dial, 1975). Herewith a short, judicious selection:

Diederich, Bernard, *Trujillo, The Death of the Goat,* Boston, Little, Brown, 1978

Friedman, Saul S., *Pogromchik, The Assassination of Simon Petlura,* New York, Hart, 1976

Gillen, Mollie, *Assassination of the Prime Minister, The Shocking Death of Spencer Perceval,* New York, St. Martin's, 1972

Havas, Laslo, *Hitler's Plot to Kill the Big Three,* New York, Bantam, 1971

Heinz, G. and H. Donnay (pseudonyms), *Lumumba: The Last Fifty Days,* New York, Grove Press, 1969

Ivanov, Miroslav, *Target: Heydrich,* New York, Macmillan, 1972

Joesten, Joachim, *De Gaulle and His Murders,* Isle of Man, Times Press, 1964

Maass, Walter B., *Assassination in Vienna,* New York, Scribner's, 1972

Mason, Herbert Molloy, *To Kill the Devil, The Attempts on the Life of Adolf Hitler,* New York, Norton, 1978

Mosley, Nicholas, *The Assassination of Trotsky,* London, Michael Joseph, 1972

And on and on. Some simply narrate. Others attempt to find out what *really* happened—John Dewey (chairman), *The Case of Leon Trotsky, Preliminary Commission of Inquiry* (New York, Harper and Row, 1937)—or have a new theory about Robert Kennedy's killer or the conspiracy behind Martin Luther King's death, or, for that matter, the Tsar—"dramatic new evidence." For the very contemporary murders we are normally left at the mercy of instant publishing: the Moro books (mostly in Italian, fortunately) were in the shops almost before he was interned. There is one remarkable exception in Julen Agirre, an emigré Basque journalist, who in *Operation Ogro: The Execution of Carrero Blanco* (New York, Quadrangle, 1975) interviewed the four ETA members who assassinated the Admiral and thus gave an intimate and highly detailed firsthand account of the operation.

The major difficulty with the single-assassination genre is that a murder at a particular moment is snatched from history. In fact, some academics have made use of the technique in an attempt to link political murder to other factors by quantitative methods: Ivo K. Feierabend, Rosalind L. Feierabend, Betty A. Nesvold, and Franz M. Jaggar, in "Political Violence and Assassination: Cross-National Assessment," William J. Crotty (editor), *Assassination and the Political Order* (New York, Harper and Row, 1971), used data from eighty-four countries for 1948 through 1967 with uncertain results. Perhaps such an attempt is no more futile than the case histories strung together or the quick journal article on assassinations in the Middle East or Africa or wherever. Few have the skill and technique to focus on the meaning of murder as did Bernard Lewis in *The Assassins: A Radical Sect in Islam* (New York, Basic Books, 1968) or Mousnier's *The Assassination of Henry IV.* In a real sense assassination is simply a political technique that becomes relevant only within a particular context, while the *idea* of assassination has a more general history. And for those unable to talk directly to the involved, a quick introduction can be found to the theorists of the idea of political murder in Walter Laqueur's *The Terrorism Reader* (Philadelphia, Temple University Press, 1978). As for the *real* sources, they have been the involved, the killers, the victims, the bystanders, the involved.

index